170°E

40°S

ABEL TASMAN
NATIONAL PARK

MARLBOROUGH
SOUNDS
MARITIME
PARK

NELSON LAKES
NATIONAL PARK

PAPAROA
NATIONAL PARK

ARTHUR'S PASS
NATIONAL PARK

MT COOK
NATIONAL PARK

WESTLAND
NATIONAL PARK

MT ASPIRING
NATIONAL PARK

FIORDLAND
TIONAL PARK

45°S

170°E

Hope this will help everyone.
to understand New Zealand a
bit better.
21st FEB 1989.

love Stewart

HERITAGE

HERITAGE
THE PARKS OF THE PEOPLE

DAVID THOM

LANSDOWNE PRESS

Editing: Richard King
Art: Kate Greenaway and Chris Elliot
Cover Design: Chris Elliot
Indexing: Felicity Stewart
Typeset in New Zealand by Typocrafters Ltd, Auckland
Printed in Hong Kong by Everbest Printing Co. Ltd

Published by Lansdowne Press, Auckland
a division of Weldon Pty Ltd
59 View Road, Glenfield
Auckland, New Zealand
© David Thom 1987
First published 1987

ISBN 0-86866-109-0

Contents

Foreword

New Zealanders have every reason to celebrate the 100th anniversary of the creation of the first national park. It marked the beginning of the present comprehensive system of specially protected areas all over the country. This network ensures that future generations will be able to enjoy their rightful heritage of New Zealand's great natural beauty and its unique endowments of wild plants and animals.

In the early days the Maori way of life did not seriously threaten the natural environment, but when the first Pakeha settlers arrived it was inevitable that they should exploit the natural resources as a means of survival and the creation of wealth. They were all too efficient and but for the foresight of some enlightened Maori and Pakeha leaders, the destruction of the forest and the erosion of the hills might have gone a great deal further. The opportunity to protect or restore a representative example of a flora and fauna which exists nowhere else could have been altogether lost. It is right that their foresight is recognised and appreciated.

The national parks have enabled countless New Zealanders to appreciate the splendour of their native country, but this opportunity must be used with care and discretion. The natural environment is not indestructible. The native ecosystems are not resistant to unlimited disturbance and encroachment.

The creation of national parks and other protected areas serves two purposes. It allows the people of New Zealand to know their country better, but it also allows the native wild species of plants and animals to hold their own against development and exploitation.

The National Parks Service can look back with considerable satisfaction on a century of achievement. Much of this is due to the dedication and enthusiasm of the members of the service themselves, but it also reflects the interest and concern of many ordinary citizens. Without the support of public opinion, the development of the system of national parks would have been very different. I hope that future generations of New Zealanders will show an equal, if not a greater, concern for the survival of their natural heritage so that further areas of natural value can be brought under proper protection.

H.R.H. Prince Philip
Duke of Edinburgh

Preface and Acknowledgements

If I can trace the initial idea for this book to any particular place and time, it would be to Bali at the third World Congress on National Parks in 1982. A senior manager from an African national parks administration told me that if a park guard was asked about his duty the reply would be, 'I am guarding the wealth of the nation'. In the African context this meant the animal wealth of the wonderful parks of that continent.

After thirteen years in New Zealand parks administration at that time, I felt that 'wealth of the nation' could be accorded a different but equally valid interpretation, and that an attempt should be made to relate the hundred-year story of national parks in New Zealand. I did not expect to find how deeply interwoven into history our parks and reserves are, or that they would represent milestones in a journey of land understanding.

In preparing the book I have had some wonderful and devoted help — all from the generation that will be next to assume responsibility for the management and protection of the parks; in order of their association with the project: David Rees, Sue Weston, Andrea Holm, Mary Neazor, Eric Alexander and Felicity Burton. Without their research and their enthusiasm, professionalism, advice, concern and whole-hearted involvement, the task would not have been possible.

David's preliminary research opened up the scope of the work. Sue and Mary, the backbone of the research effort, spent two years researching libraries, archives, museums, galleries and national park information sources, and travelled many hundreds of kilometres in the process. Mary covered history up to 1890 and Sue the period beyond. Andrea did some checking in the United States, and in libraries and with the Countryside Commission in the United Kingdom. Eric carried out a checking assignment in the final stages, while Felicity also checked and was editorial assistant and secretary during the hurly-burly of typesetting and illustration.

Friends and colleagues, both present and formerly in national park work, have given tremendous help. At an early stage I sought notes and recollections from Lance McCaskill. 'This will rejuvenate me!' said the wonderful old man, in ill health, walking with a stick and totally undiminished in mind and spirit. Pages of typewritten notes arrived in due course. My friend and former colleague Rod Syme was equally generous with notes and recollections of the 1920s to 1960s era. Ray Cleland gave invaluable information about his experiences as a ranger in the 1950s and subsequently.

It would require another book adequately to record and acknowledge the information and notes provided, the conversations held and the time given by many others in reading and commenting on drafts. Patrick O'Dea, Charles Fleming, Priestley Thomson, Brian Jones, Les Hutchins, Jim McFarlane, Alan Mark, Les Molloy, Lindsay Stewart, Tupi Puriri and Ivan Jamieson are all colleagues associated now or formerly in national parks administration, to whom I am deeply indebted for wisdom, advice, recollections and comment.

I have had equally generous support from former colleagues in the Department of Lands and Survey: Bing Lucas, George McMillan, Paul Dingwall, Dave McKerchar, Darcy O'Brien, Dave Bamford, Gavin Muirhead, Jay Davison, Peter Croft, Mal Clarborough, Gavin Rodley, Ian Whitewell and Roger Still have all contributed generously — information delving, offering advice and commenting on drafts. Many other friends, formerly in the Department of Lands and Survey and now with the Department of Conservation, provided information and located file material.

To the rangers whose names are identified with the photo essays and who so readily took up the concept, I owe special thanks. They know the parks best, and together we wanted to say more about events and values, and even management, than is often said. Each essay is a comment about all the parks, as well as its particular subject. The individuality and the perceptions of the authors comes through, along with their practicality and their poetry.

There are many many others to whom I am indebted for a comment, review of a draft, the provision of a valued piece of information or some well-judged and constructive advice or criticism: Tom Durrant, John Shaw, Peter Wardle, Janet Davidson, Bruce Biggs, John Mazey, Tipene O'Regan, Margaret Mutu-Grigg, Te Warena Taua, Koro Wetere, Venn Young, Roger Fyffe, Murray Hosking, Michael Roche, Geoff Park, Mike Barnes, Craig Potton, Peter Mounsey, David Collingwood, Gerry McSweeney, Gerard Hutching, Harold Jacobs and Pat Sheridan.

As a means of scoping the final chapter about the future, I wrote to a wide circle of people whom I knew to be concerned and interested, and received thoughtful, considered replies: Ralph Adams, Ian Atkinson, David Bamford, Ray Cleland, Kevin O'Connor, Jay Davison, Alan Edmonds, Keith Garratt, David Given, Paul Green, Les Hutchins, Charles Fleming, Bruce Jefferies, Brian Jones, Geoff Kelly, Jim McFarlane, Brian Molloy, Gerry McSweeney, Alan Mark, David McKerchar, Geoff Rennison, Geoff Park and Guy Salmon.

It is appropriate to record appreciation to the libraries who have been so helpful: to Moira Long in the National Library of New Zealand, Sherrah Francis in the National Archives, Mary Beaven in the library of the Commission for the Environment, and librarians in the Auckland Public, University and Institute and Museum Libraries, the Canterbury Museum, the Hocken Library and libraries and museums in Nelson, Taupo, New Plymouth, Gisborne, Napier, Wanganui, Westport and Hokitika.

Friends abroad have generously given time to the review of chapters dealing with events remote from New Zealand. Ann and Myron Sutton were authors of the centennial book on Yellowstone National Park and very kindly reviewed and commented on chapter three. James Thorsell, of the Commission on National Parks and Protected Areas of IUCN, provided a similar service for chapter seventeen.

My grateful thanks for their helpfulness and genuine interest go to those on the publishing staff who worked so hard in the final stages; to Barbara Nielsen, the editorial wisdom of Richard King and the design skills of Kate Greenaway and Chris Elliott.

Finally, I would like to pay special tribute to Sir Hepi Te Heuheu for time given so willingly to consultation and review, and for his very particular and personal contribution to the opening of the book.

Introduction

Some eighty million years ago and long, long before the period of the earliest humans or their identifiable forbears, the ancestral land mass of present-day New Zealand began to break away from its parent Australian continent. Another fifty million years went by. Somewhere, probably on the plains of Africa, our primitive forbears emerged — a part of nature, a species living within the web of ecology and evolution. Further immense spans of time passed; tens of millions of years. Evolving humans began to use the simple stone tools that made them more effective hunters. The fashioning and use of the tools, and an increasing ability to reason would one day create the technology that would lead to dominance over natural things.

About seven hundred thousand years ago, as the earliest species of humankind was emerging, something upset the climatic balance. There was a gradual cooling, and then the ice ages began. Ice sheets expanded from the polar regions. As the ice advanced and thickened, sea levels fell. Land bridges formed across the North Sea, the Dardenelles and the Persian Gulf. England was joined to Europe; East Asia and North America became linked across the Bering Sea; Australia and New Guinea were connected. Hunters followed the animals across the land bridges. They were able to move into North America and Australia, and eventually to spread throughout the whole of the continental world.

The oceans and seas defining the continental world were the limits to expansion; a barrier awaiting the technical developments in the construction and navigation of ocean-going vessels, which were as yet tens of thousands of years in the future.

The ice ages came in cycles of cooling and warming. As the chill of the first two glacial advances bit more deeply, it seems likely that people migrated to warmer climes. But by the time of the third advance, about seventy-five thousand years ago, humans had discovered fire, the weapon to be one day employed in vast assaults on nature. Fire enabled people to live through the third ice age without migrating.

By the end of the ice ages humans had spent some half a million years in what is called the Old Stone Age. It was an immense period, two hundred and fifty times as long as the Christian era, two thousand times as long as the period of industrial and scientific development that has followed the Industrial Revolution. Their economy for the whole of that period had been that of the hunter. Humanity had been a part of the ecology, part of nature itself, living within the constraints imposed by nature.

A warming period set in about twenty thousand years ago. Plants grew, forests spread and game multiplied. The cave refuges of the great chill could be vacated. Food gathering could supplement hunting. Tribal units clustered where food sources were abundant, often near marshes and rivers. Fish was the first staple food.

Life flourished in the warmth, which set the stage for a quickening in the pace of development. The Mesolithic, or Middle Stone Age period, was ushered in. The character of hunting changed as the prey changed. Huge animals, like the mammoths of the ice ages, were reduced in numbers by hunting, travelled north and became extinct. The game of this warmer climate was smaller, fleet and numerous: deer, birds, pigs. The hunter needed more cunning, less force and new tools, like the bow and arrow. Hunting and fishing were not the only sources of food in these warmer regions. Plants, nuts, berries and fruits could all be eaten — in season. Some could be stored. Not only this; plants could be cultivated and animals tamed.

Then, in the warm, lush crescent that sweeps from Egypt up the coast of Lebanon and curves down into the valley of the Euphrates, skills were drawn together with the invention that was eventually to change the face of the earth. Agriculture was the magic carpet that would carry humanity away from the millions of years as a part of nature and wilderness and give time to develop ideas, language, writing and art.

Agriculture provided the means to concentrate the growing of food. The city became possible, and sometime between 3500 and 2500 B.C. the first true cities grew near the Tigris and Euphrates Rivers. Here, with the civilisation of Sumer, history began because people learned to write. They also learned how to craft metals, engage in commerce and make war, to consider their role in the world and relationship with nature. There was time to explore the world of the creative and the imaginative, to create art.

Within a thousand years of the flowering of Sumeria, the cities, the arts and the agriculture of two more brilliant civilisations had arisen in the valleys of the Nile in Egypt, and the Indus River, far to the east. Ideas and techniques spread across the Mediterranean Sea to Crete, whose culture would eventually merge with that of the Mycean Greeks.

The organising ability of the Romans who followed extended their influence over much of the region that had been the cradle of civilisation. A vast area, extending from the Indus, through Mesopotamia and Palestine to North Africa and the Italian and Grecian fringes of the Mediterranean, had been greatly changed by the time the Roman Empire had reached the zenith of its power at the beginning of the Christian era. Harvests of cereals were gathered from the shores of the Rhine to the banks of the Nile, and vines and orchards festooned the hillsides of Syria, Greece and Italy.

Both the forests and the wild beasts were in decline through the whole of the vast region. The forests — the habitat of the animals — were reduced to make way for crops or to provide the timber needed for cities and ships. To the north, in Europe, where Roman influence extended as far as the Rhine and the Danube, vast forests covered the land. The nomadic peoples, Celts and Scythians, who ranged the forest and the steppes of Asia had acquired agricultural skills, but love of the nomadic life, particularly of hunting, induced some conflicts with the settled existence promoted by agriculture. Hunting and warfare were central themes of Celtic existence. The forests were the dominating element of their environment. In these forests lived red and fallow deer, wild boar, bears, birds and wolves. As the forests reduced, and animal numbers declined, hunting became the prerogative of the powerful. Hunting reservations were established by the kings, and a body of forest law evolved, so important that its own administrative hierarchy descended from the king. This was the law taken to England by William of Normandy and sternly overlaid on the forest law already imposed by the English kings.

By this time, one thousand years into the Christian era, the fruitful lands that had been the granary, orchard and garden of Rome were, in general, exhausted and infertile. Overused, overgrazed and denuded of forest, their soil mantle exposed to the elements and eroding, they could no longer support a flourishing population, let alone the demands of a high civilisation.

Until some two centuries before William's invasion of England, the land that was to become known as Aotearoa had no human contact. Through the tens of millions of years of warm stable climate preceding the ice ages it had continued to move away from its parent continent, its original life cargo and some wind-blown colonists evolving in total separation from the continental world through which people were spreading; in which they were a part of nature. The ice ages came and went; agriculture was invented, civilisation blossomed and spread, the Roman Empire rose, declined and fell. Vikings invaded southern England. The forest ecosystems of Aotearoa, devastated by volcanism in the north, related to neither humans nor any mammals. The monastery bells and Gregorian chant of Christian Europe were matched only by the pealing calls of tui, kokako and korimako. South lay the storm-driven seas of a vast ecosystem whose birds and animals gathered in abundance around southern shores and islands. North and east lay the Pacific Ocean and the Polynesian triangle. More than five hundred years before Ferdinand Magellan entered the Pacific, Polynesian sailors, navigating ocean distances far beyond the contemplation of Europeans of the time, piloted a double-hulled canoe through the surf of a New Zealand beach. The human story of New Zealand began.

The national parks, reserves and other protected areas of New Zealand contain the record of some of this human story. Indeed we understand the term 'heritage' most clearly when it is used in the sense of great human achievement from the past which informs and enriches the present. But in New Zealand we are stewards as well of a truly 'natural' heritage, of the nature that evolved without man, of a rare and separate evolution that can be traced over three hundred million years into the past. Our national parks are the largest repositories of the heritage.

In 1987 it will be just one hundred years since the gift by Te Heuheu Tukino and his people of the sacred mountains of Ngati Tuwharetoa to be the first national park of New Zealand. Tongariro was one of the first national parks of the world. The concept of 'national park' had been in 1887 just seventeen years on its journey from a talk around a campfire in the Rocky Mountains.

This American idea was adopted by a great Maori chief in an act that has no parallel in any other history. The gift emerged from the clash of two cultures, the one springing from a thousand years of residence in Aotearoa, the other an inheritance from the history of agricultural Europe. The gift was, in the words of Te Heuheu, to be 'for the use of both Maoris and the Europeans'.

In the years that have followed, the vital role of national parks and other protected areas has become appreciated as more and more wilderness has disappeared, species have become extinct, productivity has declined and the deserts have crept outwards. The relationship of civilisation to the wilderness preserved in the protected areas has become better understood. Civilisation is created from the resources of the wilderness, but civilised humanity becomes in ever greater need of the values that wilderness provides.

Other national parks have been created in New Zealand. An administration as uniquely New Zealand as the parks themselves has evolved. Other New Zealanders, Maori and European, have contributed to a remarkable story, which is, in its essence, about understanding New Zealand. Te Heuheu and his people implanted a signpost to the future. Historical timing presented New Zealand with an unparalleled opportunity, and advice, in time. What have we made of the opportunity? Who were those whose perceptions and determination constructed our reservation system? One hundred years after a great act of vision, what is the record?

The gift of the peaks of the Tongariro Mountains (1887)

The gift set in place the nucleus and core of the national park. Embracing the volcanoes and the high plateau of the central North Island, and with major extensions in 1922 and 1983, Tongariro National Park now covers more than 79,000 hectares.

Egmont National Park (1900)

The mountain and its protective forest are vital to the well-being of Taranaki. Little changed in area since the park was established, the sharp line around the mountain that defines forest and farmland embraces 33,500 hectares. The remainder of Taranaki was once similarly covered with forest.

Arthur's Pass National Park (1929)

Based on a major reservation advocated because of its botanical interest by a great scientist late last century, this park of 99,000 hectares enfolds a centuries-old route of commerce and trade as well as the headwaters of great rivers flowing both east and west.

Fiordland National Park (1952)

One of the last great wildernesses of southern temperate regions, unsurpassed as an undisturbed example of fiord systems, the Fiordland National Park was declared a World Heritage site in 1986. Not only rich in its Maori associations, but also of great significance in very early European history, the magnificence of this vast area claimed early recognition. An area of 800,000 hectares was reserved for national park purposes in 1905. Finally constituted as a national park in 1952, Fiordland today covers 1.2 million hectares. In this view across Dusky Sound, Resolution Island lies in the centre of the picture beyond the Acheron passage.

Abel Tasman National Park (1942)

The smallest of New Zealand's national parks (22,500 hectares), Abel Tasman was opened three hundred years to the day from the visit of the Dutch navigator. Famous for the beauty of its coastline, the park includes islands offshore, as well as high, rugged, granite country inland.

Mount Cook National Park (1953)

This elongated, narrow, 70,000-hectare segment of the Southern Alps includes New Zealand's highest mountains and largest glacier. Reservation dates from 1887 and 1890, but a national park was not declared until 1953. Mount Cook and Westland National Parks abut each other along the Main Divide and together were declared a World Heritage site in 1986. The photo shows the Hooker Valley and Mount Sefton.

Urewera National Park (1954)

Growing consciousness over decades of the need for forest and water-catchment protection, led eventually to constitution of the Urewera National Park in 1954. This greatest tract of native forest in the North Island covers 213,000 hectares. Te Urewera is the home of the Tuhoe people and is rich in its heritage of Maori history and legend.

Nelson Lakes National Park (1956)

Smaller in scale than the other parks of the alpine chain, this park, with its lakes, its forests of beech, its mountains and sparkling rivers, is a complete sample of alpine landscape. Extension in 1983 increased the area of the park to almost 102,000 hectares.

Westland National Park (1960)

Containing 117,550 hectares in 1987, and designated a World Heritage site, Westland National Park, like many of the others, was based on large reserves made decades earlier. A major addition in 1982 extended the park 'from the mountains to the sea'.

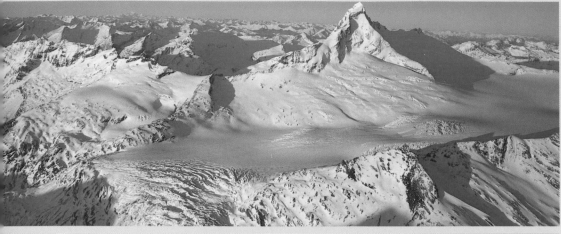

Mount Aspiring National Park (1964)

The beauty of the alpine wilderness of the Mount Aspiring area had been recognised long before it became the last park on the Main Divide. The largest and least developed of the alpine parks had been the scene of much exploratory effort associated with the gold era of early European history.

Hauraki Gulf Maritime Park (1967)

The maritime park concept, which links forty-seven islands with reserves on the coast and gathers together history, scenery, recreation and nature reservation, became a reality in the marine playground of the Auckland region in 1967.

Marlborough Sounds Maritime Park (1972)

Marlborough Sounds was the second maritime park, embracing some one hundred and forty reserves and 52,000 hectares. Reservation dated to the early years of the century. The history of the area reaches back to centuries of occupation by Maori people.

Bay of Islands Maritime and Historic Park (1978)

Smaller than the other maritime parks, Bay of Islands is focused on the bay named by Captain Cook which became the centre of early European history. The park's fifty-five reserves, islands as well as important reserves on the mainland, are contained in 4000 hectares.

Whanganui National Park (1986)

A river famous in its Maori history and associations and scenically renowned in the early years of the century was enfolded, but not included, in the 79,000 hectares of lowland forest of the Whanganui National Park in 1986. The reservations that protected the gorges through which the river flows date to the early years of the century.

Paparoa National Park (1987)

The last national park of the century, situated between Greymouth and Westport, includes the 'pancake' rocks of Punakaiki and the forested limestone country inland and to the north. Selected for its scientific and ecological values, its impressive canyons, limestone topography, cave systems and exquisite small-scale beauty, Paparoa National Park encompasses 30,000 hectares.

3779—TE HEU HEU—AT TOKAANU—LAKE TAUPO—KING COUNTRY.
BURTON BROS. DUNEDIN

Te Heuheu IV Horonuku

Tapuaeharuru, Taupo
23 Hepetema 1887.

Kia Te Paranihi
Ki te Minita
mo te taha Maori
Kei Poneke.

E Pa,

Tena koe — He kupu atu tena ki a koe, ara, he whakaatu, kua maha nga
ra e korerorero ana matou ko Te Ruihi mo te rahui whenua ka
whakatapua nei mo te Iwi ki Tongariro — No te mea e mohio ana matou
he mea nui rawa taua mea, a, i te mea hoki kihai ano nga whakaaro o
etahi o nga tangata o taku iwi i tino marama ki taua mea.

Na kua oti te wehe atu o taua whenua e te Kooti Whakawa Whenua
Maori, a, kua whakataua nga tihi o Tongariro me Ruapehu ki toku ingoa
anake, ki te tangata nona teenei whakatauki 'Ko Tongariro te maunga, ko
Taupo te moana, ko Ngatituwharetoa te iwi, ko Te Heuheu te tangata'.

E hoa, kua hainatia e ahau te pukapuka i homai nei e Te Ruihi ki toku
aroaro, hei whakapumau i te tukunga atu o taua whenua hei whenua tapu
mo te Iwi katoa kia rite ai ki te hiahia o te Kawanatanga me taku kupu
hoki i whakapuakina nei e au ki a koe i Rotorua. Engari e rua aku kupu
hei whakaatu ki a koe.

Tuatahi — Ko taku papa ko Te Heuheu Tukino i horongia nei ki Te
Rapo kei runga i taua maunga e takoto ana, a, e mea ana ahau me
whakaneke mai ia ki tetahi wahi ke atu. Ko taua tangata, otira e mohio
ana koe, he rangatira nui rawa, a, he mea tika kia mahia e Te
Kawanatanga tetahi urupa kohatu mona i te mea kaore ahau me toku iwi
e kaha ki te mahi mea pera mona. Kua whakaae te hoa, a Te Ruihi, ki
tenei kupu aku, ana whakaae mai hoki koe.

Taku kupu tuarua — Koia tenei — kua kaumatuatia ahau, a, ko nga
whakahaere mo toku iwi kai taku tama kotahi kai a Tureiti Te Heuheu
Tukino, a, ko taku hiahia me whakamana, ara, me whakahua tonu tona
ingoa ki roto ki te Ture Whakamana i te Whenua Ka whakatapua nei mo
te iwi, ara, ko ia tonu te Kai-Tiaki hei riwhi mo toku turanga kai-tiaki, i
runga i taua maunga ana mate ahau — a kua whakaae mai hoki a Te
Ruihi ki tenei kupu aku, ana whakaae mai koe.

Koia ena aku kupu ki Te Kawanatanga i taku tuhinga ara i taku
hainatanga i te pukapuka tuku atu i Tongariro me Ruapehu hai Whenua-
Tapu mo te iwi katoa, Pakeha me te Maori.

Heoi ano na
to hoa na

Te Heuheu Tukino

Tapuwaeharuru, Taupo
September 23rd, 1887

To Te Paranihi
Minister of Native Affairs
Wellington

Sir,

Greetings. This is to inform you that my people and I have spent several days talking over with Mr Lewis (Under Secretary, Native Department) the subject of making Tongariro a National Park, because we regard it as a matter of great importance, and besides, the minds of some of my people are not clear on the subject.

A division of the land has been made by the Native Land Court and the same Court has awarded the tops of the mountains, Tongariro and Ruapehu to me alone because I am the person to whom the following proverb applies: 'Tongariro the mountain; Taupo, the sea; Ngati Tuwharetoa, the tribe; Te Heuheu the man.'

Friend, I have signed the deed laid before me by Mr Lewis for the purpose of confirming the gift of that land as a National Park in accordance with the wish of the Government, and to fulfil my word spoken to you at Rotorua.

'I have, however, two words to make known to you. First — my father, Te Heuheu Tukino, who was overwhelmed at Te Rapa, is laid on the mountain, and it is my wish that he be removed to some other place. He was, as you know, a chief of very high rank, and it is right that the Government should erect a tomb (urupa kohatu) for him because both my people and I are unable to do so. Your friend, Mr Lewis, has agreed to this word of mine, subject to your approval.

The second word is, that I am an old man and the affairs of my people are conducted by my only son, Tureiti Te Heuheu Tukino. It is my wish that he be authorised, that is to say that his name be inserted in the National Park Act; this is that he be a trustee appointed after my death. Mr Lewis has also agreed to this word of mine subject to your approval.

These are my requests to the Government on my signing the deed giving Tongariro and Ruapehu to the Government as a National Park, for the use of both Maoris and the Europeans.

From your friend

(Signed) Te Heuheu Tukino

One of my ambitions has been to instil in my young people's endeavours the need to fully understand the responsibilities that attach to ownership of land in whatever tenure — be it communal holdings, such as marae papakainga or family interests in undivided lands, or in private ownership, such as a family home or a private or family trust.

The major responsibility as I perceive it is that the land be passed on to the following generation in better condition than that in which it was received and thereby give renewal to the feelings of 'turangawaewae' and 'tangata whenua'.

And as with my people, where the ownership of land is a serious concern, so should the pride of ownership in our nationally owned lands be in us all.

The gifting of Tongariro symbolises for me the handing on of the precious 'taonga' into the care of the people of New Zealand and may it always be that all such 'taonga' will be revered and honoured by all people and then the saying

'Te Ha o taku maunga
Ko taku manawa'
(The breath of my mountain
is my heart)
will have significance to all nature lovers.

If the reading of this book instils in you a greater appreciation of the beauty and the meaning of our national parks, then the agonies and concerns of history and the growing pains to maturity for our nation will be accorded their proper place. I hope we can look forward to enhanced opportunities to enjoy and care for the wealth of nature and history contained within all protected natural areas in Aotearoa.

Sir Hepi Te Heuheu, chief of Ngati Tuwharetoa and great grandson of Te Heuheu IV Horonuku.

— Sir Hepi Te Heuheu.

Turangawaewae — Where a person stands or belongs; the sense of merging of a person and the land.
Tangata whenua — A person belonging to the land.
Taonga — An object of extreme value, a treasure, something precious.
Rohepotae — 'Our' sphere of influence (rohe=area; potae=hat).

Chapter 1

A Century of National Parks in New Zealand

It was Sir Hepi Te Heuheu's great-grandfather, Te Heuheu Tukino, and his people who gave the peaks of Tongariro, an initiative that led New Zealand to be one of the first countries to establish national parks. To understand this remarkable gift it is necessary to understand something of the long history of the Maori people in New Zealand. Chapter Five, 'Te Whenua, Te Iwi', tells the story of Polynesians who, travelling far from tropical islands, came to a cold, large and different land. After centuries of struggle with this land they called Aotearoa, they won through to a distinctive new culture, marked among its many attributes by a deep feeling for the land. To understand the gift it is necessary also to know about the clash with the different European cultural view of the values of land which began after European settlement.

The initiative was Te Heuheu's, but the idea of 'national park' had come from an explorer's conversation beside a campfire on the banks of the Madison River in the United States. In 1874, just two years after the Yellowstone River region had been made the world's first national park, William Fox, a former Premier with a great appreciation of New Zealand natural beauty, wrote to Julius Vogel, Premier at the time, to suggest that the Government of New Zealand should take a similar step with regard to Lake Rotomahana and its volcanic wonders, including the Pink and White Terraces.

A photograph by the Burton brothers of the Pink Terrace prior to the 1886 Tarawera eruption.

Mackinnon Pass on the Milford Track about the turn of the century.

To provide accommodation for travellers between Pipiriki and Taumarunui, a houseboat, the *Makere*, was built in Taumarunui and floated down to the junction of the Ohura and Wanganui Rivers in 1904.

Houseboat. Wanganui River. E.

Tourist guidebooks of the early 1900s advised that ladies could reach the terminal face of the glaciers around Mount Cook provided that they 'leave their fashionable high heels at home, and don serviceable boots'.

This advice aside, women were still restrained by convention to wearing shirts buttoned high to the neck, and ground-length skirts on walking expeditions. The photograph shows a Gifford party on the Tasman Glacier near Ball Hut.

In 1882 William Spotswood Green, an English clergyman, came to New Zealand to climb Mount Cook. In this *London Graphic* illustration his party is shown traversing the seracs (jumbled cubes and pinnacles of ice) of the Grand Plateau. Green said that among the peaks of the Southern Alps was work 'for a whole company of climbers, which would occupy them for half a century of summers, and still there would remain many a new route to be tried'.

Modern climbers in the Mount Cook region.

Below right: A mountain hut may not offer the comforts of home, but the warmth of the small beacon shining from the Tasman Saddle Hut in Mount Cook National Park suggests comfort, shelter and the camaraderie that belongs in the tradition of the mountains.

Below: Well laden and prepared for mountain weather, tramping club members head out from Edwards Hut in Arthur's Pass National Park.

It was the incomparable Terraces that launched tourism as an industry in the 1870s. A decade later, roads and railways facilitated travel. Other sites later to be incorporated in national parks attracted visitors, including the Southern Lakes, the Wanganui River and Milford Sound. Surveys for the Milford Track began in 1888, and by 1900 the famous walk was a going concern. Scenery and tourism were the basis of Thomas Mackenzie's argument for a 'Sounds' national park. Awareness of the potential for tourism surfaced often in parliamentary debates about national parks. The Wanganui River (not to be related to a national park until 1986) was in its heyday known as the 'Rhine of New Zealand', with a major hotel, a fleet of steamships and a houseboat in the early 1900s. One hundred years after Tongariro, the national parks, and particularly Mount Cook and Fiordland, are central to a tourist industry that earns above one billion dollars annually. The number of visits tops three million.

Climbing launched tourism at Mount Cook, particularly the exploits and writings of William Spotswood Green, who travelled from England in 1882 with the sole objective of climbing this 'splendid peak'. The original Hermitage accommodation house had been built within a few years, forerunner to succeeding Hermitages and pre-dating by decades the other famous hotels in future national park areas, like Lake House (now demolished) at Lake Waikaremoana and the Chateau Tongariro in Tongariro National Park. Green's forecast of work sufficient to occupy half a century of climbers proved a modest estimate.

In a century of climbing in the national parks hundreds of mountaineers, including names to become famous in the Himalayas, the Andes, in Europe and the Antarctic, have cut their mountaineering teeth and their first steps in the Darran Mountains of Fiordland, Mount Aspiring, the Mount Cook region or on Egmont's ice.

The last phase of exploration — that of mountaineering exploration, predominantly by New Zealanders — was ushered in by the early climbing exploits. Other ways to challenge the dangers and grandeur of the mountains and enjoy the freedom of the high country followed naturally. The alpine and tramping clubs became, for a time, the chief repository of back-country knowledge.

These clubs would in time play a major role in shaping the public input in the administration of New Zealand's national parks and reserves, which is as unique as the areas themselves. In 1987, one hundred and thirty clubs, representative of over sixteen thousand active participants in mountain recreation, are incorporated in the Federation of Mountain Clubs.

Skiing followed tramping. Suitable snow and weather at Mount Ruapehu in 1987 can in a day draw twelve thousand people to two major ski-fields. Over six hundred thousand people will, in the season, now take part in the sport pioneered on the mountain in 1913. Ski-fields in four of the other alpine national parks offer skiing variety, from long downhill running on the Tasman Glacier at Mount Cook to the family outings more characteristic of the ski-fields in Nelson Lakes, Egmont or Arthur's Pass National Parks.

A notable aspect of the history of science in New Zealand has been the efforts of scientists to recognise and explain the biological distinctiveness of New Zealand. Leonard Cockayne, one of the pioneers of ecology as a science, is closely connected with several of the national parks, Tongariro and Arthur's Pass in particular. The acknowledged significance of the scientific and ecological importance of the national parks and reserves has grown slowly, as on the one hand their distinction has become better understood, while, on the other, the world outside has become increasingly modified.

There have been scientific programmes in national parks and reserves for many years, but it was not until 1981 that scientific value became one of the criteria for the establishment of national parks. This has been a strong factor in the selection of the last national park of the century — Paparoa National Park in Westland. It is also the reason for the Protected Natural Areas programme of recent years — an effort to capture and maintain a representative sample of the ecosystems unique within each region before the opportunity is lost.

Scientific information is a base for education. The first visitor centre, providing for displays and interpretative programmes, was opened at Arthur's Pass in 1959. Interpretation and education about nature generally and the natural and scientific treasures of particular parks has grown steadily since.

Winter fun on the Hut Flat, Tongariro National Park. Here, two major ski-fields can host six hundred thousand visitors during a ski season.

Start of the learners' race. A ski meeting at Ball Hut, Mount Cook, in 1931.

Summer programmes led by rangers take visitors out into living libraries of nature. A major centre for Fiordland National Park is to be opened at Te Anau in 1987. Several national parks have live-in nature education centres. For the children from schools of the region who spend a week as guests of the outdoors, this is adventure as well as a learning experience about natural processes in the field and classroom.

To a large extent the century-old history of national parks in New Zealand is the history of conservation, and the history of conservation is the history of the forests. It might even be claimed (as suggested in the Introduction) that the history of the forests is the history of civilisation, for in the long term it is the management of the forests (particularly in a steep, unstable country) that determines the soil stability on which, ultimately, civilisation is dependent.

It was often concern about land protection that focused on 'national park' as the means to achieve this once confidence and understanding of the concept of national park as public land under statutory protection became generally understood. All the national parks have immense importance as soil and water conservation areas. The origin of at least two (Egmont and Urewera) and the partial genesis of others lies in an awakening of their role as protectors of vast areas of adjacent productive land. It was the policies of the Maori King Movement — retarding European settlement and forest clearance across a vast tract of the central North Island — that provided the time for conservation values to be better understood.

An immense surge of progress with land reservation in the period 1900 to 1920 arose paradoxically from a decade of enormous forest destruction in the 1890s. Towards the end of the 1890s scenery preservation groups had sprung up in many parts of New Zealand. In the climate of unhappy consciousness of forest loss, Harry Ell, one of the most forceful conservation leaders New Zealand has ever seen, pushed through the Scenery Preservation Act of 1903. The surveys and recommendations of the commission and board set up by the Act had, by 1920, set aside at least half of the land now contained within national parks and reserves.

It was forest damage by deer that led in the 1920s and 1930s to a growing realisation that introduced animals were a threat to the forests.

In 1921 the Department of Lands and Survey was reporting that there were seven national parks in well over a million hectares of reservation. This covered five of the areas we know today, but there was a variety of administrations and objectives were far from clear. The concept of 'national park' was not defined in legislation. By this time serious river flooding and soil erosion were driving home hard lessons about land protection. Introduced animals, especially deer, goats and opossums, emerged as a new threat to the forests on which the stability of upland New Zealand depended.

Campaigns by the Royal Forest and Bird Protection Society and the Royal Society of New Zealand promoted soil and water conservation. Two distinguished New Zealanders, Lance McCaskill and Arthur Harper, had very influential roles. Harper was the last of the mountaineer explorers and under his mana the growing band of mountain users, together with senior officials of the Department of Lands and Survey and far-sighted Ministers, shaped a remarkable piece of legislation: the National Parks Act, 1952.

The maritime parks are as uniquely representative of New Zealand's landscapes and conservation history as the national parks. It was perhaps inevitable that the involvement of an island people with the coastline and the

History and recreation in the Bay of Islands Maritime and Historic Park. Historic Kemp House and the Stone Store overlook yachts in the Kerikeri Basin.

sea should lead towards the maritime park idea when the same competition began for private ownership of recreational resources as had, decades earlier, shaped the course of policy towards national parks. Competition for ownership, subdivision and sale of the northern coastline and its islands began in the 1950s. The seagoing fraternity of Auckland were quick to insist that Crown holdings should not be surrendered. The creative partnership of citizen and administrator that had in the 1940s so greatly influenced the future of national parks emerged again to invent the assembly of functions we know today as maritime park. That such a concept could be fashioned at all, and be applied later in other outstanding areas of land and seascape like the Marlborough Sounds and the Bay of Islands, was a tribute to the foresight of the citizens and administrators who had created reserves in the earlier years of the century.

One of the truly remarkable things about national parks in New Zealand is that while the original idea was American, everything else has been as

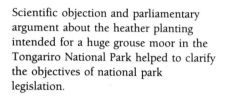

Scientific objection and parliamentary argument about the heather planting intended for a huge grouse moor in the Tongariro National Park helped to clarify the objectives of national park legislation.

indigenous and home-grown as the scenery, plants and animals the national parks protect. The ethic stated in our national park law grew straight out of New Zealand circumstances: destruction of forest, loss of native bird life, forest damage by deer, an attempt to make a huge grouse moor over land in and near Tongariro National Park.

The national parks and the later maritime parks are interwoven into the history of European discovery about the real nature of Aotearoa. It is possible to see in this story the analogy of a journey, of an alien culture being enfolded and dominated by the land as a painful 'land-learning' is worked through. The Polynesians of more than a thousand years ago brought the culture of small tropical islands and endured an arduous 'land-learning'. Eventually a distinctive and wonderful culture emerged. The national parks story, with all the symbolism of its initiation by a Maori chief, is a similar story of a clash between land and culture. It occupies an important place in our journey towards a new and distinctive culture.

Chapter 2

The Heritage Today

The gift of the mountain peaks was made in September 1887. One hundred years later on a September day there were thousands of New Zealanders skiing, climbing, tramping and picnicking among the snowfields, forests and tussockland of the magnificent national park that has grown from the gift. Elsewhere there were climbers high in the alpine wilderness of Mount Cook National Park, surfcasters on a Northland beach, and a class of children from Rotoiti Lodge in Nelson Lakes National Park out on a botanical expedition. There were deerstalkers in the Urewera forests, rafters on a tumbling river and yachtsmen threading the sounds and islands of the maritime parks.

Over the century the heritage — public land owned by all New Zealanders — has grown to become a vast estate. The national and maritime parks and the reserves now cover nearly three million hectares, more than one tenth of our country. While the mountain peaks of Tongariro National Park are representative of the volcanic power that has built and shaped much of the

Sacred mountains of Ngati Tuwharetoa, the volcanoes of Tongariro National Park suggest the latent power that has shaped northern New Zealand. Far below, the tectonic plates of the earth are in conflict.

Climbers on the summit of Mount Cook.

Classwork in natural history at Rotoiti Lodge, Nelson Lakes National Park.

landscape of northern New Zealand, the heritage has grown piece by piece to become a living record of the endless variety of our landscape, and of its formation by many geological processes.

The heritage samples this variety, but not in any systematic way. Its growth is inter-woven with the events that have made our history, and with the foresight of the individual New Zealanders, Maori and European, who have followed Te Heuheu Tukino. Perhaps it is more truly heritage because the building has been part of a historical process rather than a systematic one. From this process has come a variety of types of reserve, of legislation, and of management styles as uniquely New Zealand as the places themselves.

The scale and splendour of the twelve national parks makes them the focus and keystone of the heritage. The National Parks Act describes the essence of these, the 'crown jewels': 'Areas of New Zealand that contain scenery of such distinctive quality, ecological systems or natural features so beautiful, unique, or scientifically important that their preservation is in the national interest.'

The Act goes on to direct that such areas are to be preserved in perpetuity so that we may receive in full measure the 'inspiration, enjoyment, recreation, and other benefits that may be derived from mountains, forests, sounds, seacoasts, lakes, rivers and other natural features'.

In 1987 three of the national parks — Fiordland, the great mountain wilderness that is unique in the world, and the combined extent of Mount Cook and Westland National Parks, which links across the main divide of the Southern Alps and plunges in just a few kilometres to the Tasman Sea — have been designated World Heritage sites. Such identification of outstanding universal value is made by UNESCO's World Heritage Committee, an international group that administers the World Heritage Convention and selects and

lists the cultural and natural sites regarded as the heritage of humankind as a whole. Although there are still fewer than two hundred such sites in the whole world, the importance of our New Zealand heritage is such that other sites within New Zealand will be considered and, without doubt, selected as time goes on.

The protected area system beyond national parks is governed by two pieces of legislation, the Reserves Act and Conservation Act. The Reserves Act provides the legal basis for a range of reserves having historic, scenic, nature, scientific and recreational values. The names describe the primary purpose of each type of reserve but all contribute to the preservation either of a historical site or a sample of the plants, birds, insects and landscape that give New Zealand its original and distinctive character.

The Conservation Act governs the forest sanctuaries such as Waipoua, which protects our finest remnant of the kauri forest that once covered Northland. Forest ecological areas preserve samples of a range of forest ecosystems, ensuring that we will continue to be able to study the plant, bird and insect communities we cannot recreate, and that their gene stocks will continue to be available in the future.

The Conservation Act also governs the concept of forest park. There are, in 1987, twenty of these wonderful areas. Most of them are within original native forest, although two embrace the exotic forests that have been planted for production. The central idea of the conservation park is that New Zealanders should have every possible opportunity to enjoy their forests. The tracks, huts and other facilities that extend the opportunity of trampers, hunters, sightseers and picnickers are all provided as part of the plan for multiple-use forest management. It is essential to the idea that forest park management plans remain flexible, and that, if necessary, the scheme for management can allow timber production. Conservation parks are a very important part of the heritage today, but are not discussed further in this book, the central theme of which is the national parks.

Farm parks and maritime parks link a number of different kinds of reserve with land managed for production farming. As parts of the farms can be used for camping and access, public opportunity to enjoy the beauty and recreational benefits of the reserves is greatly enhanced. Access, however, is not always a matter of going where one pleases — some of the maritime parks

Mount Tasman, the Balfour Glacier and the western face of the Main Divide glow in evening light. The glacier falls into Westland National Park. Darkness descends on much of Mount Cook National Park, which adjoins Westland along the Divide. Together, these two majestic parks have now been recognised as World Heritage sites of outstanding natural value.

A family picnic on one of the beaches of the Bay of Islands Maritime and Historic Park.

Yachts moored, Moturua Island, Bay of Islands Maritime Park.

In Manginangina Scenic Reserve in the Bay of Islands Maritime and Historic Park is a sample of the mixed forest that once covered much of Northland. The dominant tree was the kauri, which grows only in northern New Zealand. The characteristic clean bole, like these in a magnificent grove of young kauri in Manginangina, was one of the attributes that made it attractive for masts and spars in the age of sail.

include nature reserves that can be viewed from the sea but entered only by permit.

Maritime parks collect together some of our most valued groupings of islands and coastline. The fleet of islands lying in the approaches to Russell, Paihia and Waitangi, together with bays on the coast west of Cape Brett and the beautiful kauri forest of Manginangina, are gathered together in the Bay of Islands Maritime and Historic Park. The rich history included within the park complements that of sites like Waitangi and Kerikeri.

The Hauraki Gulf Maritime Park stretches north and east from the barrier of islands guarding the entry to the Waitemata to beyond Manaia Head, sentinel at the entrance to Whangarei Harbour. It includes such outstanding nature reserves as Little Barrier Island and the Hen and Chicken Islands. The third maritime park, in the Marlborough Sounds, again brings together under one 'protect and enjoy' concept an outstanding area of islands and sheltered water.

As well as the reserves of the land, there are the reserves of the sea, the 'marine' reserves. The variety of the types of reservation may seem confusing but the name — maritime or scenic, forest or nature — will always give a clue as to the objective or central feature of the 'protected area', a term that covers all reservation. Common to all is their record of a distinctive New Zealand environment, and common also, with the two exceptions of nature reserves and scientific reserves, is the access which permits New Zealanders to know and enjoy their country. Because nature reserves protect flora and fauna that are either very rare or of great scientific interest, a special permit is required for access. Access to scientific reserves may also be restricted if control is needed.

In 1987 many elements of the heritage are linked by the cross-country routes of the New Zealand walkway system, conceived in 1975 as a chain of tracks linking to form a walk from North Cape to Bluff. Although this vision has been modified by subsequent events, many of the tracks of the walkway system connect with the tracks of the parks and reserves. Enterprising and fit New Zealanders can hoist a pack, depart from Cape Egmont, circle the lower slopes of legendary Mount Taranaki and make their way to the forests of the Wanganui River by way of the Matemateonga Walkway. They can then proceed onwards by trails of the ancient Maori to the tracks of Tongariro National

pass that has linked west and east in both Maori and European history.

Different they may be, but together the national parks record much about the way New Zealand was made, and about the evolutionary separation from the rest of the world's major land areas, which led to a unique plant life, the absence of mammals, and birds that lost the power of flight. In the forests of the national parks lies an ancient inheritance of three hundred and fifty million years of evolution, much of it as yet unstudied. In the remote valleys of Fiordland are the takahe and kakapo, last of their evolutionary line, rarer than the rarest jewels of the fabled Orient.

Fiordland, Mount Aspiring, Westland, Arthur's Pass and Nelson Lakes National Parks all contain the Alpine Fault, the surface indication that the immense tectonic plates of the earth's crust are in conflict. In the north, the volcanoes of Tongariro National Park signal another point on the line where the Pacific Plate drives under the Indian-Australian Plate.

The park areas, too, have featured in New Zealand's human history. Indeed, in some regions they are all we have to remind us today of the nature of the land the Maori came to and lived in for perhaps a thousand years before Europeans arrived. Often special, even tapu, places of the Maori, enshrined in lore and legend, and central among the cherished lands of particular tribes, they figure later in the human story as European navigators and explorers investigated coasts and hinterland. Captain Cook met friendly Maoris in Dusky Sound, in what is now Fiordland National Park, in 1773. He spent six weeks there and named every part of the sound. Other parks contain the routes of Maori commerce, the sites of battles and great events, and the history of peoples. Some relate to particular tribes: the Urewera is to the

Valley of the takahe, Fiordland National Park.

It was in Cascade Cove in Dusky Sound that Captain Cook's sailors first saw Maoris on the 1773 voyage. Cook may well have enjoyed this view out from the cove. 'There is room for a fleet of ships,' he noted.

Urewera National Park is steeped in the legend and history of the Tuhoe people. The meeting house at Maungapohatu is situated on an enclave of tribal land.

Tuhoe people what Tongariro is to Ngati Tuwharetoa. Some parks tell of the history of relationships between Maori and European, others of the exploits and perceptions of European explorers and individuals.

It is sometimes thought to be contradictory that there are only four national parks in the North Island, in contrast to the eight in the South Island. But national parks are not chosen on any geographic basis. They can occur only where the very high qualities and values of the land can justify selection. The balance is restored in the north by the farm parks and maritime parks. Both, like all our forms of reservation, are a New Zealand invention, and both look outwards to the insular New Zealanders' relationship with coasts and the sea. This relationship, as old as human history in New Zealand, is particularly strong in the warmer seas and more varied coastlines of the north.

The sign 'Scenic Reserve' is often found by a highway, perhaps where the road passes through bush, opens to a panoramic view, or invites a pause to picnic or walk in the bush. Many, but not all, of New Zealand's twelve hundred scenic reserves have been chosen because they are visible from roads and railways. Like the national parks, the scenic reserves, which today add up to almost half a million hectares, have nearly one hundred years of history. Unlike the national parks, they are often small, sometimes a fraction of a hectare. From these little fragments, perhaps securing the natural setting of a waterfall or a small but precious swampland habitat, scenic reserves can range upwards in size to thousands of hectares, like the reserves of the Waioeka Gorge in the Bay of Plenty or the Rahu Saddle in Westland.

Scenic reserves protect places of scenic interest and beauty, or fine natural features and landscape. Variety of size is matched by variety of incident — a waterfall, an attractive area of a particular kind of bush, a bog, a headland or rocky outcrop, a lake, collection of alpine plants or a field of native tussock grass.

Some of the largest of the scenic reserves lie in the spectacular gorges that often provide the main transport routes from region to region. The Mangamuka Gorge Reserve near Kaitaia in the far north, the Waioeka Gorge Reserve and the reserves of the Buller River Gorge all ensure that the original character of these typically New Zealand situations has been preserved. The value and importance of the scenic reserves continue to increase as the patches of native bush that confer character and landscape quality on so many rural landscapes continue to disappear.

The scenic reserves are the small jewels crystalising some of the diversity and detail of original New Zealand. This part of the heritage has resulted from a hundred years of history, during which opportunities were taken as they arose. Some of the reserves were gifts from Maori or European people, others were obtained as new roads were built, many were purchased with government funds as the need was disclosed. The outcome of history is an extremely varied distribution. North Auckland has a large number of scenic reserves, while an immense area of the South Island high country has none at all — an outcome of concerns with the protection of tall forest which resulted from the forest destruction that played a large part in the history of the heritage.

On mainland New Zealand the parks, forest reservations and scenic reserves constitute the major part of the heritage. Magnificent as it is, it would be much less in its value as a heritage without the nature reserves of the off-shore islands. These geographical extensions of New Zealand range from the subtropical Kermadecs, six hundred kilometres beyond North Cape, to the sweep of the subantarctic islands: the Snares, the Auckland Islands, Campbell

For a New Zealander it is natural to look outwards to the sea. This pa site in the Bay of Islands Maritime and Historical Park looks towards Cape Brett. New Zealanders of other ages have also directed their gaze out to the sea.

Left: Mangarakau Scenic Reserve on the Whanganui Inlet, north-west coast of the South Island, has a road frontage of three kilometres and some very fine coastal forest.

Below: Marokopa Falls Scenic Reserve was designated in 1913, a date indicating that it was in all probability selected by the Scenery Preservation Board.

Island, the Antipodes and the Bounty Islands. Campbell Island, seven hundred kilometres south-east of Bluff, is farthest south, a lonely and wind-swept extinct volcanic dome in the Southern Ocean.

Seven hundred kilometres east of Christchurch, and on a similar latitude, lie the Chatham Islands, scene of the efforts by the New Zealand Wildlife Service to rescue a tiny endemic bird, the Chatham Islands black robin, from extinction. Other offshore islands close to the mainland coast now provide homes for species that have been eliminated from the mainland by introduced predators and reduction of habitat. The saddleback thrives on the rugged Hen and Chickens group, and kakapo live now on Little Barrier Island, where the forest and rich bird life hint at the character of New Zealand before people arrived. Almost all the islands, and particularly those farthest from the main-land, are important for their endemic plants and birds — small records of the separate evolutionary process that has so distinguished New Zealand. Over thirty per cent of the plants of the subantarctic islands occur nowhere else in the world. The islands include some of the world's last remaining areas of vegetation unmodified by humans or introduced animals and are recognised to be of international scientific importance.

The islands are related to mainland New Zealand by geological history. The Chathams and the subantarctic islands are linked to the mainland by a sub-continental sea shelf in shallow seas. The Kermadecs lie just to the west of the Tonga-Kermadec trench, lying between the tectonic plates in the ocean floor. Many of the islands are volcanic, some recent and active like the Ker-madecs and the privately owned reserve of White Island, others are older volcanic remnants, perhaps extinct like the Campbell Islands and the Three Kings.

The human history of the islands is notable particularly for the explor-ations in the Pacific that followed Captain Cook, for sealing and whaling and

Royal albatross nesting on Campbell Island.

The subantarctic islands are important as protected breeding areas for birds and animals of the Southern Ocean. Seal colonies also exist around the mainland New Zealand coastline. This seal was photographed on the shore of the Abel Tasman National Park.

scientific expeditions, and for shipwreck, hardship and doomed attempts to found settlements.

The islands are the nesting and breeding places for the sea birds of the New Zealand region. Here is the greatest diversity of marine birds on earth, with one-third of all varieties occurring as breeders or visitors. The rat-free Snares Islands are home for up to six million sooty shearwaters, the southern tablelands of the Chatham Islands are the nesting location for the rare magenta petrel, and Campbell Island hosts the southern royal albatross, the world's largest sea bird. 'Wall-to-wall birds!' was an aircraft pilot's description of a crater in the Kermadec Islands, shelter for the boobies and frigate birds of tropical oceans. The particular wealth and diversity of the sea-bird populations of the subantarctic islands arises from their location in the nutrient-rich seas of the Southern Ocean, most productive of the world's ecosystems.

The location of these islands in the Southern Ocean is the explanation for another of their distinctions in the realm of natural science. The notion that indigenous large animals are part of our fauna would surprise many New Zealanders, but the subantarctic islands are the haul-outs, part of the habitat and the sheltered nurseries for fur seals, elephant seals, leopard seals and Hooker's sealions. Some of the whales of New Zealand's extended economic region, in which they are protected, use sheltered waters like Carnley Harbour of the Auckland Islands as a calving and nursing area.

These are some of the great natural values of the offshore component of the heritage, values that have justified the additional protection and standing conferred by the designation of 'national reserve' for the subantarctic islands.

Scenic, nature and scientific reserves, or historic reserves which protect values of national or international significance can be declared 'national reserves'. Such reserves are the finest of their class and especially important in the values they protect. The whole or part of a reserve can, on the declaration of the Governor-General by order in council, be given national reserve status, which is such a high level of protection that its designation can only be changed by Act of Parliament. This level of protection equates to that of a national park.

National reserves are selected by the evaluation of candidates representing the finest of a 'theme'. The themes used as the basis are lakes, rivers, maritime/coasts, mountains, forests, archaeological heritage, discovery, architectural heritage, colonial events, natural heritage, natural wonders, islands and wetlands.

New Zealand's first national reserve, in the beautiful beech forest and mountain scenery of the Lewis Pass, was declared in 1985. In addition to the Lewis Pass and the subantarctic islands, other national reserves will be declared in the future. It is a comment on the quality of the heritage that selection is a difficult process of detailed evaluation and comparison.

Such is the heritage today, one hundred years after the gift: magnificent, diverse and of many values. Its economic potential grows each year as truly original nature the world round is further reduced. But it is the intangible values that far outweigh economic factors: the inspiration conferred by majestic scenery or by the beautiful small things of nature, the scientific programmes enlarging our knowledge of natural systems, the opportunities to meet nature on nature's terms, the education of young New Zealanders about their own distinctive inheritance, and the landscapes that have no parallel elsewhere because they are the product of a unique natural history.

Chapter 3

The World's First National Park

The rolling grassland basins of Yellowstone National Park lie mostly in the state of Wyoming, cradled in the Rocky Mountains, one thousand kilometres from the west coast of the United States. It is vast — nearly nine million hectares in area, each side of a rough square being about one hundred kilometres. While most of the park lies north-east of the continental divide, the northern and eastern boundaries lie in mountains. The Yellowstone River flows north into the state of Montana through its famous canyon from Yellowstone Lake. Leaving the park, it drains on to the north before swinging east to join the Missouri. Other rivers find their way west into Idaho and the Snake River, which joins the Columbia River's run to the Pacific Ocean.

The Grand Canyon of the Yellowstone River.

Sir Frank Fraser Darling called Yellowstone 'a great window on a panorama of nature'. Its wonders — roaring geyser basins, mountains of black glass, travertine terraces, canyons of coloured earth — had not been encountered by a person of European descent until 1807, when an explorer named John Colter left his expedition to explore and trap on his own. His stories of fire and brimstone were believed no more than those of other trappers in the decades that followed.

Yellowstone is a vast wildlife reserve in which the grizzly bear is king. Just below him in the ecological pyramid are the ungulates — bison, deer, moose, bighorn and the elk (or wapiti) — which roam the mountains in summer and descend to the basins during the frigid, unforgiving winters of blizzard and deep snow. The predators, other than the grizzly, include black bears, wolves, mountain lions, coyotes and badgers. Monarch of the world of birds is the bald eagle. The lakes and rivers of Yellowstone are the scene of the crashing dive of the magnificent osprey, or fishing eagle. With the ice thaw of spring, the waterways, marshes and islands become host to a horde of migrants — trumpeter swans, pelicans, gulls, cormorants and terns — which come to breed in the solitude and to feed on the life of the productive waters.

Yellowstone remained relatively unknown until the late 1860s, even if westwards expansion had brought in a flow of adventurers after the decline of trapping in the 1840s. It was not until the summers of 1869, 1870 and 1871 that three successive expeditions were able to describe and communicate its upland grandeur. Cook, Folsom and Peterson of the 1869 expedition climbed up to the accompaniment of howling wolves, bugling elk and roaring mountain lions. They were overwhelmed by the magnificence of it all, and cautious in their telling of it. The credibility of Yellowstone stories was still a problem. Nonetheless, the idea of preserving the Yellowstone wilderness began to be

The terraces at Mammoth Hot Springs, Yellowstone National Park, are some of the largest travertine formations in the world.

The Great Fountain Geyser, Yellowstone National Park. Charles Cook, of the 1869 expedition, described their first view: 'The setting sun shining into the spray and steam drifting towards the mountains gave it the appearance of burnished gold, a wonderful sight. We could not contain our enthusiasm; with one accord we all took off our hats and yelled with all our might.'

discussed. In fact, Cook and his two companions had talked about it while in camp. An idea that had been centuries on its journey was ready to burst.

It was a year later, by a campfire in the same region, that it was finally stated. The expedition of 1870 was an able and influential group. Its leader was Henry Washburn, Indiana congressman, former major-general of the Civil War, and appointed by President Ulysses S. Grant to be Surveyor-General of Montana. He led a team of nineteen, which included Nathaniel Langford, a banker and protagonist of the Northern Pacific Railway, and Cornelius Hedges, a lawyer and correspondent. Protection from possible Indian attack was the role of a military escort commanded by Second Lieutenant Gustavus C. Doane, who had more than the attributes required of a soldier. He was a sensitive and accurate observer, and he could write. Even now, the Yellowstone he saw can come vividly to life. But history states that it was Cornelius Hedges who at last expressed the idea, at the first camp after leaving the lower Geyser Basin: '. . . when all were speculating which point in the region we had been through would become most notable when I first suggested uniting all our efforts to get it made a national park, little dreaming such a thing were possible'.

Washburn, Hedges and Langford not only had an idea, but also conviction and the means of spreading it. Washburn and Hedges wrote newspaper articles about the Yellowstone and what they had seen and done. Langford wrote also, and next winter gave a series of lectures in the East. One of those who heard his messages was Ferdinand Hayden, head of the Geological Survey of the Territories. Hayden sought an appropriation of forty thousand dollars from Congress for a survey of the area.

So in June 1871 Hayden, at the head of an expedition that included two talented visual artists, moved into the Yellowstone for what proved to be a successful and productive summer. The photographer William Jackson and artist Thomas Moran recorded events and scenic wonders.

The climax was swift. Action was needed if growing commercial interest in the area was to be forestalled. In both Congress and the Senate, in

Where it all began. Participants at an international seminar run by the US National Park Service hear about the camp-fire site on the opposite side of the Madison River, Wyoming, where the idea of reserving Yellowstone was proposed.

December 1871, Yellowstone was reserved 'from settlement, occupancy, or sale under the laws of the United States, and dedicated and set apart as a public park or pleasuring-ground for the benefit and enjoyment of the people'. President Grant signed the reservation into law on 1 March 1872. The idea's time had come, in a landmark victory of preservation over exploitation. Even in the nineteenth century, given traditional European and American attitudes to nature, the Yellowstone reservation was nothing short of remarkable.

The reservation of wild land was by no means a new idea. In the third century B.C. in India the Emperor Ashoka gave protection to fish, animals and forests. Small parklike areas were set aside for the preservation of modified forests and herds of hoofed animals in China centuries ago. During the Middle Ages sovereigns and princes of central and western Europe forbade hunting and lumbering in certain forest domains. Aztec rulers and African monarchs had made similar edicts. But the idea of reservation 'for the benefit and enjoyment of the people' was the outcome of centuries of turmoil and change.

From the earliest days of Western civilisation the wilderness had disappeared as agriculture spread and humans exploited the natural environment for their own purposes. Forests made way for crops, trees were felled

Lily pads growing in Riddle Lake, Yellowstone National Park.

to build ships and cities. If wilderness areas were protected, it was for hunting — a pastime that, arguably, has more to do with exploitation than preservation. Underlying these attitudes and practices was the axiomatic belief that people were superior to nature and thus had a right to impose their will upon it. It was a view upheld by Christian thought, which taught that God gave humanity 'dominion over the beasts of the field and the fowls of the air'.

The Pilgrim Fathers who landed at Massachusetts Bay in 1620 carried with them the farming practices of the English countryside and a Christian view of the world. Their 'Great Ponds' Act of 1649 was about the people's rights to enjoy public lands: 'Great ponds are . . . the property of the Commonwealth and fishing in them is free to the public.' Time saw the expansion of the colonies towards the Appalachian Mountains in the south and eventually west of the Hudson River in the north. As the settlers pushed west, their agrarian, European culture came into full-blown conflict with the land that had been the home of the American Indian for fifteen thousand years. Inevitably, the Indian nations were displaced from their land and the forests were eliminated to provide timber and space for crop growing. However, by 1763, vast as the colonies of the east had become, they were still largely contained within the Appalachian Mountains and a line east of Lake Erie, Ontario and the Saint Lawrence River.

It was a small part of the immense North American continent. Westwards lay the wilderness, dark, gloomy and untamed; known to be the haunt of Indians and wild animals, if not ogres and demons. This was the Biblical view of the wilderness — cursed, desolate, the opposite of a garden, a 'howling waste'. As it was a place of great hardship, the wilderness could also be a place of testing and purification. Driven by an agricultural culture and supported by their Christian view of the world, the pioneers set out to tame it.

Hunting, with its severe mental and physical challenges, frustrations and rewards, suited perfectly the wilderness ethos and the pioneer way of life. On the frontier, hunting was a necessity as well as a pursuit. But to hunt and fish was also the essence of a freedom to enjoy the natural world, which was to be an American. Hunting was not a privilege of class, as it was in Europe. Nevertheless, in the South, and elsewhere, shooting wild fowl, stalking deer and riding after hounds were soon the favourite recreation of wealthy land-owners.

It is apparent that in terms of humanity's relationship with its environment, colonisation was bound up in old values — values that put people before nature, farm ahead of forest and restricted enjoyment of the wilderness to sport. Before anything like a concept of reservation or park could evolve, the validity of these values would have to be challenged.

In ancient Britain and Europe centuries of forest laws had set aside wildlife and forest areas for the exclusive use of kings and the aristocracy for hunting. In contrast, the reservation of Yellowstone created a park open to all Americans. Embodied in the legislation was the notion of social equality — a relatively recent idea that had its origins in the French and American Revolutions. In 1776 this democratic ethos was enshrined in American law. The Declaration of Independence, less than a hundred years before Yellowstone, established one of the basic principles of national parks. It spoke of freedom and equality and of government proceeding upwards from the people. Notions about aristocracy were flatly rejected, as was, by implication, anything to do with aristocratic reservations for hunting — the cause of nature reservation in Europe, England and Africa.

The European philosophers Edmund Burke and Immanuel Kant in the late eighteenth century expressed thinking that made it possible to regard wild nature as aesthetically agreeable. Burke felt that terror and horror could stem from exultation, awe and delight. An English aesthetician defined 'picturesque' as the pleasing quality of nature's roughness. The deists accorded wilderness, as pure nature, special importance as the clearest medium through which God showed His power and excellence. This contrasted with cities and rural countryside, where humanity's works were imposed on those of God.

Romanticism and Primitivism contributed other perspectives to these changes of attitude. Romantics preferred the wild and rejected the ordered garden. The Primitivists believed that people's well-being decreased in proportion to their civilisation. Retreat to wilderness could be beneficial. Enthusiasm for noble savages and the wild in nature became popular amongst literary people. English poets attacked the 'smoky cities'. Daniel Defoe's story of Robinson Crusoe on his island was an immense success. Jean Jacques Rousseau argued persuasively that people should incorporate primitive qualities into their presently disordered lives.

The Indians and the vast forests of the New World attracted these romantic reactionaries of a civilisation from which wilderness and forests had departed. The North American wilderness was visited and written about. Byron, in *Don Juan*, wrote of 'pleasure in the pathless woods, rapture on the lonely shore'.

These sentiments would have cut little ice with most of those engaged in pushing back the frontier. But there were a few behind the line, from the cities, literature and the professions, who could identify with this thinking. Among them were surveyors, scientists and military men whose duties carried them into back country, city persons and literary folk who went to see for themselves. The Europeans had provided the eye for a new view of wilderness, and a vocabulary for describing that view. Occasionally it came from the frontiersmen themselves. 'No populous city,' declared Daniel Boone, 'with all the varieties of commerce and stately structures, could afford so much pleasure to my mind, as the beauties of nature I found here.'

Young nationhood, after independence and the national feelings it inspired, gave still more focus to the long reappraisal of the values of wilderness. There was Europe, rich in history, art and culture; wilderness was long departed. In the wilderness of nature the United States was unmatched. Scenery albums began to appear, and American poets and novelists turned their perceptions and their pens to the praise of natural America. Among the most famous of these was James Fennimore Cooper, whose stories were set in the plains and forests of the west. Thomas Cole, an artist from frontier Ohio, expressed the insights of the writers in his landscapes. He became famous as a celebrant of natural America, but his view was not total; rather, that an ideal society has its roots in both civilisation and wilderness, the one for culture, the other for vigour. Cole had spent three years painting in Europe. Perhaps he had noted that the Vandals who sacked Rome came from the wilderness.

Other artists followed. Thomas Moran, an exponent of huge canvases and dazzling colours, and the artist of the Hayden expedition, made his own very direct contribution to the birth of the national park idea. His paintings helped in the establishment of Yellowstone.

Onto the platform of ideas, perceptions, and changing attitudes stepped three figures whose prescient shadows reach us today: Henry David Thoreau, George Perkins Marsh and Frederick Law Olmsted. The contribution of each was different; the collective power of their thinking about the importance of wilderness to society remains stunning.

In character and career the three were disparate. Thoreau noted the spread of forest destruction moving west from a Massachusetts that had become like England. Attracted to wilderness, he went, in the spring of 1845, to live by a large pond near Concord in Massachusetts. His purpose was 'to transact some private business with the forest obstacles . . .' He built a log cabin and lived there for eighteen months. The essays in which he described life at Walden set out a philosophy of civilisation and wilderness, the inspiration and nourishment of civilised people. 'In wilderness,' said Thoreau, 'is the preservation of the world.'

The versatile and highly educated George Perkins Marsh related the observations of his early life on the frontier in Vermont to what he saw later in his extensive travels as American representative in Turkey and Italy. Land poverty, erosion and decline of productivity had destroyed the great civilisations that had been cradled in Asia Minor and Mediterranean Europe. His *Man and Nature*, he said, 'makes no scientific pretensions and will have no value for scientific men.' In fact, it exercised enormous influence. In his 1864

William Fox painted several scenes at Yosemite, including this watercolour of the Cathedral Rocks, on one of his visits to the United States in 1853 and 1875.

edition Marsh suggested that 'the invasion of New Zealand by people, plants and animals, the South Island' could be the subject of a study. By 1868 *Man and Nature* was exercising its influence in New Zealand, being read and quoted by Thomas Potts, Arthur Dudley Dobson and other observers of events on the New Zealand frontier.

In 1864, the year in which *Man and Nature* was published, the American Congress granted to the state of California a tract of land of about ten square miles, which included the spectacular canyons of the Yosemite Valley. The express condition of the grant was that 'the premises shall be held for public use, resort, and recreation; shall be held inalienable for all times'. The overture to the Yellowstone decision was being played. The conductor was Frederick Law Olmsted, first superintendent of Central Park in New York City, and driving force of the new idea of the park as a playground for the nation. 'Great public parks,' said Olmsted, 'must be managed for the benefit and the free use of the people . . . unless means are taken by government to withhold them from the grasp of individuals, all places favourable in scenery to the recreation of the mind and body, will be closed against the great body of the people.'

The Yosemite Valley and its giant redwoods had been threatened by private exploitation in the 1860s. The Congressional grant placed the land under state control.

So far, so good, but what responsibility was the state to exercise? Olmsted, one of the recently appointed commissioners of the new park, was in no doubt. His advisory report was a powerful argument that the state of California had a 'duty of preservation'. With state acceptance, a further step had been taken. At this point the concept of 'national park' was but a step away. The idea awaited its situation, and found it in the valley of the upper Yellowstone in the Rocky Mountains.

The idea was brand-new, untested, unexplored, and to some, unacceptable. One hundred years later we know much more about its difficulties and complexities, that it can be interpreted in different ways and that there will forever be a built-in tension between the ideal of preservation and the benefit and enjoyment of people.

GEORGE PERKINS MARSH (1801–1882)

From a modest beginning on the frontier of Vermont, Marsh fought against personal difficulties to become one of America's most respected men. He had a distinguished political career, serving as a member of Congress, helping establish the Smithsonian Institution and becoming United States Minister to Turkey and subsequently to Italy.

Marsh's diplomatic positions in Europe gave him an opportunity to travel, collect plants and animals for the Smithsonian and compare the Old and New Worlds, observing human impact on the landscape. He became aware of the inevitably damaging effects on the environment of such processes as forest clearance and water pollution.

His influential work *Man and Nature* was the first book to dispute the popular belief in nature's superabundance and to advocate the need for conservation of natural resources. The work begins with an examination of the decay of the territory of the Roman Empire. While some natural factors may have been involved, the major cause of disaster is 'man's ignorant disregard of the laws of nature'. Marsh agreed that there was much uncertainty about the relative effects of natural factors and those induced by man, and suggests that the careful observation and study of recently colonised areas, such as the South Island of New Zealand, could throw light on the subject. In 1868 *Man and Nature* was cited by Potts in the New Zealand House of Representatives in moving in favour of 'steps to ascertain the present conditions of Forests of the Colony, with a view to their better conservation'.

The book was widely acclaimed for its compelling argument for the prudent management of the thin earth skin on which all life depends.

Lone Star Geyser in Yellowstone
National Park in maximum eruption.

As always, the label of 'national park' immediately attracted visitors. 'National park' is the seal of quality, a national guarantee of the finest and most representative nature. So tourists came to Yellowstone, not really knowing what they could do, any more than an administration starved of resources knew how to manage. Elk, bison and bears were shot by hunters who believed they were in a game reserve. Bandits held up stage coaches, ranchers brought in cattle, and sightseers damaged the thermal areas, souveniring encrustations and liberally soaping geysers and hotpools in the expectation of eruptions. Indian resentment of the changes led to attacks.

The idea almost foundered, administration sagged, and in 1886 the Army was brought in to run the park. It did so for thirty years. Misuse was controlled but there was still a great deal to be learned about the management of nature in 'natural' places. When there was concern at the population levels of bison, elk and deer, their predators — mountain lions, wolves and coyotes — were shot. Modern management of ecosystems would intervene in a normally functioning predator-prey situation only if a natural cycle was seriously imbalanced by unusual events, as when elephants are culled to limit forest destruction in some of the African parks. In Yellowstone, first lessons in wildlife management were being learned.

In this laboratory of an idea, objectives and management were sorely tested, clarified, won through and achieved public support. Congress declared other national parks: the towering ice-carved granite walls of Yosemite, the giant ancient redwoods of Sequoia, the forests, meadows and high volcanic

Winter is hard in the central Rocky Mountains. A bison forages in the Yellowstone River valley.

peak of Mount Rainier, the multi-coloured walls and blue splendour of Crater Lake, the dramatic stalactites and stalagmites of Carlsbad Caverns, Mesa Verde with its human heritage record of the cliff-dwelling Indians, the Grand Canyon and the grizzlies and bighorn sheep of Glacier National Park in the Rocky Mountains on the Canadian border. The US National Park Service was set up in 1916. Forty years' hard experience clarified the legislative directions to the new service: 'To conserve the scenery and the natural and historic objects and the wildlife therein and to provide for the enjoyment of the same in such manner and by such means as will leave them unimpaired for the enjoyment of future generations.'

Chapter 4

The Parks and New Zealand's Natural Heritage

The term 'national park' means just that — especially the designation 'national'. It means scenery, plants and wildlife that are distinctively a country's own. While on continents, plants and animals may cross national frontiers and be common to whole regions; in New Zealand, 'distinctive' is especially pointed as so much here occurs nowhere else. More than eight in every ten of our native flowering plants, fish and insect species are found only in New Zealand. The ability of birds to cross oceans means that the proportion of endemic species is lower: six in ten.

Even if some very important sections are missing, the parks and reserves are living libraries of the natural history of the 'ancient islands'. In their forests live much of what we have left of the endemic plants and animals. Their scenery illustrates the immense forces that have shaped the present-day New Zealand landscape. Here is Aotearoa as the Maori knew it. The way national parks are selected means that they include our finest scenery and the best examples we have left of different types of forest, alpine vegetation and wetland. Scientific work in the parks studies ecosystems that are the product of millions of years of evolution.

How does one use this library to understand the extraordinary story of New Zealand evolution the parks have to tell? Much is done to help by park handbooks, displays in the visitor centres and lectures and interpretative programmes given by the rangers. There are scientific papers and bibliographies for those who wish to delve more deeply. One preliminary step, however, will help greatly. To understand best it is necessary to grapple with a different dimension of time than the one we customarily use.

How long is eighty million years? The mathematically inclined might like to relate this problem to distance. Assume, for example, that you are standing and looking at an object one kilometre away. If the kilometre is made to represent eighty million years, the whole of the thousand years of human presence in New Zealand is represented by the last twelve millimetres, or half-inch, of time. Events in this mere fraction of time have had a profound effect on the rest of the kilometre. And that kilometre is really only a small part of the overall distance. The ancestral line of our podocarp forests dates back almost four kilometres. It is sixty kilometres to the formation of Planet Earth.

Those who prefer to feel rather than think the time dimension could do no better than to go into one of the parks. Let us choose, say, a spot in Fiord-

Visitor centres are provided to contribute to the pleasure and interest of coming to the park. Displays offer information about the history and nature of the park region. This one describes plants and points of interest to be found on walks in Egmont National Park.

Summer programmes of talks and guided excursions by the park rangers are very popular. This talk by a ranger at the visitor centre in Urewera National Park has clearly captured the interest of the audience.

land National Park, a little off the Milford Track in the valley of the Arthur River on a still, warm day in early summer. It will be wet on the ground, so relax against your parka on a tree. Let your mind float off into space, and feel time, millions and millions of years of it . . . endless. Whether you sense or hear the indefinable background of the stirring of the beech forest mingled with echoes of a hundred waterfalls, you will not know. But then — sound unmistakable — the rattle of a stone falling down a scree slope. There is no one there! That booming distant noise of thunder was an avalanche. The planet is going about its work. It is work that has once already reduced to sea-washed plains the mountains thrust from the ocean floor to form land that geological investigation but neither shape nor position can recognise as ancestral New Zealand.

But another very important idea must be added to the time dimension before the detailed story told by particular parks can be properly appreciated. This is the idea of the movement of continental plates.

Concealed under the world's oceans, and virtually circling the globe, lie mountain chains, called mid-oceanic ridges. Along these ridges the earth's crust is being torn apart, forming rifts thousands of kilometres long. Hot lava from below wells into the rifts, solidifies and splits again. New lava enters and the process cycles on. This is 'sea floor spreading' and the vast plates of the earth's crust are 'rafted' by this process. The presence of great trenches in the ocean floor, complementary to the oceanic ridges, explains why the world is not continuously expanding. Near the trenches, the moving sea floor, with its accumulated layers of sediments from land erosion, sinks down towards the heat of the earth's core. The mixture begins to melt and the molten product finds its way to the surface in volcanic activity, which can be extremely violent.

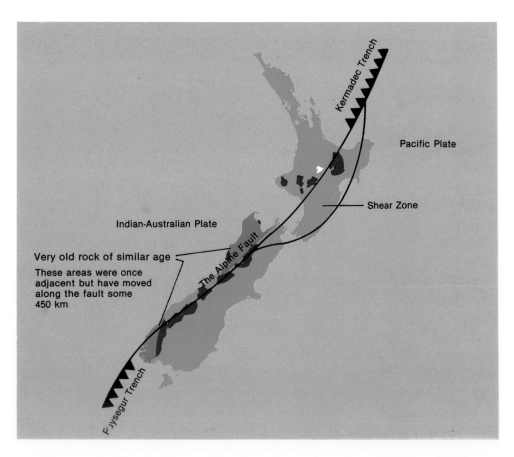

Parks and Plates.

New Zealand lies on the meeting place of two of the rafting plates, the Indian-Australian Plate to the west and the Pacific Plate to the east. The volcanoes of Tongariro National Park are visible evidence of events in the north, where the Pacific Plate sinks down (subducts) under the Indian-Australian Plate, but in the south it over-rides, driving up the Southern Alps.

The movement between the plates is a huge shearing action, with the Australian Plate going north and the Pacific Plate to the south. The result is the Alpine Fault, a gigantic feature of global size running along the western side of the Southern Alps, then swinging north-east through Nelson Lakes National Park to link with fault systems in the North Island by way of the Wairau Valley and Cook Strait. Several of our parks, therefore, have an additional dimension of interest because of their position near the meeting place of two of the earth's crustal plates. In the north, the boundary above which the Tongariro volcanoes sit extends north-east to the sea and into the subduction zone of the Kermadec Trench. In the south, the Alpine Fault leaves the land near Milford Sound to connect into the Puysegur Trench.

All the parks in the North Island are examples of a volcanic history that has contributed much to scenery, not only in its molding of the land, but also in the production of fertile volcanic soils, which have shaped natural as well as human history. The volcanic features of the Bay of Islands Maritime and Historic Park range in age up to twenty million years. Those of the Hauraki Gulf Maritime Park include the classical symmetry of Rangitoto, where evidence suggests that eruptions began only eight hundred years ago with the most recent events being just over two hundred years into the past. The major volcanoes of the Tongariro National Park have been active for about one million years, while the volcanoes of Egmont National Park range from the youthful Mount Egmont (Taranaki), perhaps only seventy thousand years old and last in eruption a little over three hundred years ago, to the progressively older Pouakai and Kaitaki volcanoes, eroded by the action of ice and water to much lower than original levels. Both the Whanganui and Urewera National

The impressive outcrop of St Pauls Rock Scenic Reserve, Bay of Islands Maritime and Historic Park, stands above the township at Whangaroa Harbour. The reserve protects a remnant of volcanic activity of about twenty million years ago.

Ngauruhoe in eruption provides visual confirmation of volcanic power. The mountain has been erupting intermittently for about two thousand five hundred years and is still in its cone-building stage.

In this view the Alpine Fault runs north-east along Speargrass Valley in Nelson Lakes National Park. In the distance it swings further east across the northern end of Lake Rotoiti and into the Wairau Valley.

Parks have at times been mantled by ash and pumice from great explosions in the Taupo region.

So the geological interest of volcanoes in the North Island parks belongs firstly to their association with a feature of global scale, and secondly to a variety that is a product of age difference, the effect of erosion and the differing composition of the eruptive material thrown out by the volcanoes.

Like the parks of the North, the alpine parks of the South Island have the additional interest of the great conflict of the plates. In other respects the contrast is total. There are no evident volcanic features. The Pacific Plate is overriding, not subducting. The mountains, and the Alpine Fault at their western toe, are perhaps even more striking evidence than northern volcanoes of the titanic scale of the crustal conflict. The Alpine Fault is clearly evident in Nelson Lakes National Park. As it runs south-east it passes through Lewis Pass National Reserve, to the west of Arthur's Pass National Park, west of Mount Aspiring National Park and out to sea in the north-western corner of Fiordland National Park.

Volcanoes shape the land with great cones like Ngauruhoe, with the materials ejected, to be carried by wind or flow as lava or lahars (mud flows) across the countryside. Erosion by wind and water shapes, carries and distributes the soft ashes and pumices. All these processes are interpreted and can be observed in the North Island parks.

Again, there is a contrast with the South. The rocks of the Alps may in places be volcanic in their origin, or deposited once as sediments on the sea floor, to be then compressed into rock by accumulating weight, or hardened and changed in composition by combinations of heat and pressure. Even so, they are generally hard and resistant to, if eventually conquered by, the erosion processes that shape the alpine landscape.

A névé, where the snows collect and compress into the ice that feeds the glacier. The head of the Dart Glacier in Mount Aspiring National Park.

A graphic example of glacial action. The path of a former glacier in Nelson Lakes National Park, with the lateral and terminal moraines clearly evident.

The sense of glacial movement is captured in this photograph of the Volta Glacier in Mount Aspiring National Park.

Nature's erosion battery is formidable and the results of its work extremely visible — the freeze-thaw splitting of rock into the fragmented slopes known as screes, the avalanches, the mighty bulldozing of glaciers, the buzz-saw action of rivers whose whole beds become alive in flood, and the fiendish fury of a mountain storm.

The achievements of the erosion battery are evident in all the southern parks, but particular parks provide individual examples. While Arthur's Pass National Park is now the northern limit of active glaciers in the South Island, the work of the great glaciers of the ice-age period of the past two million years can be seen throughout the South Island and in all the alpine parks. As might be expected, the great U-shaped valleys, the hanging valleys and the fiords themselves in Fiordland National Park demonstrate ice-age sculpture at an enormous scale. The national parks of the Main Divide — Mount Aspiring, Westland, Mount Cook and Arthur's Pass — all provide working examples of the whole sequence of glaciation, from the huge snowfields feeding the ice rivers to the moraines where debris collects at their feet. Westland National Park, extending from the mountains to the sea, also encompasses the ice-laden rivers — in fact, the whole of a huge glacial drainage system. It also surrounds vast forest-covered moraines, the legacy of the ice-age period when glaciers extended well beyond the modern-day coastline.

Glaciation is, of course, but one facet of the work of water. In storms all the national parks provide dramatic examples of this primary agent of erosion at work. There is no more impressive environment than Fiordland National Park in heavy rain. Far above the walker on the Milford Track, the bare, dark mountain slopes are festooned with falling veils of water, whipped into spray by the wind. Collecting torrents plunge into streams alongside the track. The streams disgorge into foaming rivers. The world becomes confined by torrential rain and thundering water.

Water at work. A waterfall in the valley of the upper Arawata River, Mount Aspiring National Park.

Shingle beds of the mighty Arawata
River, with Mount Aspiring National
Park on the left (the Haast Range) and in
the distance.

New Zealand has been described as a 'geological textbook' because the landscape is young and the processes that shape it are very evident. The national parks, with the interpretation of events provided in the visitor centres and by the full-scale working models outside, are like the illustrated pages of the textbook.

Beneath the young landscape, however, lie rocks that vary greatly in geological age, and from which geologists can read a story stretching over aeons of time; erosion, volcanism and mountain building being the dominant processes. Included within the Paparoa National Park is an area composed of possibly the oldest rock in New Zealand, formed from sediments deposited on the ocean floor seven hundred million years ago, in what is known as the Pre-Cambrian geological period. In contrast, the sandstones and mudstones ('papa' rock) of the Whanganui National Park are geologically young, varying in age from a youthful thirty million years inland towards Taumarunui, to geological infancy, just a few million years, nearer the still-rising coastline.

Why the difference beneath the surface of the land we see and use today? In all the national parks this 'story of the rocks' is told — the stranger-than-fiction history of the errant land mass, once part of a great supercontinent called Gondwanaland, which was split apart by sea-floor spreading some eighty million years ago.

The supercontinent of Gondwanaland embraced South America, Africa, Australia and Antarctica. Prior to the onset of sea-floor spreading, New Zealand was an area on the adjacent ocean floor. Collision of the crustal plates then thrust ancestral Aotearoa above the ocean. The Tasman Sea formed as

the land rafted eastwards over the period of eighty to sixty million years ago, then becoming fixed in relation to Australia while sea-floor spreading developed between Australia and Antarctica to form the Southern Ocean.

Of course, the New Zealand raft had a cargo on board — the plants and animals that were themselves the result of millions of years of evolutionary history on the supercontinent. Carried away from the vast continental region in which they had evolved, and across which they had dispersed, increasingly isolated as the voyage continued and no longer part of future continental evolution, they became the raw material for a separate island-confined evolution.

The plants and animals of the voyage related particularly to the Australian and Antarctic continental areas that had adjoined the sea basin from which ancestral Aotearoa had emerged. The plants were the ancestors of New Zealand native forest, including kauri, the podocarps (miro, totara, matai, kahikatea, rimu), the beeches, manuka, rata, proteas, tree ferns and shrubs.

The travelling animals were few: ratite birds (moas and kiwis), perhaps takahe, kakapo, weka and a few others; reptiles — tuatara and geckos; large land snails, frogs and a range of insects, of which the most interesting and ancient were the wetas. Of immense significance to subsequent evolution was the absence from the cargo of predatory and browsing mammals. The only mammalian representatives were two species of bat. Most of the mammalian order were yet to evolve.

Sixty million years ago the raft came to anchor. In the inland environment birds grew larger and the colour of some species tended to darken. The absence of predators encouraged loss of flight and promoted diversity in the insect world. Bird colonists flew in at intervals, mostly from Australia, and the range of bird species increased.

Over the vast time span that elapsed before the coming of the Polynesians,

Stories in the rocks. Originally laid down under the sea, then uplifted to be exposed to the eroding action of waves and wind, the pancake rocks of Paparoa National Park reveal a small facet of the geological epic.

Kiwi and moa were among the original cargo.

Several species of large and handsome native land snails are to be found in a number of New Zealand's protected areas.

Hamilton's frog. New Zealand's primitive frogs do not seem to need running or standing water. They inhabit a range of forest and grassland environments.

the cargo was subjected to land uplift and submergence, volcanic action and earthquakes, and the great climatic changes of the ice ages. The Polynesian canoes arrived on the coast of what in some respects could be called a time capsule. Except for the high mountains and areas of volcanic destruction, the islands were covered with 'dinosaur' forest.

What has happened since is the story of this book — the struggle between human needs as perceived from a cultural focus and the slow recognition of the uniqueness of the time capsule, the sensitivity of the ecology and the instability of its landscape. The significance of the national parks and reserves can be assessed more readily from an account (even if greatly condensed) of the natural history of the capsule.

As with the discussion about time and evolution, the broad grasp of two situations will help an appreciation of the value and importance of national parks and reserves as the living museums of the dinosaur forests. The first is the ecological diversity of New Zealand. This is explained simply — the country is elongated and mountainous. It covers an extensive band of latitude. The range of climate is, therefore, considerable and this range can be increased further by height. In addition, whole regions can be isolated by mountain ranges. The habitats of plants and animals can be extremely local- ised, and varied in the character of their climate and soil. In summary, this small country has nearly two hundred and seventy distinctive ecological districts and a greater ecological diversity than Australia.

The second factor relates to altitude difference. In a mountain situation, plants tend to find bands of suitable altitude. Often the highest tree species

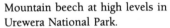

The distinctive form and beauty of beech forest of mid and lower levels is evident on the Maungapohatu road in Urewera National Park.

Mountain beech at high levels in Urewera National Park.

A fine stand of nikau at Kaihoka Lakes Scenic Reserve in Nelson lends a tropical aspect to the lowland podocarp-hardwood forest of the reserve.

in the harshest environments is the mountain beech. As altitude lowers, other beech species come in. At even lower levels the hardier podocarp species mix with beech forest. It is only in lowland areas that New Zealand forests attain their richest development in mixed podocarp-hardwood communities — the typical temperate rainforests of New Zealand.

Thus, it is not hard to understand why each national park and reserve is almost certain to be representative of a different ecological region or regions, and why the altitudinal variation of forest within a park will be distinctive in its own right. And, given the insistence of colonial development that land suited for settlement must not be reserved it is clear why the rich podocarp forests are not well represented within the protected-area system.

Since land suitable for colonial agricultural settlement was primarily the easier lowlands, it is predominantly steep-country protection forest that is left undeveloped in 1987. The lowland forests are, however, the richest habitats, for birds as well as for the insect life that is itself the staple food of ground-dwellers like the kiwi. Almost all native birds show a year-round preference for the warmer microclimates and more abundant food choices of this most diverse forest mixture.

Large continuous tracts of lowland podocarp forest are reserved only in Whanganui National Park in the North Island, and the Paparoa National Park and a coastal strip of Westland National Park in the South. While most of the other national parks have some podocarp forest at their lower altitudes, it is the hardy beech that predominates. There is one remarkable exception, which illustrates well the ecological variation that can occur from region to adjacent

Like most native birds, the kereru (New Zealand pigeon), known for its partiality to the fruit of the miro, favours lowland podocarp forest and is rarely seen in beech forest.

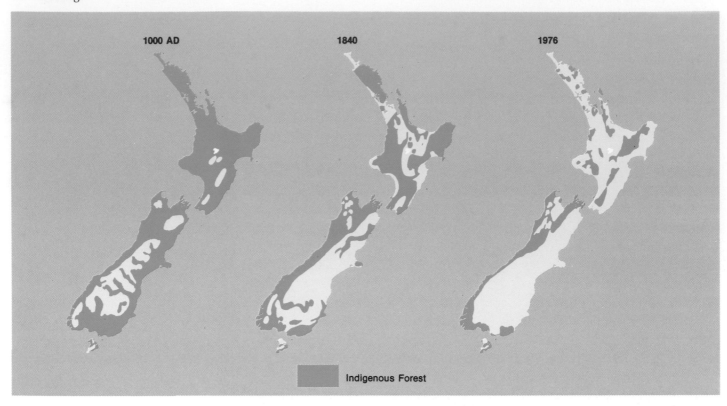

1000 AD   1840   1976

Indigenous Forest

The reduction of New Zealand's indigenous forest.

region. Egmont National Park, well endowed with lowland forest species, lacks many types of mountain trees and is totally without beeches.

The forests have been the centre of controversy for more than a hundred years, during which time there has been a growing awareness of the unique natural environment in New Zealand. But our tree species are just a fraction of the total range of indigenous plants. There are many other plants and habitats, such as tussock and native grasslands, sand-dunes and mangrove and saltmarsh estuaries, wetlands and shrublands, that should be represented in the living museums, not only for what they have to say about the essential character of New Zealand, but also for their value to science and education.

Some are included already, like the tussock grassland of the desert area of Tongariro National Park and high-country tussock and native grasslands in

Mangroves near the Waitangi National Reserve are an example of a habitat that is insufficiently represented in reservation.

This tussock grassland, with its clumps of matagouri, in Mount Cook National Park is an example of the once extensive but now under-represented tussock lands.

the South Island parks. The grassland representation, however, is small, for the same reason that lowland forests are under-represented. The grasslands were well suited to the needs of a farming culture. Burnt, grazed and fertilised, their ecology and composition were greatly changed. The Protected Natural Areas programme discussed in Chapter 15 is the response of the 1980s to the challenge of a reservation system intended to sample the greatest possible range of the diversity of original nature.

Beautiful and magnificent as are the parks, it should not be assumed that they are the image of pristine Aotearoa at the arrival of the Polynesians. Two eras of colonisation have caused extensive change in their ecosystems, native birds being affected most of all. Seven bird species have become extinct during the period of European settlement and more than twenty species are endangered or rare. Removal of forest habitat, particularly preferred lowland forest, and the depredations of some of the twenty foreign species of introduced mammals occupying forest habitats has reduced almost eighty species of native land and freshwater birds to fewer than one dozen species in abundance.

So while the call of the kiwi is heard, and the extraordinary music of the kokako, while bellbirds energetically sing their territorial songs to park visitors, who also delight in the attendance of an inquisitive and fearless robin, it is a rare and treasured occasion on which the forests ring with song as they surely did in days past.

The parks and reserves have become the last refuges of endangered species, the scene of rescue operations and of searches for the last representatives of dying breeds. The kakapo, a flightless bush parrot, clings to a precarious existence in the native reserves of southern Stewart Island, but may be doomed to extinction from attacks by feral cats. Another flightless bird, thought to have been extinct, was rediscovered in 1948 in a remote valley of

Ferrets, stoats and weasels were imported in the 1880s to help, it was thought, with the attack on the rabbit plague. They helped as well with the attack on indigenous bird life.

The rare kakapo

Takahe

Tuatara

The saddleback, while extinct in mainland New Zealand, is thriving on several offshore island reserves.

In common with species of the great range of marine birds from the oceans around New Zealand, the gannet (takapu) nests mainly on offshore islands. The Cape Kidnappers sanctuary is the only major nesting area on the mainland.

Fiordland National Park. Since then the colony of takahe has barely held its own. A breeding programme has commenced, aimed at increasing the wild population and establishing new colonies. There has been recent concern for the kea, fearless clown of the alpine regions. In the battle to save the remnants of a once abundant bird life, the national parks and reserves have a vital role.

Offshore island reserves are priceless sanctuaries for species reduced to critically low numbers on the mainland. Tuatara, the only remaining example of an order of reptiles that became extinct elsewhere about one hundred million years ago, now survive on only about twenty islands. Kakapo have been transferred to Little Barrier Island Nature Reserve and takahe to Maud Island in the Marlborough Sounds. The eradication of opossum from the Kapiti Island Nature Reserve has saved the forest habitat of one of the most important sanctuaries, host to a population of the rare little spotted kiwi as well as recently introduced saddlebacks, which now thrive on several of the island reserves.

In relation to New Zealand's national heritage, the parks and reserves may be seen as comprising four elements: the national parks, the mainland reserves, the offshore island reserves and the protected area system. These elements are complementary — each as important as the other. All contain representation of the ecological variety and genetic stock of a rare evolutionary event. Endangered bird life is protected in the offshore island reserves, whose subantarctic component is, as well, of world importance as a haven and nesting area for the wild nature of the Southern Ocean.

After one hundred years, while much remains to be done, the shape as well as the challenge of a potentially superb reservation system are both evident. In 1987 the element most in need of attention is that of protected areas, the insurance that all the ecological districts of New Zealand will have their samples and examples, the insurance that the New Zealand landscape of the future will carry the signature of its unique inheritance.

Chapter 5

Te Whenua, Te Iwi

Fiercely plies the shaft of this my paddle,
Named Kautu-ki-te-rangi,
To the heavens raise it, to the skies uplift it.
It guides to the distant horizon,
To the horizon that seems to draw near,
To the horizon that instils fear,
To the horizon that causes dread,
To the horizon of unknown power,
Bounded by sacred restrictions.
Along this unknown course,
Our ship must brave the waves below,
Our ship must fight the storms above.
This course must be followed
By chief and priest and crew,
But place our trust in Rehua
And through him we'll reach the land of light.
O Rongo-and-Tane, we raise our offering.

Te Rangihiroa (Sir Peter Buck) made a free translation of this canoe-paddling song, attributed to Ngati Ruanui, which captures well the hopes and anxieties of a long ocean voyage. It appears that the original Maori has been lost.

When, at some time in the eighth century, the people whose descendants would in the course of time become the New Zealand Maori came to a strange, steep, forest-covered land without people, their landfall was one of the last major achievements of a migrational impulse that had started some five or six thousand years before. Human beings had indeed left what is now South-East Asia between forty and thirty thousand years B.C. to establish themselves in Australia and New Guinea, but it was a 'second wave' of migrants, the Austronesians, who were to push further into the Pacific. These people also originated in Asia, but their culture had developed beyond the hunter-gatherer one of the early travellers. The newcomers had sailing canoes with outriggers, which made long journeys safer and more certain. Furthermore, they knew about root crops and pig farming, which allowed them to

---

Te whenua, te iwi — The land, the people. To fully understand the gift of the Tongariro mountain peaks, one must appreciate that to Maori people land and people can be one. Te whenua means the placenta, or afterbirth, as well as the land.

settle areas that could not support a hunter-gatherer way of life. From these migrants evolved the Melanesian and Polynesian peoples and cultures of later times as their movement continued, with stops and starts and long intervals, across the Pacific, expanding to north and south but always following one general direction — to the east.

Archaeologists have established that an Austronesian-type culture was present in New Caledonia around 2000 B.C. Fiji was settled some five hundred years later, and Tonga and Samoa shortly after that.

When, over a thousand years later, 'the most daring of neolithic navigators and explorers in the history of mankind', to use the words of Elsdon Best, once more sailed their great canoes towards the morning, their occupants carried with them a culture that had become distinctively Polynesian. The earliest settlement yet discovered east of Tonga/Samoa is in the Marquesas, and probably occurred some time in the first centuries A.D. From this group further voyages fanned out throughout east Polynesia to Easter Island (A.D. 400), Hawaii and the Society Islands (both A.D. 600) and finally to New Zealand (about A.D. 750). Other settlements, such as the atolls of Tokelau and Tuvalu, were probably later still — the Tokelaus in A.D. 1000, the Ellice Islands perhaps as late as A.D. 1400.

These forebears of the Maori, then, inherited a tradition — tested and shaped by experience — of voyaging to make a life in a new land. This determined much of their response to the new environment of Aotearoa in which they found themselves.

First, it is certain that they did not arrive in New Zealand as the result of an unplanned 'drift' journey. Indeed, most significant travel within the Pacific seems to have been planned: at least in the sense that the travellers prepared

Pacific settlement

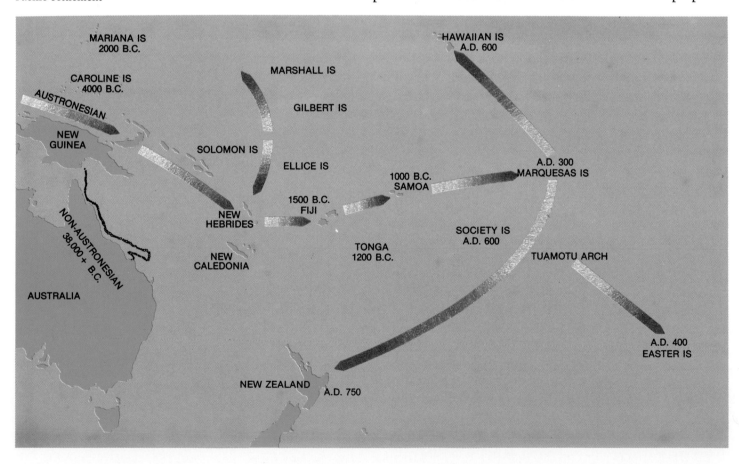

deliberately, even if they were not sure what they would eventually find. Recently it has been shown that many of what are now the region's staple food plants are not indigenous to central and eastern Polynesia and must have been deliberately introduced as carefully packed tubers or rhizomes. Dogs, pigs and chickens were also taken from a homeland to the new territory. The kumara, yam, taro, gourd and paper mulberry were brought by the Maori to New Zealand as the result of forethought and intention to settle whatever land was found.

Probably these people had other food plants with them too — sugar cane, breadfruit, bananas — but found they soon died in a comparatively cold, harsh climate. That these, and pigs and chickens, were not known to the Maori of later times, suggests that return voyages for new stocks could not be made, in spite of the probability that comprehensive Polynesian seamanship had navigated the outwards journey. As a result of this and other evidence, scholars and archaeologists now discount earlier theories of a voyage of exploration, followed by a return home and the setting-out of a 'Great Fleet'. The archaeological signs point to one or more independent migrating groups from the same region, forced to leave their land of origin perhaps by over-population and a scarcity of resources, by war, or the hostility of another group. While the 'canoe traditions' of the Maori may well have originated not from actual boats but from movements within the country after their ancestors reached New Zealand, or from the star-paths used as navigational aids, their importance in Maori oral history and in whakapapa, or genealogies, is in no way lessened.

As the wave of Polynesian settlement fanned out over the Pacific Island groups, a definite social pattern had emerged, which can now — through the efforts of archaeologists — be retraced. This pattern holds good in Tonga, Samoa, the Marquesas and Society Islands, in Hawaii and, with significant differences, in New Zealand.

First came the 'initial settlement' phase. The voyagers landed, settled in the most favourable locations (on the coast, near river mouths, on flat land) and established horticulture. If need be, forest was cleared and burned. After a few hundred years the pressure of a growing population on limited resources would lead to movement into the interior and areas that were more difficult to cultivate. This was the second or 'expansion' phase. Evidence of warfare begins to be found, demonstrating perhaps that local populations were large enough to cause friction. The third or 'elaboration' phase occurred when a certain density was reached in the ratio of land to population. Social energy could no longer move outward into further settlement, since most cultivable land was taken up. Instead, it worked internally to produce social stratification, evidenced by elaborate religious ceremonies and hierarchies and the emergence of supraterritorial leaders and policies. Centuries later, at the time of European contact, many of the island groups had well-defined aristocratic and priestly castes who were able to command a lower-ranking population, with a slave class at the very bottom. In our own time, archaeologists have uncovered the huge temples and ceremonial structures built by order of the ruling class, which used labour and resources from distant localities. That none of this occurred in New Zealand can be attributed to its physical differences — of climate and topography — and especially its much greater extent.

The initial settlement period began the moment those first travellers stepped ashore, to find themselves in a very different environment from the one they had left. The climate was much colder, the land thickly forested, the soils heavy. Here, nevertheless, they struggled to establish the horticultural food economy that had supported them in the homelands. Although the tropical or subtropical Polynesian island groups were far more hospitable, they contained a great variety of local environments, which meant that different techniques were needed to grow even one crop in different places. Adaptability and experimentation were familiar concepts in Polynesian horticulture, and the new settlers were accustomed to the idea of careful techniques to help crop growth and storage.

Horticulture could only be practised, of course, after careful preparation. The early Maori would have cleared the bush using traditional slash-and-burn techniques, thus beginning to modify the hitherto untouched environment — burning-over affects soil, regrowth, and the plant sequence that is eventually re-established. In their gardens (often very extensive), they practised soil improvements — using drainage, mulching, water control and gravel to improve soil structure. Stone walls provided shelter as well as defining different crops and activities. The ground was carefully picked over to ensure that no weeds became established, and at certain times of the year temporary huts were built so that continuous attention could be given to the crops.

The continuous food production of the tropics was not possible here — something the new arrivals probably realised after their first winter. The food plants that survived and became important were those reaching maturity in the shortest time, and even these had to be stored over the cold months to ensure both an immediate food supply and seed for re-planting next spring. The kumara, which matures in only five months, became the staple crop. To preserve these root vegetables, familiar storage techniques — such as those for yams — were adapted and reapplied in new ways, and an entirely new method, pit storage, was invented.

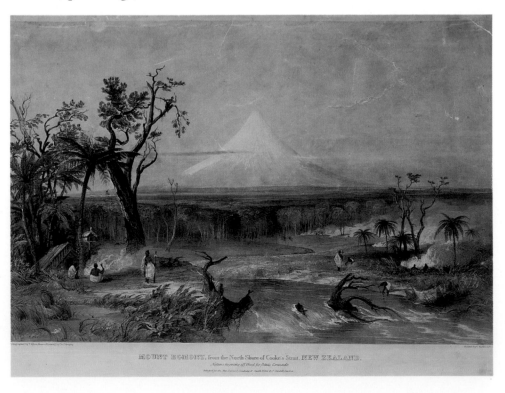

'Mount Egmont from the North Shore of Cooke's Strait' — Charles Heaphy, 1842. Burning off for potato grounds was a common method of preparing ground for cultivation. Explorers from Captain Cook's time onward noted evidence of fires that often continued for days.

These photographs show clearly the traces of ancient Maori horticultural systems. Artificial lines or ridges dividing the garden plots can be seen, as can the stone mounds. The mounds were sometimes merely the result of clearing the ground, but might also be deliberately constructed over a core of humus as a device to grow kumara.

Maori gardening involved significant modifications to the natural environment, including soil drainage, soil modification through the addition of ash or gravel and provision of pits, mounds and walls to provide the best crop-growing conditions.

Horticulture remained, as it was throughout Polynesia, a food source that could be guaranteed by hard and continuous work. Owing to its seasonal and partial nature in a temperate climate, however, its relative importance declined and that of other resources increased.

Early settlement was established, no doubt, in the most favourable locations — as near to as many food sources as possible, on flattish land and close to avenues of transport and communication. These requirements were usually best met on the coast and/or near a river mouth. Here it was possible to take food from river, sea and forest.

The bounty of the sea, the 'kai moana', was always present — fish, crayfish, shellfish and porpoises. There were eels in the rivers and birds in the forests, wetlands and on the coasts. Eels, sea fish and shellfish could be preserved by drying, while rats and birds could be stored, surrounded by fat in gourds or kelp bags.

For the first few centuries, and particularly in the south, seals and moa were a very important food resource. Moa, in one or more of its species, from the three-metre-tall *Dinornis* to the much smaller *Euryapteryx*, was present in most regions. But by the fourteenth century it was becoming scarce in most regions, and by the sixteenth had been almost eliminated, although some may have survived in the interior of the South Island until the eighteenth century. By this time seal species, too, had been reduced in numbers. Even the fur seal, which the first settlers had found breeding all around the New Zealand coasts up to and including the far north, were now rare except in the remote south.

Even before the moa had gone, hunting had eliminated some distinguished bird species such as the bush eagle, a pelican and a flightless goose. As many as forty species, a whole range of bird life, were extinguished in the longer term by hunting and the extensive use of fire.

The wood pigeon (kereru) was an important item of Maori diet. The water trough with snares, while not the only means of catching pigeons, illustrated well the care and skill that alone ensured success in food gathering to a people with limited technical resources but with great powers of observation. After feeding on the fruit of the miro, pigeons would become thirsty. As the birds raised their heads after drinking, they would be caught in nooses.

Fish, shellfish and other kai moana were important items in the diet of coastal groups; an importance that can be gauged by the dozens of specialised terms relating to the ocean, the shore, fishing activities and the species of marine life. As with other food sources, they were exploited with care when at their prime, after which the hapu would move on until the next year or season.

Large shell middens, however, like this one in Northland show that the tribe might take full advantage of this resource at the right time.

Plants native to New Zealand were also utilised, although they did not receive the intense cultivation of the introduced crops. The new country was not, after all, a totally alien environment; a number of plant genera found in Polynesia are found here as well. The Maori noted this, as was demonstrated by their occasional transference of words used in the Pacific Islands for one species to another within the same genus. Such an 'overlap' meant that they could adapt their knowledge of traditional 'famine foods' — eaten on islands after a natural disaster had destroyed crops — to wild products such as tawa and hinau fruits and the roots and trunks of cabbage trees, which needed prolonged preparation to render them non-poisonous and edible. Fern root, pounded and cooked, became as much a staple as the kumara, especially since fern or bracken was often the first regenerative growth on a burnt-over area.

The hunting and gathering which thus supplemented horticulture were based on a ceaseless and minute observation of nature. Dozens if not hundreds of Maori words and terms described every natural aspect of the environment — plants, birds, insects, the sea and its shores. The people of Foveaux Strait, for instance, distinguished twenty separate winds. Kai Tahu, the southern tribe, had at least fifteen different terms for the varieties of alpine snow, and other tribes developed their own vocabularies to describe and reflect their local environment.

It was this scrutiny which, as the Maori realised that food resources could in the long run be non-renewable, enabled them to put in place a protective system of rahui (temporary ban) and tapu. This ensured that a particular food — flora or fauna — would only be exploited when its population and/or stage of growth ensured that some would be left for the future. River banks, for example, might have imposed on them during the eel-spawning season a rahui that was removed only when the eels reached maturity. Similar measures prevented harmful practices that might destroy a given resource. It was forbidden to open shellfish on the seashore and throw the offal in the place where they had been taken, because it was observed that if this occurred the shellfish population disappeared as a result of pollution. The Maori *did* modify the natural environment to suit their needs, but they could not afford to cause massive dislocations within it. Exploitation of resources occurred within carefully prescribed limits and was responsive to local conditions and fluctuating circumstances.

The second or expansionist phase of Maori history began around A.D. 1200. Initial coastal exploration and settlement had been fairly rapid, both South and North Islands being occupied at about the same time. Once horticulture and storage techniques had been mastered, a movement inland to quite different environments could begin. However, there were significant changes to the Maori food economy, and therefore the way of life based on it, in different regions, especially in the South Island. Owing to the much colder climate, horticulture could not be established south of Banks Peninsula on the east coast, and not at all on the west. As a result, the people who settled in the south and west became entirely dependent on hunting and gathering. Their year became organised around a seasonal trek from one food source to another, a more extreme version of the lifestyle further north, where a hapu (subtribe) would tend its gardens part of the year and at other times visit the river or seashore, or send hunters into the bush at the appropriate times for taking food. Although these southern people depended far more heavily than did horticulturalists on such a major food resource as the huge flightless moa, they did not belong to a separate culture — the term 'moa hunter' is quite inaccurate. Nor were they in any way culturally 'simpler' or more 'primitive' than more settled groups. Horticulture in New Zealand did not follow on a hunter-gatherer culture; instead, semi-nomadic hunting and gathering evolved as a complete way of life from one in which it had complemented gardening; it was an appropriate adaptation to local conditions.

As is the case elsewhere in the Pacific, the signs of military activity can be traced in the archaeological record from about the middle of the expan-

Pa were usually located in a carefully chosen defensive position, perhaps on hills or cliffs with good oversight of surrounding land. Their role as a fortress was sometimes their only function, but usually they were the heart of all communal activity, in both peace and war, and central to the prestige of the tribe.

A sketch in 1844 by the artist G. F. Angas of Motuopuhi, a pa on a headland extending into Lake Rotoaira, portrays the strength and thoroughness of the palisaded defence system of a typical pa.

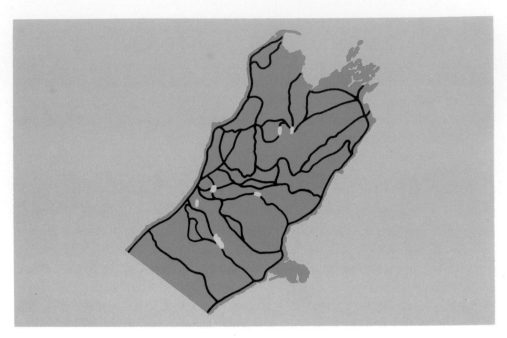

Routes of Maori trade in the northern South Island.

sionist phase, that is, around the fifteenth century. Fighting had undoubtedly occurred earlier, but it seems to be at this time that the formidable fortified pa began to appear, with their defensive systems of ditch, bank and palisade. This indicates that local populations were now large enough to cause friction, and settled enough to rely on permanent military structures. Very few pa have been discovered in the south or west of the South Island, which indicates that the smaller, mobile populations there did not settle their differences in the same way.

Although Maori culture and society thus far followed the familiar pattern of Polynesian settlement, it did not really enter the third or elaboration phase. The social stratification, religious ritual and rulers with extended power bases found elsewhere in Polynesia had not developed by the period of sustained European contact that occurred at the end of the eighteenth century. Each tribe or hapu acknowledged only its own chiefs, and the mana of those chiefs was dependent on their personal qualities as much as their lineage or birth status. They worked like everybody else — although perhaps at more exalted tasks, such as carving or tattooing — and while among the warriors and elders they could *suggest*, they did not command. Slavery existed, but not to such a degree that there was a large class kept in bondage. This loose, indeed anarchic social structure seems to reflect the fact that New Zealand is much larger than the Pacific homelands: the 'critical mass' stage of population in relation to land and resources had not been reached. Certain aspects of Polynesian culture such as tapu, on the other hand, were developed to a degree seldom seen elsewhere, presumably because they proved useful social tools.

Exploration of the country would have preceded, or at least accompanied, expansion; an exploration of untracked and forested New Zealand that was as thorough as it was difficult. A small, bold, energetic population walked the coasts, battled through the dense understorey of the forests, forded, swam, and rafted the great rivers, found its way through river gorges, and crossed alpine passes. As time went on, the best routes were established. Trails ran along the coasts and followed the rivers inland through gorges and passes, streams were bridged, pegs driven for footholds, and ladders, ropes and vines provided for cliff descents.

These routes, often with extended canoe voyaging complementing the trails, became the highways of commerce once local skills with particular materials evolved, and trade in worked stone as well as in food and plant materials developed. In the twelfth or thirteenth centuries, people from Mount Camel in Northland were using obsidian and basalt from Mayor Island and Coromandel. The prized materials and artefacts from the specialised centres of production of particular regions found their way to the ends of the country. Nephrite, the greenstone found in localised areas of the central and western South Island, became the most prized stone of all. By the seventeenth century, greenstone artefacts from remote parts of Westland were being passed from group to group, carried through the passes and canoed across the straits, some eventually reaching the far north of the North Island.

Maori geographical knowledge — as European explorers found centuries later — was extensive and detailed, although people naturally knew their own locality most intimately. Such geological and geographical information as the sequence of rivers in a water system, of peaks in a mountain range, or the various types of greenstone was frequently 'fixed' by oral maps in the form of legends. In the South Island the story of Tama and his daughters, for instance, contained information about various types of greenstone and their location as the father transformed his children into varieties of the semi-precious stone.

Such a 'map', however, was at the same time a story with characters and events. To the Maori the natural world was not something 'out there', alien, non-human and therefore valueless. The material and spiritual were entirely integrated — much as the 'new physics' of the twentieth century teaches that mass and energy are not separate, but that mass is merely a form of energy. The physical form of the country embodied the gods and ancestors. Mount Taranaki, for instance, did not merely symbolise but *was* the ancestor and god of the Taranaki people. Since the ancestor was frequently identified with the current head of a tribe or hapu, and the chief and his people with each other, such enduring features of the physical world brought about 'a fusion of men and ancestors and a collapse of distance in space-time' for the Maori. The people of the present day were no more separated from their past in time than they were from the land in space. Nor were history and myth differentiated; living men and women identified themselves with the divine ancestors and traced their genealogies back to the beginning of time or beyond.

Since land was identified with the physical body of the ancestor, it shared the strong tapu attached to the human body. This was symbolised in many place names, such as 'the place where Rangi rested' (had contact with the land) or 'so-and-so's hair' for a clump of flax bushes. Since the tapu of the ancestor was bound up with that of his or her descendants, intense feelings of shame, despair and loss of mana were likely to result if the land was invaded or taken. (Modern Maori people, as Aila Taylor, of Te Ati Awa, has observed, consider the old tribal boundaries as still in force, although the land may be legally 'alienated'. One cannot be cut off from one's own body.) Nevertheless, although land was held under a recognised form of communal ownership — rights being maintained by continued use of the land and its resources — it was not owned absolutely in the European sense. The ancestors, and Papatuanuku, the Earth Mother, could not thus be sacrilegiously dismembered by their children.

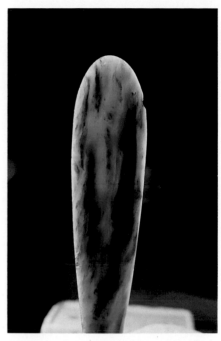

The patu of Te Wera, celebrated chief of Ngapuhi, from Teahuahu. Donated to the Waitangi National Trust board in 1952 by a descendant of Te Wera.

The patu is made from nephrite, one of the several kinds of greenstone found only at a few areas in the South Island. Local tribes specialised in quarrying and working the stone, which was then carried throughout the country on a network of trade routes. Highly skilled and respected specialists worked the stone into ornaments, tools and weapons.

In this prow carving on Te Toki a Tapiri, the great war canoe now in the Auckland Museum, Tumatauenga, the atua (spirit) of war, tells Tangaroa, atua of the sea, he is coming.

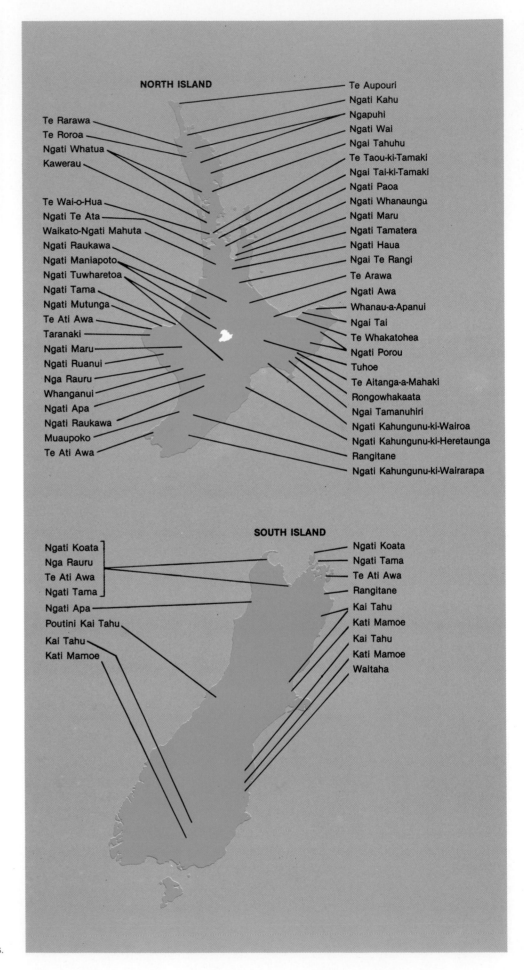

NORTH ISLAND

Te Aupouri
Ngati Kahu
Ngapuhi
Te Rarawa
Ngati Wai
Te Roroa
Ngai Tahuhu
Ngati Whatua
Te Taou-ki-Tamaki
Kawerau
Ngai Tai-ki-Tamaki
Ngati Paoa
Te Wai-o-Hua
Ngati Whanaunga
Ngati Te Ata
Ngati Maru
Waikato-Ngati Mahuta
Ngati Tamatera
Ngati Raukawa
Ngati Haua
Ngati Maniapoto
Ngai Te Rangi
Ngati Tuwharetoa
Te Arawa
Ngati Tama
Ngati Awa
Ngati Mutunga
Whanau-a-Apanui
Te Ati Awa
Ngai Tai
Taranaki
Te Whakatohea
Ngati Maru
Ngati Porou
Ngati Ruanui
Tuhoe
Nga Rauru
Te Aitanga-a-Mahaki
Whanganui
Rongowhakaata
Ngati Apa
Ngai Tamanuhiri
Ngati Raukawa
Ngati Kahungunu-ki-Wairoa
Muaupoko
Ngati Kahungunu-ki-Heretaunga
Te Ati Awa
Rangitane
Ngati Kahungunu-ki-Wairarapa

SOUTH ISLAND

Ngati Koata
Ngati Koata
Nga Rauru
Ngati Tama
Te Ati Awa
Te Ati Awa
Ngati Tama
Rangitane
Ngati Apa
Kai Tahu
Poutini Kai Tahu
Kati Mamoe
Kai Tahu
Kai Tahu
Kati Mamoe
Kati Mamoe
Waitaha

Maori tribal locations.

High, close to Rangi, the Sky Father, and difficult to climb, mountains were specially venerated. Within the territory of each tribe was a special mountain, a tapu place, sometimes thought to be the home of spirits. Such mountains could give signs foretelling the future. The bones of those of chiefly rank would be laid to rest in hidden places on the tapu mountain.

Greatly feared and venerated among the sacred mountains was Tongariro, tapu mountain of Ngati Tuwharetoa, ancestor mountain of the chiefs of the tribe who traced their ancestry to Ngatoro-i-rangi, high priest of Te Arawa, one of the original canoes. It was Ngatoro-i-rangi who had brought fire to the mountain when on his journey of exploration he had climbed to the top, and, perishing with cold, had cried for fire to his sisters in Hawaiki.

Perhaps eight centuries of interaction between the land which had been without people, and the 'tangata whenua', the people of the land, had brought into being a culture distinctive in its customs and its warfare, its art and architecture, its language and its poetry.

In December 1642 the Ngati Tumatakokiri people, who at that time lived in the area now known as Abel Tasman National Park, saw two enormous vessels approaching, white sails above of a shape never seen before. Two local canoes went out in the evening to reconnoitre. Their crews called out and blew blasts on the shell trumpet used by night sentries. Strange noises, seemingly in reply, came from one of the alien vessels, contact was broken off and the Ngati Tumatakokiri canoes returned to shore. In the morning another double-hulled canoe paddled out, to be followed by seven more. They positioned near one of the vessels, and when a small boat was passing between the two, a Tumatakokiri canoe, paddling furiously, rammed the boat, assaulted its crew with spear and clubs and killed four.

The Dutch seamen who died belonged to the crew of the *Zeehaen*. The

Natural hot bath — G. F. Angas, 1844.
Natural hot baths or mineral springs occur in several regions of New Zealand. If used for bathing (perhaps even as a 'spa'), they were sanctified for that purpose. Other hot springs were reserved for cooking only.

It is probable that the canoes that attacked Abel Tasman's seamen came from a pa on Taupo Point in Golden Bay. The point is now included within Abel Tasman National Park.

commander of the expedition, Abel Janzoon Tasman, sailed his two ships away from Whariwharangi Bay without effect on Maori history, culture or society. A sketch by his sailing master was all that was recorded. More than a hundred years were to pass before European sails would again be coming in from the unknown vastness of the Pacific and lifting above the horizon of the rolling waters of Hinemoana, the Ocean Maid.

Chapter 6

European Rediscovery and Settlement

Tasman had been told to head south from the East Indies and west of Australia. Once in the prevailing westerly winds of the Roaring Forties he was to run to the east, where, according to the centuries-old belief of European map-makers, he might find the Great Southern Continent.

The tumultuous seas of the Southern Ocean were trying on ships and men. Edging north in search of easier weather, Tasman discovered Tasmania. Storms then forced him towards the coast of the South Island of New Zealand. On 13 December 1642 he noted, 'Towards the middle of the day we saw a great land uplifted high. We had it S.E. of us, about 60 miles away.'

Tasman turned north, sailed up the coast, rounded Farewell Spit and came to anchor in Tasman Bay on 18 December 1642. Next morning came the bloody encounter with Ngati Tumatakokiri. The Dutch hauled up their anchors and set sail, passing up the west coast of the North Island to sight Three Kings Islands on the Epiphany, 6 January, 1643. Eventually, by way of Fiji and Tonga, they returned to Batavia.

One hundred years later a new seafaring nation was prominent in Europe and was, like Spain, Portugal and Holland before her, extending her economic

'A view of Moordaerer's Bay, as you are at anchor there in 15 fathom' — Isaac Gilsemans, sailing master on *Zeehaen*, 1642.

Tasman's encounter with Ngati Tumatakokiri probably took place in Wainui Bay off Whariwharangi Beach. Gilsemans' drawing provided information about the dress and equipment of Maori people of that time but Maori society remained unaffected by the contact.

JAMES COOK (1728–1779)
JOSEPH BANKS (1743–1820)

The names of James Cook, navigator, and Joseph Banks, botanist, are closely associated with New Zealand's early history. The two men, who with a hundred others shared the tiny, cramped *Endeavour* on Cook's first visit to the South Pacific, were very different people.

James Cook had the humblest of beginnings as the son of a agricultural labourer in Yorkshire. He progressed from a shop-hand, to apprentice on a coal ship, to the Navy and finally, in 1768, to the command of the *Endeavour*.

His three visits to the Pacific lasted nearly a decade. He discovered new parts of the Pacific, proved conclusively that the Southern Continent did not exist, charted New Zealand and the eastern coast of Australia and ventured further into Antarctic waters than had any other man to that time.

He was stubborn, persistent and patient, and largely self-educated. His attitude towards indigenous people was conservative and humane. On his second voyage to the Pacific (1772–75), Cook made his own experiments. Perhaps he was stimulated to do so by his contact with men of science — Banks on the first voyage, the Forsters on the second. His journals reveal wide-ranging and accurate observation, whether of people or the natural environment. His death in Hawaii cut short his career at the early age of fifty.

Many of the islands Cook named on his voyage round New Zealand are now reserves. Two places associated with him — Ship Cove and Dusky Bay — are among New Zealand's most important sites of its European history.

Captain James Cook — an engraving of a painting by Nathaniel Dance, 1776.

Joseph Banks became a wealthy man in his early adulthood, able to pursue his interest in natural history at Oxford University, and on an expedition to Newfoundland and Labrador. Becoming a member of the Royal Society in 1766, he learned soon afterwards of Cook's forthcoming expedition to the South Pacific. Thanks to the help of influential friends he was appointed botanist, organising equipment and a party of scientists and artists at his own expense.

Aged only twenty-four on the trip's departure, he responded to the pleas of friends and family that he should undertake instead a Grand Tour of Europe with the comment, 'Every blockhead does that; my Grand Tour shall be one round the whole globe.'

In New Zealand he was unable to botanise as much as he would have liked, but still produced many observations of plant life and Maori customs. Banks and Daniel Solander, the Swedish naturalist, returned with a large collection of plants, fishes, birds and insects, none previously described by science. Unfortunately, they were never to publish their discoveries.

Banks's career as an explorer was short-lived. After refusing to go on Cook's second expedition because he considered that there was inadequate space for his expanded suite, he made a botanical trip to Iceland. The remainder of his long life (he died in 1820 aged seventy-seven) was devoted to the study of science in Britain. He was president of the influential Royal Society for over forty years and played a vital role in transforming the royal gardens at Kew from a pleasure garden into a scientific one. His knowledge, influence and money enabled him to expand greatly the Kew and British Museum collections through a network of world-roving collectors.

Rather than being a great scientist himself, although he was certainly competent, Banks was a dynamic man who could inspire and organise others.

Sir Joseph Banks — an engraving of a painting by Thomas Phillips.

and political power. With Britain, though, the casual empire building of private enterprise was both restrained and strengthened by a careful government, which used ostensibly apolitical enterprises to test the water for its own ambitions: thus, in 1768–71, an unusual astronomical voyage to the South Pacific took place.

So the next European sails came in from the east. They belonged to His Majesty's Bark *Endeavour*, commanded by Lieutenant James Cook, R.N., in the vanguard of an exploration that had different objectives from the mercantile aims set for Tasman by Governor Anthony van Diemen of the Dutch East India Company in 1642.

Cook's purpose was to observe the transit of the planet Venus, which would allow calculation of the distance of Earth from the sun. It was a scientific body, the Royal Society, not the Navy or any other official organisation, that petitioned King George III for money and a ship to carry out the observation. The society was then given help by the Admiralty, and it was decided to combine astronomy with determining whether the Great Southern Continent did really exist.

Piercy Island, lying off Cape Brett in the Bay of Islands Maritime and Historic Park, is one of the many island reserves originally named by Captain Cook.

On board, along with the ship's complement of Cook, his officers and crew, was a small group of scientists. These were led by Joseph Banks, one of the 'gentlemen amateurs' of the eighteenth century whose money and social standing allowed them to pursue their interests — in Banks's case natural history. Another natural historian, Daniel Solander, was second to Banks in the little group, which was rounded out by Herman Sporing, Banks's secretary, and two draughtsmen, Sydney Parkinson and Andrew Buchanan.

Their presence was indicative of the changes in European thought since Tasman's time. The Age of Enlightenment was stimulating scholars to observe, catalogue and classify the world, in the hope of discovering rules and patterns that applied across the spectrum of nature. It was no longer enough to discover new lands. They must also be investigated as carefully as possible.

Historical chance, therefore, meant that from the earliest sustained European contact, New Zealand was being observed, mapped, drawn — its people, plants and animals all described in writing. After Cook's first voyage Europeans formulated ideas and expectations of this new country, which then shaped the ways in which they approached it.

The *Endeavour* with its crew of 'observers' first sighted land on 6 October 1769, landing two days later near present-day Gisborne. For the next six months Cook, his scientists and artists recorded their observations of the people and nature seen during their circumnavigation of the islands.

Banks and Solander, full of excitement and industry, observed a biology unlike any seen before by Europeans. They made the first collection of New Zealand plants, identifying some three hundred and sixty species. Parkinson and Buchanan sketched plants, birds and fish and drew the people who came to the ships.

On leaving Poverty Bay, Cook went south across Hawke Bay to Cape Turnagain before putting about. The numerous bays on the east coast provided ample opportunity to observe, collect and trade as well as to replenish water supplies. After bad weather in the north *Endeavour* passed Tasman's Three Kings and turned down the west coast, recording the Kaipara but missing the rich and densely populated Tamaki isthmus. Mount Taranaki was sighted, and called Egmont. 'A very high mountain and in appearance greatly

On 15 January 1770 the *Endeavour* entered Ship Cove around the north end of Motuara Island. The people in the pa at the western end 'came to the palisades and brandished their weapons'. Cook raised the Union Jack on the highest point of Motuara and claimed the surrounding lands 'in the name and for the use of His Majesty'. Cook appreciated the natural beauty of Ship Cove and its abundant supplies of timber, water and fish.

We 'entered . . . by a channel scarcely twice the width of the ship; and in a small creek, moored head and stern, so near the shore as to reach it with a brow or stage, which nature had in a manner prepared for us in a large tree whose end or top reached our gunwale.'

It is thought that this is the tree referred to by Captain Cook and still to be found in Pickersgill Harbour, Dusky Sound.

resembling the peak of Tenerife,' said Cook. In January 1770 they came into Ship Cove on Queen Charlotte Sound. The visitors were entranced by the bird life, none more so than Banks. He thought the bird song 'the most melodious wild musick I have ever heard, almost imitating small bells'.

Ship Cove became the strategic base of Cook's Pacific exploration — he was to return there four times. By the middle of March they had sailed the east coast of the South Island. Going north on the west coast they sighted the wide-mouthed bay with a line of islands which Cook called Dusky Bay, 'behind which there must be shelter from all winds'. On 16 March, Banks noted a curious thing — two hills of a brick colour — the Red Hills, west of Mount Aspiring. In the great chain of mountains piled high they could see valleys covered in snow — the glaciers of Westland.

When the success of the first voyage conjured a second to investigate discoveries in more detail, the commander (promoted to the rank of captain), was an inevitable appointment. Less inevitable was the company of Banks and Solander. Instant fame led Banks to demands the Lords of the Admiralty were unable to comprehend fully, particularly the need for two French horn players in a retinue of fifteen. A hard-working father and son combination, Johann and George Forster, offered a substitution not less competent and a great deal less costly. Johann Forster was a professional who needed money, in contrast to Banks, the amateur, who did not. Natural talent had been sharpened by sustained and systematic application.

The two ships of the second voyage, *Resolution* commanded by Cook and *Adventure* by Tobias Furneaux, sailed first to Cape Town, and headed south into Antarctic waters late in November 1772. In the next four months Cook took them around the Antarctic ice. The ships lost contact in bad weather, and Furneaux headed on a more northerly course for their pre-arranged rendezvous at Ship Cove. *Resolution* stayed south in all the dangers of icebergs and sea ice, of fog and gale, until mid-March. Then 'I shaped my course to New Zealand' and '. . . was not backward in carrying sail,' said Cook. They entered Dusky Sound late in March 1773.

The six weeks in Dusky Sound were a prelude to a remarkable phase of its history. On the point above *Resolution*'s snug mooring, trees were cut to allow observations by Wales, the astronomer. The Forsters had an extremely

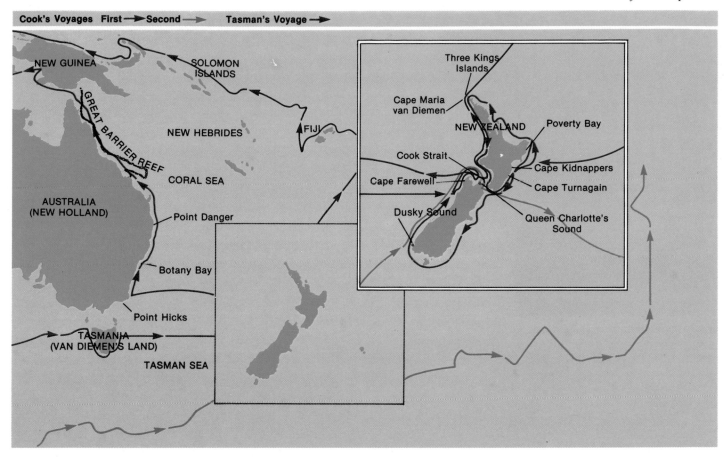

Cook's Voyages First → Second →   Tasman's Voyage →

busy and, for natural history in New Zealand, intensely valuable period. The foundations for ornithology in this country were established, along with a wealth of other observation about the botany and zoology of the area. Cook and his surveyors must have been very busy indeed. Every part of Dusky Bay was mapped and named.

They met *Adventure* at Ship Cove. At Motuara Island, just offshore, Furneaux had established a hospital and planted gardens. But Cook was not happy to idle away the winter months in Ship Cove. Early in June, New Zealand lay astern and to the west. He was beginning a great sweep into the unknown Pacific to the east and north. Then it was back to Ship Cove and off into Antarctic waters to south and east. A year later he was again in Ship Cove, making ready for his return to England. He was to see Ship Cove once more.

The second voyage lies near the origin of two diverging strands, both of which feature strongly in subsequent conservation history. On the one hand scientific evidence of something unusual was accumulating. And on the other? There were Furneaux's gardens in Motuara Island, and other gardens planted by Cook in various places. Attempts, if unsuccessful, had been made to establish goats, sheep and pigs. The ship rat was undoubtedly ashore. The long story of European plant and animal introduction had begun.

Cook's account of his voyage shaped the whole of subsequent history in New Zealand and the South Pacific Ocean. A great deal of information about New Zealand became available in Europe. Navigators of many nations followed in the wake of the great explorer, with copies of his journals open on the chart-room table. Cook's sojourn in Dusky Bay and the information he provided about it led others there. For decades the Sound was the centre of

NAVIGATORS AND NATIONAL PARKS
For clarity, only Tasman's voyage, Cook's first voyage and an early stage of his second are shown. Navigators Vancouver and Malaspina are also associated with Fiordland National Park. Dumont d'Urville is associated with Tasman Bay and Abel Tasman National Park. Bellingshausen, a Russian navigator-explorer called at Ship Cove.

In 1827, on his way from Tasman Bay to survey the east coast of the North Island, d'Urville sailed the *Astrolabe* through the dangerous waters of French Pass, now within the Marlborough Sounds Maritime Park.

European activity. Among those who came was George Vancouver, who had served as a midshipman on the *Resolution* voyage. As an explorer-commander in his own right, Vancouver returned to Dusky Sound for refreshments. His surgeon and naturalist, Archibald Menzies, studied and collected ferns and mosses.

In 1793, two years after Vancouver's visit, a Spanish expedition, led by Captain Malaspina, was off Dusky Sound, which could be recognised 'by the exact details which Captain Cook, with his usual accuracy, has given'. Don Felipe Bauza, a senior officer, took an armed boat into Doubtful Sound, past the island that now bears his name, and sailed up Malaspina Reach. Echoes of Cook continued. A Russian expedition on a voyage of scientific exploration arrived in Ship Cove in May 1820. This venture was in the Cook model: Bellingshausen, the commander, had scientists, observers and artists on his two ships.

Almost the last of the distinguished line of navigator-explorers, and second only to Cook among those who came to New Zealand, was Dumont d'Urville. His first visit was as executive officer of the *Coquille* in 1824. Commander in 1827 of the *Astrolabe* (the re-named *Coquille*), d'Urville went to Tasman Bay with the express purpose of completing Cook's chart and became to Tasman Bay what Cook is to Dusky Sound. Then, with skill and daring, he took *Astrolabe* through French Pass and sailed on to chart the east coast of the North Island. With his wonderfully documented *Natural History of the Voyage of the 'Astrolabe'*, which he wrote on his return to France, further information about plants and animals, at least those of the coasts and coastal waters, was recorded. Most of the *Astrolabe*'s exploration and nature collection was on the coastal fringes of Astrolabe Bight, on the western side of Tasman Bay.

Within a year of Vancouver's visit to Dusky Sound, a sealing gang was landed there by Captain William Raven of the *Britannia*. Cook's accounts of the abundance of whales and seals on the Southern Ocean, and reports of the large numbers of whales seen from convict transports bound for New South Wales, had greatly interested the whaling and sealing industry.

Ironwork and sails were left with the *Britannia*'s party so that they could build their own ship if their parent ship did not return. First, however, they constructed New Zealand's first European house. When *Britannia* did return, a vessel of some sixteen metres was almost completed. The *Providence*, as she

JULES-SEBASTIEN-CESAR DUMONT D'URVILLE (1790–1842)

Dumont d'Urville visited New Zealand twice in the 1820s and again in 1840 on French expeditions to the South Pacific. His most important visit to New Zealand was in early 1827, when, in command of the *Astrolabe*, he arrived with instructions to pass through Cook Strait and survey several points on the north-east of the North Island.

D'Urville had a patriotic and personal desire to improve upon Cook's charts, so he extended his New Zealand stay.

The Nelson area was of special interest to him and he was pleased to find that Tasman Bay was much larger than Cook had indicated. His voyage is remembered in a number of places — such as D'Urville Island, Croisilles Harbour and French Pass.

After sailing through Cook Strait and up the east coast of the North Island, he entered the Hauraki Gulf, where he realised the potential of the Auckland isthmus with its two harbours. Further north, d'Urville spent a week in the Bay of Islands. He was a keen botanist and his collection contained many new

specimens from New Zealand. This study surpassed in importance any work done since the voyages of Cook.

D'Urville's third visit, in 1840, was made at the end of a long exploratory voyage that ranged south to the Antarctic. His stay in New Zealand was brief, as it had become a British colony several months before. He returned home to enjoy promotion and fame. Sadly, d'Urville, his wife and only surviving son were killed in a train crash in France in 1842.

was called later, was indeed providential for a certain Captain Bampton, who arrived in the Sound in October 1795 on an ancient and quite unseaworthy East Indiaman named the *Endeavour*. The complement of *Endeavour* and the accompanying brig *Fancy* amounted to some two hundred and fifty souls. All were eventually returned to Australia on *Fancy*, *Providence*, an American whaler, *Mercury*, which called later at Dusky Sound, and *Resource*, built from a converted longboat. *Endeavour* herself lay rotting on, and eventually beneath, the waters of the Sound.

Sealing spread around the southern coast and on to the islands further south. By the 1830s, the seal population of the Southern Ocean had been almost destroyed. Twenty years later a similar decline in whale populations had been hastened by the setting up of stations for shore whaling. Of this the Fiordland coast had its share when a base housing sixty men was established in 1829 in Preservation Inlet, south of Dusky Sound.

By 1810, Europeans were in frequent contact with Maori people on the coast, particularly in the north. As well as the sealers and whalers, ships came to procure flax and timber. Maori people supplied vegetables, prepared and

One of two cannon lifted from the bottom of Dusky Sound by a marine expedition in 1984, 188 years after their weight had upset a raft transferring gear from Captain Bampton's decaying *Endeavour* to a base ashore in readiness for removal to a new vessel, the *Providence*, built by sealers in Dusky Sound in 1792.

Astrolabe Roadstead provided a sheltered anchorage for d'Urville's vessel. The French commander wrote that it 'offered the most picturesque landscape as well as the promise of all sorts of discoveries to our eager eyes'. In just one week he accurately surveyed and explored the district, replenished his supplies and made contact with the local Maori.

traded flax, cut timber for spars and crewed on the European vessels. Contact enhanced neither the reputation of Europeans nor relationships between the races. These deteriorated, the cause on some occasions being offence against customs, on others, trickery or ill treatment. Utu, or revenge for insult, was long-established Maori custom. Repayment could be harsh and violent, as was the destruction of the *Boyd* in Whangaroa Harbour in 1809.

These contacts had, however, only a limited impact on life in New Zealand. Certainly the trade goods offered began to change the pattern of Maori life as the various local hapu concentrated on supplying commodities to obtain them. But the Europeans lived largely on Maori terms, often dependent on Maori people for food — since they seldom grew enough of their own — and sometimes becoming more or less completely integrated into Maori life through marriage or liaison with local women.

With the arrival of missionaries who, from 1814 on, began to settle in the north, mainly in and around the Bay of Islands, a new and different situation developed. These first true European settlers brought with them their families and their faith. As they brought also the intention of converting the heathen to Christianity and a 'decent' hard-working life, they were well armoured against the possibility of succumbing to Maori influences. Rather than temporarily exploiting a resource and moving on, as the sealers did, the missionaries bought land for settlement and food production. A substantial eighty hectares were purchased by Samuel Marsden after his famous first sermon in New Zealand on Christmas Day 1814.

Like the sealers and shore-based whalers, the missionaries were dependent on the Maori. Social exchanges and missionary teaching began to influence Maori life in the north. New elements were integrated into traditional patterns: muskets were used in long-standing tribal quarrels and Christianity cross-fertilised Maori beliefs. In the same way, the Maori adopted the new animals and crops being introduced by missionaries on farms established in the north in the late 1820s and the 1830s. Potatoes, maize, pumpkins and other vegetables could be fitted into the horticultural system without difficulty. (Potatoes in particular, being much easier to grow than kumara, quickly became a staple.) Some experiments were made with fruit trees and a few chiefs began to run their own herds of dairy cattle. Neither pastoralism nor

Lancing a sperm whale.

Waitangi Treaty House, Waitangi
National Reserve.

agriculture could be called widespread — there were too few European settlers
and the Maori way of life remained semi-nomadic, unsuited to the intensive
year-round attention needed — but both were established in New Zealand in
1840.

Other, less beneficial settlers were establishing themselves. Charles
Darwin, visiting the Bay of Islands in 1835, noted reports that the Norwegian
rat had, in two years, annihilated 'kiore' in the north. 'In many places,' he said,
'I noticed several sorts of weeds, which, like the rats, I was forced to own as
countrymen.'

During the 1830s, missionary activity expanded as far south as Rotorua
to the east and Kawhia to the west. Marsden made notable journeys of exploration, as did Henry Williams, who arrived to take charge of the work Marsden
had begun. To at least some of the missionaries, the wild unfamiliar landscape
was an image of the unregenerate heathen souls they had come to save. To
Richard Taylor, the desert near Tongariro was a world blasted by sin.

By the late 1830s, social change and change in the natural environment
were both occurring. The process had been gradual in extent and variable in
location. Quite suddenly, pressures that had been building for some time
precipitated a decisive event: the annexation of New Zealand as a British
colony.

The event was not predictable — the policy of the Colonial Office of the
British Government was, at the time, one of 'minimum intervention'. On the
one hand it was easier to let private and semi-official interests do the work;
on the other, New Zealand was not particularly attractive: a small, remote, difficult country with only a few useful products and a war-like native people.
Further, it was accumulating a particularly lawless European element, notably
in the whaling and trading centre of Kororareka. The concern of the missionaries at the influence of this den of iniquity on local Maori people registered
clearly with highly placed officials in the Colonial Office.

By 1839 the Colonial Office had decided to try to gain sovereignty over parts of New Zealand. The decision to act was made more urgent by the activities of Edward Gibbon Wakefield's New Zealand Company, which had furthered its aims of colonisation by sending out a preliminary expedition to buy land in May 1839. The Government was forced to take action to prevent a private interest from acquiring the upper hand.

On 29 January 1840 Captain William Hobson arrived in the Bay of Islands carrying official instructions to conclude a treaty with the Maori that would give the British Government official standing in New Zealand. On 6 February at Waitangi about fifty of the northern Maori chiefs signed the Maori version of a treaty of cession. The document was then carried around the country to be signed by chiefs in other districts. The treaty, described by historian Ruth Ross as an 'inexpertly drawn-up [document], ambiguous and contradictory in content, chaotic in its execution', marked a new phase in the relationship between European and Maori. Shortly before this the first group of New Zealand Company settlers landed in Port Nicholson (the harbour of the future city of Wellington). On 21 May 1840 Hobson proclaimed Queen Victoria's sovereignty over the whole of New Zealand. The British colonisation of New Zealand had officially begun.

Chapter 7

Settlement and Development 1840–1870

The arrival of New Zealand Company ships heralded a marked increase in the hitherto gradual pace of environmental change. The *Aurora* was in Wellington two weeks before the signing of the Treaty of Waitangi. In October 1841 *Arrow*, *Whitby* and *Will Watch* were anchored in the Astrolabe Roadstead of Tasman Bay. In the following month settlers of the offshoot Plymouth Company were landing in New Plymouth. A European population of perhaps two thousand before the Treaty of Waitangi had risen to over twenty thousand by 1850.

The divergent strands of conservation history — imported cultural change on the one hand and a slowly accumulating knowledge of the real nature of the country on the other — were evident in European exploration of the time. That concerned with New Zealand Company interests was to find usable land. In contrast, there was exploration to discover and observe more about the nature of the country and its people; a kind of inland extension of the work done by Cook and d'Urville around the coasts. Both types of exploration were greatly dependent on the assistance of Maori people.

Three of the North Island journeys of observation involved country that in the distant future would become national parks. In 1839 John Bidwill, with a team of Maori helpers, set off from Tauranga for the interior. From Taupo he saw 'Tongadido' glistening at the end of the lake. Once on the volcanic plateau Bidwill said he was going to climb to the summit of Ngauruhoe. His companions objected. Firstly, the mountain was tapu; secondly, it had been making a noise in the night. So Bidwill went on alone persisting to the top of Ngauruhoe in spite of an eruption. He peered down into the 'most terrific abyss I ever looked into, or imagined'. A few days later there was a tense interview with the great chief Te Heuheu Tukino (Mananui), who was angered by Bidwill's desecration of Ngati Tuwharetoa's sacred mountains. The unrepentant explorer and botanist returned via Rotorua, Tauranga and the Thames Valley with a collection of plants that was forwarded to Kew Gardens, the first from the high central region of the North Island.

Ernst Dieffenbach, appointed naturalist to the New Zealand Company, had arrived in the company survey ship *Tory*. His exploratory travels took him through much of the North Island. When he wished to climb Mount Egmont he met with similar objection from Maori companions. Like Bidwill, he persisted and with James Heberley, a whaler, climbed beyond the snowline. But

'Lake Howick' — William Fox, 1846.

On their first expedition, in 1846, we find Fox, Brunner and Heaphy speculating about the recreational future of the Nelson lakes. According to Heaphy's journal, they 'Discussed the probability of the Howick [Lake Rotoroa] becoming the future resort of East Indian diseased-liver invalids; of the propriety of having pleasure boats on the lake, with a tontine hotel at the Gowan, and mules for excursions to the surrounding mountains and points of view.'

he was unable to climb Tongariro. After Bidwill, Te Heuheu Tukino had laid a solemn tapu on the mountain.

Dieffenbach's *Travels in New Zealand*, published in 1843, was packed with detailed observations about people, nature and geology. A review of botanical study up until that time concluded that the greater number of botanical species was peculiar to the country and that New Zealand was a botanical centre.

William Colenso's early botanising in the north was followed by the first of many great journeys of botanical exploration. Late in 1841 he sailed for Hicks Bay, to tramp down into Poverty Bay and find his way inland to Lake Waikaremoana, where he spent a freezing Christmas. Then it was on to Rotorua and Matamata, by canoe down the Waikato River and across the Manukau to the Kaipara. From the Kaipara he crossed to the east coast and returned to Paihia. His large collection of plant specimens was sent to the herbarium at Kew Gardens. Although Joseph Banks had died in 1820, the long shadow of his influence reached out to connect Colenso's arduous journeys with those days on Cook's *Endeavour*.

The need to find farming land for the Nelson settlement inspired explorations by New Zealand Company surveyors. Early in 1843 John Cotterell and a party tracked through a break in the encircling mountains and discovered a large lake, completely filling up the pass, with wooded hills rising from the

WILLIAM COLENSO (1811–1899)

William Colenso's life spanned most of the nineteenth century and encompassed the pursuits of printer, missionary, explorer, botanist and politician.

In the 1830s Colenso was based as a missionary-printer at the Bay of Islands, where he met briefly with Charles Darwin during the visit of the *Beagle*. Longer association with Alan Cunningham and J. D. Hooker, both closely connected with Kew Gardens, extended his botanical knowledge. He perceived the challenge and opportunity for botanical exploration. In time, his journeys made him the most notable European explorer of the North Island.

In 1844 he was transferred to Hawke's Bay and over the next decade he made several crossings of the Ruahine Ranges, as well as travelling across the Onetapu Desert on the eastern side of Mount Ruapehu. His alpine plants collection from this trip was the first major one made in New Zealand. Like his other collections, this one was sent to Kew Gardens.

In later years Colenso devoted himself to botany and in 1866 he became the first New Zealander to be elected to the Royal Society. In his lifetime he published over a hundred papers on scientific matters.

'On the grass plain below Lake Arthur' — William Fox, 1846.
The 1846 expedition set out to find suitable land for sheep farming. Despite the implied area of grasslands in Fox's painting, the party discovered that hopes for a vast interior plain were unfounded.

water's edge. Further exploration was organised by William Fox, who was then company agent at Nelson, and in 1846, in company with Charles Heaphy, Thomas Brunner and guide Kehu, he explored the region. A fortnight after their return Brunner, Heaphy and Kehu set off once more to find the mouth of the Buller River.

They endured five months of hardship, but even this paled beside Thomas Brunner's epic that was to follow. With Kehu and other Maori help, he set off down the Buller. Today, travellers in the Buller Gorge enjoy the magnificent scenery of some of New Zealand's finest reserves. For Brunner it was a journey of appalling difficulty: 'The river is quite worthless and offers no room for a journal, saving many days' hunger, the danger of crossing its tributary streams, and the apparently interminable labour of making our way through so frightful a country, and in continual heavy rains.'

The party had endured almost ten months of heavy rain and thick bush when they reached Okarito. Here they could look across the forests that are now in Westland National Park to the snow-capped wall of the Southern Alps. At Tititira Head, further south, Brunner suffered a severely sprained ankle. This forced his decision to return. He had been away more than five hundred days when he again reached Lake Rotoiti. The greatest journey in the history of New Zealand exploration was almost completed.

The racing expansion of sheep farming across the Canterbury Plains following the arrival of Canterbury Association settlers at the end of 1850

THOMAS BRUNNER (1821–1874)

Thomas Brunner's 550-day return journey from Nelson to South Westland ranks as New Zealand's greatest single exploration by a European.

In December 1846, with his Maori guide, Kehu, he made his way to the Buller and then headed down the West Coast as far as Paringa (south of what is now known as Westland National Park). Kehu's detailed knowledge of the region and its food resources was essential for Brunner's survival, as no Europeans lived in South Westland in this pre-gold rush era.

His journey yielded little of direct worth for the Nelson settlement, in contrast with the rich and more accessible grazing lands then found on the eastern side of the Alps. Less than twenty years later, however, the gold rushes hit the West Coast, making it a boom region.

Brunner had modest recognition during his lifetime, receiving the Medal of the Royal Geographical Society. He later became Chief Surveyor and Commissioner of Public Works in Nelson.

Otira Gorge — William Fox.

initiated a new phase of land exploration. By 1855, those wanting new grazing land had to explore beyond the mountains. Samuel Butler, arriving in 1860, searched the great valleys and tributaries of the Rakaia, Waimakariri, Rangitata and Hurunui Rivers.

The search for gold promoted alpine exploration as it also encouraged interest in potential alpine crossings. It introduced a geological dimension into the understanding of natural New Zealand, hitherto concentrated mostly on botany and to a lesser extent on zoology. A West Coast gold rush was triggered by discovery in 1864. The Canterbury Provincial Council perceived an urgent need for a superior connection through the mountain barrier. The provincial engineer, Edward Dobson, was instructed to investigate. His son Arthur had been surveying on the West Coast and he 'knew all about the Coast'. He was familiar with the pass discovered by Leonard Harper, and had already discovered another crossing to the south of Harper's from the Waimakariri River over the Divide, and down precipitous slopes into the Otira. After evaluating all the possible routes of the area, Arthur's elder brother George reported to his father that 'Arthur's Pass was the best . . .' A road was hammered through in rain, sleet, snow and frost.

Canterbury was aware of the implications of gold discovery for the provincial economy. A commission for the geological survey of Canterbury was at once offered to Julius von Haast. He decided that the Upper Waitaki region was the best gold prospect. Early in 1862, with Arthur Dobson as surveyor, he was among the glaciers of the Mount Cook region, exploring, surveying, studying the geology and collecting botanical specimens. People who now visit Mount Cook National Park meet many features named by Haast for eminent scientists; the Hooker and Mueller Glaciers and the Hochstetter Icefall among them.

Another surveyor-engineer had viewed Mount Cook four years earlier. 'Mount Cook,' wrote John Thomson, provincial surveyor of Otago, 'the monarch of southern mountains, was full in view, distant about 25 miles, and towering 13,000 feet above the sea, was clothed in snow from its tapering peak to its base, and supported as it is by rugged precipitous sides, surrounded by desert and utterly barren mountains and valleys.'

ARTHUR DUDLEY DOBSON (1841–1934)

Arthur Dudley Dobson began his surveying career in the young Canterbury province in 1859. Over the next few years he travelled widely, including a trip with geologist Julius von Haast to the Tasman Valley in 1862, and seven months spent surveying the West Coast the next year. He is best remembered as the European discoverer of the pass from the Waimakiriri in 1864. Named in his honour, it soon became a busy route to the flourishing West Coast.

Dobson went on to become chief surveyor for the Nelson province. As Nelson provincial engineer he wrote a paper on the connection between high-country forest clearance and flooding, with special reference to the town of Nelson. He was one of a small group of men who urged conservation measures at this time.

After private engineering work in Christchurch and Australia, he became city engineer for Christchurch City until his retirement in 1921. Appropriately, in 1929, some sixty-five years after discovering the pass, he was appointed to the board of the new Arthur's Pass National Park, which was created in that year out of two large reserves set aside in 1901.

James McKerrow, one of Thomson's assistants, completed the reconnaissance surveys of Otago between 1861 and 1863. With the discovery of gold the province had boomed. The Provincial Council sought a road and rail connection and a West Coast harbour to connect the province with Australian markets. Two passes from branches of the Routeburn had been discovered by prospectors. In 1863 the Otago provincial geologist, James Hector, and two companions tramped up the Matukituki Valley to cross the Divide into the valley of the Arawata River. This adventure amongst the glaciers, avalanches, rockfalls and weather of the Mount Aspiring area needed all Hector's skills, learned in the Canadian Rockies, to keep the party alive. Further south, another successful crossing to the West Coast had been made alone by P. Q. Caples, a determined and resourceful miner. Charles Cameron crossed the Haast Pass into Westland early in 1863, to be soon followed by Julius von Haast.

Compared with the North, geographical knowledge of the South Island had been patchy until 1850, but by the early 1860s the land- and gold-driven investigations had redressed the balance. Geological description was underway and botanical study had advanced greatly.

Ernst Dieffenbach had described parts of Queen Charlotte Sound on the basis of scrambles around Ship Cove, when the *Tory* arrived in New Zealand. But it was M. E. Raoul, surgeon successively to two French vessels based in Akaroa, who was first to investigate the plants of the eastern side of the South Island in the early 1840s. Botanical studies of the Nelson area were made by

'From centre of Tasman Glacier' — Julius von Haast, 1862.

Haast wrote of this area: 'It is impossible for me to describe in adequate words the majestic scenery . . . the weird mountain chains with their crowning peaks in stately forms, and numerous tributary glaciers on their flanks, often broken into innumerable screes . . . and the wide ice-stream itself carrying slowly its enormous load of debris to its terminal face . . . all this impressed our minds with deep admiration.'

JULIUS VON HAAST (1822–1887)

Julius Haast arrived in New Zealand in late 1858 to report on immigration prospects for a shipping firm, but stayed to become a distinguished geologist and founder of the Canterbury Museum.

Haast's arrival in New Zealand coincided with the visit by Austrian geologist Ferdinand von Hochstetter, who made the country's first professional geological survey in 1858–59. Geology focused on locating products useful to an isolated young colony — especially gold and coal. Haast was soon working in the Nelson province, making a long trip down the Buller and Grey Valleys seeking suitable farmland and accessible passes, and re-examining the Greymouth coalfields discovered by Brunner some fourteen years previously. He also found the Westport coalfield, and detected traces of gold in West Coast rivers.

In 1861 he became provincial geologist for Canterbury and set off for the wilder regions of the South Island, in company with the young Arthur Dudley Dobson. He was the first European to venture up the Tasman Valley and, with Dobson, climbed to over two thousand metres on Mount Cook. Further south, he was one of the earliest Europeans to cross the pass named after him. Later in his career Haast established the Canterbury Museum and became its first director. The museum remained his main interest in later life.

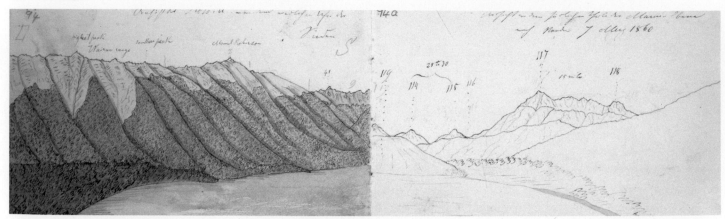

'Wairau Range from Lake Rotoiti' —
Julius von Haast, 1860.

Haast was enthusiastic about the
Nelson lakes region. He felt certain it
would 'become the favourite abode of
those whose means and leisure will
permmit them to admire picturesque
scenery'. His sketch captures the
essential character of the garment of
beech forest that clothes and protects the
skeletal mountains.

John Sinclair, who had been Colonial Secretary and had already collected
extensively in the North Island.

The survey of the New Zealand coastline from 1847 to 1851 by H.M.S.
Acheron, commanded by Captain J. L. Stokes, was more than nautical charting.
Acheron's surgeon-naturalist, David Lyall, an experienced botanist, extended
previous work in the sounds of the south-west and also botanised in the
Foveaux Strait area.

In 1853 Joseph Dalton Hooker published *Flora Novae-Zelandiae*, by far the
most comprehensive description of the New Zealand flora to that time.
Hooker had himself visited and collected in New Zealand. Available to him
were the collections of the Kew Herbarium. The explorations in the mountain
areas of the South Island that followed in the 1850s and 1860s greatly
extended knowledge of alpine botany.

In the early 1860s the South and North Islands presented a total contrast.
Sheep, grassland and gold had impelled development and prosperity in the
South, relatively unhindered by problems of land acquisition. The North was
completely bogged down and on the verge of war. It is not the purpose of this
book to attempt a historical account of the tangled web that led to the Land
Wars of the 1860s. But to understand fully how the gifting of the Tongariro
Peaks belongs in the mainstream of New Zealand history, it is necessary to
know something about the Maori King Movement and its policies, and to
locate some particular engagements of the Land Wars.

The conflict originated from the settlers' frustrations in obtaining land;
whether as arrivals in the first ships in Wellington to discover that the New
Zealand Company did not own the land they had been promised, or in
finding they could not purchase directly from Maori owners because the
Government had a pre-emptive right to purchase and resell, or just being
unable to get land because supply was nowhere near demand. In time they
were able to observe that Maori policy, in the face of disenchantment with
the Treaty of Waitangi and increasing concern at land loss, was hardening and
that the prospect of ownership was receding. There was a succession of acute
land problems and tensions in Taranaki. It was in that province that co-
ordinated Maori resistance to land sale began to take shape.

In 1854 the southern Taranaki tribe of Ngati Ruanui convened a meeting
in a large council hall specially built and named 'Taiporohenui'. This could
be translated as 'the finishing of the work' — that is, the work of colonisation.
While there was talk about withholding land from sale, an important and
related idea evolved from this meeting — that of 'kotahitanga', or unity under
a Maori king. Shaped by many meetings and the statesman-like direction of

'Burning the bush, Taranaki' — William Strutt, 1856.

This sketch gives some idea of the scale of the fires used by settlers to clear the dense bush of the New Zealand forest, where a thick undergrowth made work with axes a slow, tedious business.

As early European explorers noted, the bushfires lit by themselves and by the Maori often became uncontrollable and raced over vast areas for days, leaving behind widespread devastation.

Wiremu Tamehana, the idea developed and the search for a candidate proceeded. In 1856 the kingship was offered to Te Heuheu Tukino (Iwikau). Iwikau declined but nonetheless supported the policies of the King Movement. At the same time he was able to maintain good relations with European administrations and to keep Ngati Tuwharetoa from involvement in much of the conflict that followed.

The first phase of the war began in Taranaki in 1860. A truce followed a year of confusion, but hostilities flared up once more in 1863. The Maori forces in Taranaki were defeated by General Cameron, who returned to Auckland with most of his troops and invaded the Waikato. The final engagement of the Waikato War, the famous action at Orakau Pa, involved Tuhoe people from the Urewera, and one of two Tuwharetoa units from the Taupo area. This group, under chiefs from southern Taupo, had fallen in with some Tuhoe and Ngati Kahungunu warriors. Meeting Rewi Maniapoto, a senior commander of Waikato forces, they persuaded him against his judgement to build the Orakau Pa. The pa was taken; the unconquerable spirit of the defence has a special place in history.

The second Tuwharetoa unit was led by Te Heuheu Tukino (Horonuku), who had succeeded Iwikau in 1862 and felt under obligation to support his Waikato kinsfolk. Arriving at Orakau after the British forces had surrounded the pa, he was compelled to become a distant witness to the action.

After a short Bay of Plenty campaign, the focus moved once again to Taranaki and a phenomenon that transformed despair to new hope for Maori resistance. 'Pai Marire', or 'Hauhau-ism' as the Europeans called it, merged Christian doctrine with Old Testament morality and Maori mysticism. The boldness it engendered was the credo of the small-scale guerilla war that dragged on until 1872 in the Taranaki and Wanganui districts, the East Coast and Hawke's Bay. In 1868 the talented and ruthless Te Kooti Rikirangi burst like a storm cloud on settlements in Poverty Bay. Three years of pursuit followed, punctuated by Te Kooti's swift attacks from the forested confusion of the Urewera highlands. Government columns entering the mountain labyrinth, while having limited success, compelled Te Kooti to move towards the Lake Taupo area and the support he anticipated from a section of Ngati Tuwharetoa and perhaps even from the King Movement as a whole.

At the end of September 1869 Te Kooti built a pa at Te Porere. When this was attacked and captured he escaped, but the defeat at Te Porere marked the beginning of the end for the guerilla leader. In the light of later events in the Land Court in Taupo in 1881, related in Chapter 9, the particular interest of the engagement at Te Porere is that one of the attacking units was Wanganui led by Major Kepa te Rangihiwinui, and that according to Kepa, Te Heuheu Tukino with a section of Ngati Tuwharetoa was present but did not engage in the battle.

With the end of the Land Wars the confiscations of land that followed, along with less direct legislative devices for its acquisition, opened up the way for European-style development in the North, with the exception of the 'aukati' — the area of central New Zealand still controlled by the King Movement.

In the South, the land changes induced by the imported farming practices of the settlers were already extensive. Great fires had raced across the tussock grasslands of the South Island. Wherever they were, the settlers sought the things of home. They wrote disparagingly of gloomy forests, barren plains and dismal coasts. Unfamiliarity and loneliness deepened the already sombre tones of native New Zealand bush. The crops, fruits, berries and birds of the English countryside were as essential to the recreation of 'Home' as they were to farming practice imported from the downs of England. By the 1860s acclimatisation societies were bringing in field birds, gamebirds, waterfowl

---

TE KOOTI RIKIRANGI
(1830–1893)
Ngati Maru/Rongowhakaata

Te Kooti was born about 1830 near Gisborne. Following a Wesleyan Mission education at Waerenga-a-hika, Te Kooti worked for many years as a small trader and master on Maori-owned coastal schooners. In 1865 he fought with the government force that laid seige to the Hauhau pa at Waerenga-a-hika, but was arrested some months later on trumped-up charges and deported to the Chatham Islands.

Over the next two years Te Kooti gained the leadership of Hauhau prisoners in the Chathams and persuaded them to adopt a new religion, the Ringatu faith. This new religion drew heavily on the Bible — Te Kooti identified their imprisonment with the plight of the Jews in Egypt. The schooner *Rifleman* provided an escape from their land of bondage and in 1868 Te Kooti and his followers landed near Gisborne.

For the next four years Te Kooti fought a remarkable campaign on the East Coast and in the Urewera. After the capture of Te Porere redoubt in 1869 he was forced on the defensive.

In 1872 Te Kooti retired to the King Country, under the mana of King Tawhiao. He was pardoned in 1883 and spent the remaining years up to his death in fully developing the tenets of the Ringatu faith.

Rikirangi Te Turuki, Te Kooti

'George French Angas.'

'Te Heuheu and Iwikau' — G. F. Angas, 1847.

Te Heuheu Tukino II Mananui was paramount chief of Ngati Tuwharetoa until 1842, when, with his eldest son, he was killed in a landslide. Renowned for his wisdom and stature, he exercised great power and influence in the central North Island. His brother Iwikau succeeded him as paramount chief until his death in 1862.

and plants from the four corners of the earth. The following decade saw the arrival of hares, hedgehogs, brown trout and deer.

Despite the predominance of forest in the North Island, it was those of the South that were utilised first. Settlers lived in a world of wood. They made everything they could from it: houses, furniture, ships and fences. Once timber near a settlement had gone, transport called the tune. The cheapest and often the only transport was by sea. Hence, it was forests accessible by sea that were milled. The Marlborough Sounds supplied Wellington and Wanganui, Banks Peninsula timber went to Christchurch and that from the Catlins to Dunedin. The gold industry was soon biting into the forests of Westland.

Within the forests a less obvious change was taking place. A bird life that had never known animal attack, was being eaten out by introduced predators. The Norway rat, as the Maori observed, had eaten the Maori rat. It was unlikely to stop there. Julius von Haast, sitting at his camp fire near Mount Cook, could not help but observe it; he was knocking rats over with a stick. Some beaches crawled with them. Many explorers took bird dogs to help them to live off the land. Brunner, having eaten his own dog, noted the absence of kiwis: 'They are now nearly extinct by the dogs of the bush.' Dieffenbach commented both on wild cats and wild pigs, which he said had

'Te Heuheu's old pa of Waitahanui at Lake Taupo' — G. F. Angas, 1847.

This pa, on the eastern shore of Lake Taupo, preceded Waihi as the principal residence of the paramount chief of Ngati Tuwharetoa.

over-run the north: 'The introduction of the carnivorous dog and cat into New Zealand has had a curious and fatal effect on the feathered races.'

But in the North exploitation had been retarded by a loyalty to land — the fruit of a thousand years of occupation. You might say that a type of conservation had been applied. More than half of the North Island was still in Maori ownership. South of the Puniu River was the 'aukati', the 'world not taken away'. It could be dangerous to enter. From Taranaki to the Raukumara, and from the Waikato Heads to Hawke's Bay were the mountains and forests of untouched New Zealand — unmodified as yet by the exploitive European. The thirty years of delay was, by an accident of history, giving time for an idea to generate, in the aftermath of a great civil war, on another frontier — that of the United States.

Chapter 8

Utilitarian Conservation
1870–1887

The year 1870 was just one generation removed from the arrival of the New Zealand Company ships. In thirty years the new settlers had explored most of the land, with the exceptions of the far south-west of the South Island and parts of the central North Island, particularly the King Country. Settlement in the South Island had forged ahead. Christchurch had its elegant Provincial Buildings, the Lyttelton rail tunnel had been opened, and Dunedin could be described as a city of some grandeur.

In striking contrast was the situation in the North Island. While the major battles of the Land Wars had finished by 1865, the Taranaki chief Titokowaru had caused great alarm in 1868 and Te Kooti was still at large. The North was in a profoundly nervous state and the economy of the whole colony was in recession.

A new premier, William Fox, had taken office. In 1870 his treasurer, Julius Vogel, unfolded an ambitious proposal to an astonished House. Recognising that settlement was isolated and still largely coastal, he proposed the con-

A railway siding in the 1880s.
The expanding railway system promoted forest exploitation. Initially the timber was extracted for milling. Further clearing paved the way for dairy farming.

struction of railways through both islands, together with roads in the north to open up land. Hand in hand went immigration. More people were needed to help with the work and expand the economy. The gold to promote a new boom would be borrowed. Loans would be serviced and repaid from operating profits from the railway, and from the income of a national land estate to be set aside along the roads and railways.

These proposals, somewhat modified, won the support of the House and the country. The immigration and public works programme began to move. Within ten years the population would be half a million — double that of 1870. For the next few years the dominant figure in colonial politics, Vogel, had his hands full defending, adjusting and promoting his policies. In 1873, at the age of thirty-eight, he became Premier. And in the same year he appeared to become converted to the cause of forest conservation.

This was raised first in the House of Representatives in 1868 by Thomas Potts with the motion 'That it is desirable Government should take steps to ascertain the present condition of the forests of the Colony with a view to their better conservation.' Potts was given strong support by the botanist W. T. L. Travers and Charles O'Neill, the Member for Thames, but Vogel had not shown much sympathy, claiming that 'the invariable rule in a new colony is the lavish use of native forest'. Nothing was done about Potts's motion, although the debate about forest destruction continued.

Charles O'Neill returned to the attack in 1872, and the Government promised a Bill on the subject. There was no Bill in 1873. O'Neill did not pull punches: 'A measure for the conservation of the forests of the Colony was one which would require the careful consideration of the House and the Government, so that history might not be able to relate that they received a fertile country, but, by a criminal want of foresight, transmitted to posterity a desert!' The Committee on Colonial Industries recommended to the Governor that the provincial governments should be invited to 'consider how best to prevent the wasteful destruction of the forests of the Colony, and to supply statistics and recommendations for the consideration of Parliament'.

Outside the House, the Wellington Philosophical Society had in 1871

THOMAS POTTS (1824–1888)

Thomas Potts has the distinction of being the first parliamentarian to press for forest conservation in New Zealand. He was concerned with future timber supplies and also with forest removal as a cause of flooding. He referred in his speech to George Perkins Marsh and the connections between forest clearance and flooding established in *Man and Nature*.

Potts typified the busy Victorian gentleman with a wide range of interests. In addition to his role in national politics, he was also a member of the Canterbury Provincial Council, the local philosophical and acclimatisation societies, the Christ-church Domains' Board and the Canterbury Museum.

Nature study was his passion — whether roving the back country or cultivating his extensive garden. An acute observer, he published in 1882 *Out in the Open*, a compilation of articles covering a range of topics, including a plea for national domains — the forerunners of national parks.

Potts made clear his concern at the speed of change to the New Zealand environment since European settlement, from forest clearance and introduced animals to the depredations of hunters and even museum collectors. His suggestion that Resolution Island in Fiordland be set aside as a reserve was realised in 1891.

considered a paper on 'The results of forest destruction in the basin of the River Wolga at Astrakan'. In the same year Arthur Dudley Dobson read a paper to the Nelson Association for the Promotion of Science and Industry on the 'Destruction of land by shingle-bearing rivers', which looked at the situation in New Zealand. 'The enormous devastation occasioned by the indiscriminate destruction of forest in the Old World is so clearly shown by Mr G. P. Marsh in *Man and Nature*,' said Dobson, 'that I must refer to his work . . .'

Now the cause had attracted the most able politician of the day. Vogel asked the provinces for information and recommendations but the replies did not bristle with conviction. Some did not reply at all, while others clearly favoured continuing forest clearance. Only Vogel's former province of Otago provided the information sought. Taranaki promised judicious clearing and that no vegetation would be disturbed within four and a half to five miles of Mount Egmont. This policy preserved the future option for a national park.

Undeterred, Vogel introduced the New Zealand Forests Bill in 1874. 'The Bill,' he said 'embodies a definite proposal for the establishment and management of State Forests.' A recent visit to the southern provinces had forcibly presented to his notice 'how very large was the demand for timber which arose from our railway works and our telegraph construction and maintenance; how very great were the injuries caused by floods, and how much deterioration our climate was liable to sustain, from the destruction of forests'. There was no other subject more important for New Zealand.

Vogel had gathered his information from around the world, emphasising the United States 'because we are apt to think of America as possessing exhaustless forests . . .', and referring to a report on forest management in Germany, Austria and Great Britain by Captain Inches Campbell-Walker. It

WILLIAM FOX (1812–1893)

William Fox is probably best remembered for being Premier of New Zealand four times between 1856 and 1873. His significance in the national parks' story relates to two of his other achievements — as explorer and artist.

In 1846 Fox joined with two other New Zealand Company employees, Thomas Brunner and Charles Heaphy, on an exploring mission in the Nelson province. They were probably the first Europeans to sight Lakes Rotoiti and Rotoroa.

Fox's paintings of the Nelson lakes were among the first of a long series recording many of the spectacular areas now protected in national parks.

Until recently his work received little attention but he is now recognised as one of the first painters to portray the New Zealand landscape in natural and unpretentious manner. This ability is also seen in some of his overseas

paintings — he was a keen traveller who visited the United States in 1853 and again in 1875, when he painted at several locations including Yosemite.

Fox was interested in the Yellowstone National Park concept and in August 1874 he wrote to the Premier, Julius Vogel, suggesting that a similar idea be applied to the thermal springs district of the North Island. He envisaged Government purchase and development of areas such as the Taupo and Rotorua townships as health resorts in order to stop uncontrolled private speculation. In particular, he was keen to prevent tasteless development of the Terraces at Rotomahana, noting that overseas tourist spots, such as the Great Pyramid and the summit of Mount Sinai, were strewn with litter.

This request was the forerunner of the Thermal Springs District Act (1881), and a direct link with the creation of Tongariro National Park in 1887.

was a fallacy, he argued, that the timber supply of the world was inexhaustible. All evidence pointed to the necessity of forest conservation: 'Many countries of the East, which at one time played large parts in the history of the world, have literally been destroyed . . . by the destruction of their natural timber' and the indirect effects of flooding, destruction of watercourses, and washing away of soil. Turning to New Zealand, he quoted approximate figures, provided by Dr James Hector, showing that a quarter of the New Zealand forests had been lost between 1830 and 1868 and that the rate of destruction was increasing.

Vogel's proposal was to establish state forests, and if the provinces would allow three per cent of the whole of their land to be set apart as forest land, the Government would propose the release of the provinces from the obligation of paying for the sinking fund for the railways. The forest land would be selected so as to make the forests useful to the population likely to settle in their vicinity, and so as to give shelter to the neighbouring country.

Vogel's concluding remarks contained visionary ideas far removed from the parochial concerns of the provinces, and concepts of distinctive character

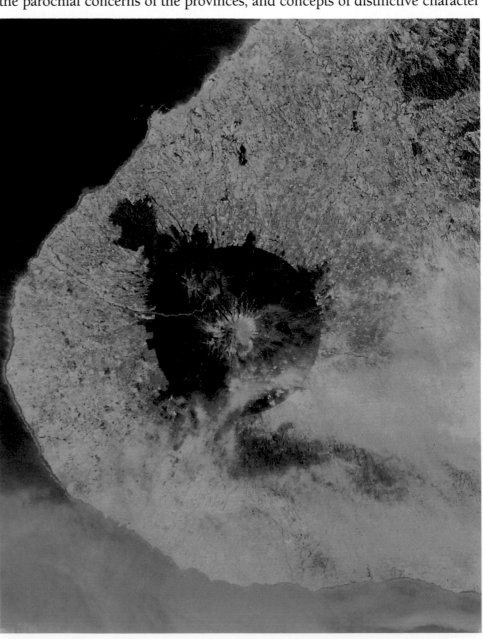

The camera of a Landsat satellite records the circle of forest around Taranaki/Mount Egmont and a policy of protection that dates from 1875.

and intrinsic value that would not receive legislative expression for eighty years.

'I plead on behalf of New Zealand,' he said, 'that whilst we are laboriously endeavouring to improve the country by means of great public works, we shall not overlook the value and importance of those great natural features, without care for which, however attractive we may otherwise make the country, we cannot make it attractive as the home of an industrious population, nor can we hope to preserve its character and its intrinsic value. New Zealand entirely unsettled — New Zealand in its old wild state — might be very much more valuable, clothed with forest, than New Zealand denuded of forest and covered with public works constructed at enormous cost and with enormous labour . . . The question involved in this forests matter is of something for New Zealand to cling to for generations; to shape its future; to decide its climate, its adaptability for settlement, its commercial value, its beauty, its healthfulness, and its pleasure-bestowing qualities.'

It was but two years since the Yellowstone National Park had been created 'as a public park, or pleasuring ground for the benefit and enjoyment of the people'. Vogel had realised that there was, and is, character that is uniquely New Zealand, that such character has intrinsic value and that great natural features have values of themselves.

Such notions in 1874 were of limited appeal. The Bill was changed greatly in its stormy passage through the House. Conservation was fine in principle but the need for it was not apparent in New Zealand. Vogel was challenging deep-seated beliefs that the forests were really an impediment to development. Clearance was considered vital to the creation of farms and, ultimately, an economy.

The real intent, said some, was the taking of land from the provinces. The remnants of the Bill, as passed into law, allowed ten thousand pounds a year for forest management, the appointment of a Conservator of Forests and the conditional setting up of state forests. Two years later, an attempt to repeal the Forest Act failed, but its financial provisions were rescinded.

The Conservator of Forests, who thereupon left New Zealand, was Campbell-Walker, who had been quoted in Vogel's speech of 1874. He had surveyed the situation in both islands and prepared a report confirming the anxieties of the conservationists. The kauri forests could be destroyed in forty years. 'We cannot be wise too soon,' he said. In the decade to 1874 perhaps one and a half million hectares of forest had been eliminated. There were, however, some positive results from Vogel's New Zealand Forests Act of 1874. Most important was the reservation of Mount Egmont in 1875, and the vesting in the provincial council of the eight-kilometre radius that the council had already undertaken to protect. Faint, and still far away, the national park idea was approaching, perhaps by way of the influence of William Fox. It was two weeks after a discussion with Fox that the Provincial Superintendent issued an order reserving from sale all the forest and mountain land within the radius.

The Land Act of 1877 added machinery that could be used for forest conservation, permitting reserves to be made for parks and domains. It repealed a large number of provincial statutes and dealt uniformly with the lands of the Crown. Most of the reserves established were at the headwaters of forested catchments, to stem soil erosion, flooding and the waste of timber. The

'Felling kauri, showing men having billy tea' — John Backhouse *c.* 1880.

Many kauri trees were tragically destroyed in fires for land clearance. Settlers soon realised, however, the value of the timber and kauri milling became an industry of primary importance for New Zealand's economy. The sawn timber was used for buildings of all kinds, boat-building and cabinet-making. Men contracted to fell the kauri spent long, hard months living out in the bush.

Egmont reserve, having lost its protection under provincial legislation, was brought under the Land Act in 1881, with a radius at that time of nine kilometres and an area of over twenty-nine thousand hectares.

The railways were not only making a large demand on the forests, they were changing the basis of the timber industry. Access from the sea and rivers was giving way to access from railways sidings. By the mid-1870s large and previously inaccessible areas that could be farmed when the forest had been cleared were being utilised in regions like Southland and the Manawatu. Timber was a large component of railway freight, not only as a sawn product, but also as poles and fencing. By the mid-1880s most of the forests accessible from the sea had been worked out. The exception was the northern kauri, still a water-based industry, but, because of export markets and the superb special qualities of the timber, maintaining a vast output.

Vogel's Bill had been nullified, the first Conservator of Forests had resigned and forest destruction was continuing unabated. Nonetheless, through the early 1880s the need for forest conservation was kept persistently before the Assemblies. Towards the end of 1884 Thomas Kirk was commissioned to examine the forests 'with a view to reporting on the best means for their preservation'. In August 1885, Vogel's second Forests Act was passed, setting aside state forests, and providing for conservation and skilled management. Thomas Kirk was appointed Chief Conservator at the end of the year. In his first week he reserved one hundred and thirty-eight thousand hectares of Southland forests, and in his second week over three thousand hectares of Auckland kauri.

Excursions to the Pink and White Terrace of Lake Rotomahana, near Rotorua, had started before the fledgling tourist industry gained impetus from the new roads and extending railways. The first tourist handbook appeared in 1872; those of each succeeding year were able to describe improved services, better accommodation and more attractions. Soon adventurous travellers could visit the Sounds and the Southern Lakes. But the Terraces were the dominant, irresistible attractions.

In the summer of 1873 William Fox spent several weeks in the hot springs district. In August 1874 he wrote to Julius Vogel reviewing the possibilities

Despite their delicate lace-like appearance, the Pink and White Terraces were solid formations. Tourists, like this party on the White Terraces, climbed them for a hot dip in the thermal pools at the top.

of the major thermal sites from Tokaanu to Rotorua. It was a crisp, lively letter. Fox the artist had been painting that summer, and Fox the writer could also bring the scenes to life. Compared with Whakatipu, Te Anau and Wanaka, he did not think Taupo, even if 'a grand sheet of bright, transparent water' could be assigned a first place in 'lacustrine scenery'. The Huka Falls would be considered a fine attraction in any part of the world. The Waikato River, 'after brawling in rapids and eddying in reaches for a few miles, is suddenly pent in between perpendicular walls . . . Between these the whole descending river rushes for a distance of two or three hundred yards, churned into a mass of snow-white foam, and roaring with the hoarse voice with which great cataracts are gifted, till the confining walls suddenly receding, it shoots forth as if out of the barrel of a gigantic gun . . .

'. . . It is not my intention to dilate on the wonderful and beautiful which abound in connection with Rotomahana and its terraces. I wish rather to draw attention to the different groups of springs, with a view to their sanitary use. At the same time, the idea that these majestic scenes may one day be desecrated by all the constituents of a common watering-place, has something in it bordering on profanity . . . that they should be surrounded with pretentious hotels and scarcely less offensive tea-gardens; that they should be strewed with orange-peel, with walnut shells, and the capsules of bitter beer bottles (as the Great Pyramid and even the summit of Mount Sinai are), is a consummation from the very idea of which the soul of every lover of nature must recoil. The Government of the United States had hardly become

THOMAS KIRK (1828–1898)

English-born Thomas Kirk emigrated to New Zealand in 1863 and tried his hand at the different occupations of timber merchant, surveyor and pioneer farmer before being appointed secretary, curator and later, council member of the Auckland Institute and Museum. He made botanical explorations of the Auckland province and of surrounding islands, including Little Barrier, sending gifts of native plant collections to museums all over the world.

Kirk may have had an unusual opportunity to influence Vogel to pass the first New Zealand Forests Act (1874). His small home in Tinakori Road, Wellington, was without water and for some time he had to borrow buckets of water from the Vogel establishment directly opposite.

In 1874 he became professor of natural sciences at Wellington College and followed this position with a short spell as a biology and geology lecturer at Lincoln College. In 1885 he was appointed Chief Conservator of State Forests, a poorly paid position. Despite recurrent ill health, he threw himself into his work, travelling long distances to make recommendations on forests all over New Zealand. He was responsible for the formation of the Forest and Agriculture Branch of the Lands Department and the initiation of the protection schemes for native forests. During his term 320,000 hectares were set aside as forest reserves. In 1888 he was compulsorily retired when an economic recession closed his section of the department. In spite of his valuable service to the colony, he died a poor man.

His research, including a study of the impact of introduced flora and fauna on native species, appeared in various scientific journals. His major work, *Forest Flora*, was published in 1889. He wrote over a thousand letters a year to settlers, students and botanists in many parts of the world.

Thomas and Mrs Kirk

'Boiling mud pool near Te Tarata, Rotomahana' — William Fox, 1864?

Fox was so impressed by the thermal attractions of the Rotomahana district that he suggested to the Government that the area be protected from tasteless exploitation.

acquainted with the fact that they possessed a territory comprising similar volcanic wonders at the forks of the Yellow River and Missouri, than an Act of Congress was passed reserving a block of land of sixty miles square, within which the geyers and hot springs are, as public parks, to be for ever under the protection of the states; and it will doubtless take care that they shall not become the prey of private speculators, or of men to whom a few dollars may present more charms than all the finest works of creation.

'I beg to suggest to the Government of New Zealand that as soon as the Native title may be extinguished, some such step should be taken with regard to Rotomahana, its terraces, and other volcanic wonders. It is to the credit of the Maoris that they have hitherto done all in their power to protect them, and express no measured indignation at the sacrilegious act of some European barbarians who, impelled by scientific zeal or vulgar curiosity, have chipped off several hand's breadth of the lovely salmon-coloured surface of the Pink Terrace.'

With this letter the national park idea in the Yellowstone model officially entered New Zealand. The objective of the letter was, however, 'to draw the attention of the Government to the great value of the sanitary provision which nature has made in the district described . . . The country is almost worthless

The Tarawera eruption of 10 June 1886 was New Zealand's largest volcanic event since Maori settlement. The eruption tore a deep rent across Mount Tarawera, blew apart the famed Pink and White Terraces and buried the surrounding landscape in sticky volcanic mud. More than a hundred and fifty people lost their lives, principally in the Maori settlements around Lake Rotomahana. This photograph by the Burton brothers shows 'Mr Hazard's Home'.

for agricultural or pastoral or any similar purposes; but when its sanitary resources are developed, it may prove a source of great wealth to the colony . . . What is required is simply practical skill enough to make water run in pipes . . . the engineer who designed the baths of Caracalla or Nero cannot now be got; but I doubt not that there are tradesmen . . .'

Late in 1880 an agreement was signed between the Crown and representatives and chiefs of the Ngati Whakaue people, who generously gifted twenty hectares containing the medicinal springs along the southern shores of Rotorua 'for the benefit of the people of the world'. In 1881 the Thermal Springs Districts Act was passed. Government involvement with facilities at thermal springs commenced at Rotorua and Te Aroha, where another gift of land was made by the Maori people of the locality. Thermal springs continued to be the focus of government expenditure and interest until well into the twentieth century, reflecting the world-wide interest of the wealthy in spas and watering places. The Rotorua Spa was planned in emulation of Vichy, Carlsbad, Bath and Harrowgate.

With a spa now complementing 'Te Tarata', the tourist centre grew. The Terraces were billed as 'the eighth wonder of the world' — painted, photographed — New Zealand's pre-eminent tourist attraction. On 10 June 1886 they ceased to exist. Mount Tarawera erupted with a volcanic blast that, according to the *New Zealand Herald*, was apparently heard all over the North Island. As for the Terraces, said the *Herald* 'They are gone, and their site is the scene of a raging volcano.'

Tragedy as well as destruction attended the explosion. At first it seemed that the whole future of Rotorua, including its tourism, was in doubt. There was an initial fall in the number of visitors, but as the 1887 Report of the Lands and Survey Department pointed out: 'There are still plenty of attractions for invalids and tourists — splendid baths, fountains, ornamental grounds, geysers of Whakarewarewa and Tikitere, and even in the grandeur of desolation of the great fissure, craters and ejecta of the volcanic eruption itself.' The town was not sinking, as had been feared, attention was drawn to other thermal areas of considerable beauty, like Waiotapu, and the road network from Rotorua towards the Tongariro Mountains allowed the more venturesome to explore further afield.

Indeed, that prospect had been developing for more than a decade. A coach service from Rotorua to Taupo commenced in 1875, extending the Taupo to Napier service, which began in 1872. Of very much greater consequence, the first surveys were commencing for the vital link in Vogel's grand plan — the North Island Main Trunk Railway. Between the railheads of Te Awamutu and Marton lay more than three hundred kilometres of rugged, part-forested 'terra incognita'. In 1883 surveyors C. W. Hursthouse and John Rochfort set out from Te Awamutu and Marton respectively; Hursthouse to prospect a route to New Plymouth, Rochfort to go through the centre of the island. Their adventures and frustrations reveal much about the King Country of that time — the people as well as the topography were resistant to the railway.

Other surveyors engaged in triangulation work through the King Country 'enjoyed' similar experiences, but a few venturesome travellers whose business attracted less suspicion fared well enough. Early in 1883 an explorer-writer named Kerry-Nicholls set off from Auckland on a thousand-kilometre journey to the King Country. He wanted to satisfy his personal curiosity, and to make known 'more fully that portion of it which was virtually a blank on the maps, and thus to add, as far as lay in my power, to the geographical and geological knowledge of a vast and important region'.

From Rotorua he travelled to Taupo via the Terraces and the new hotel at Wairakei, thence along the eastern shores to Tokaanu. From Tokaanu he made a circuit of the mountains and continued to the west of the lake into the northern King Country. With his companion interpreter, he ascended Ngauruhoe and Tongariro and twice climbed Ruapehu.

'Never,' said Nicholls, 'had I seen a more varied and enchanting scene. I had beheld a wider expanse of country from the summit of the Rocky Mountains, gorges and precipices more stupendous in the valley of the Yosemite, and I had gazed over land very similar in outline from the summit of Fujiyama

---

ALFRED KINGCOME NEWMAN (1849–1924)

After completing his studies as a medical student with excellent results, Newman chose to leave the profession to enter the commercial field as partner in a firm of general merchants. In 1884 he was successful in his second attempt to be elected to the House of Representatives and served several long terms as the Member for Thorndon (1884–90), Hutt (1890–93), Wellington Suburbs (1893–96) and finally Wellington East (1911–22). From 1922 to 1924 he was a member of the Legislative Council. He was the first parliamentarian to promote the idea of a national park and continued throughout his long political career to bring the matter before successive Governments.

Newman maintained an interest in civic affairs, serving on such bodies as the Wellington City Council, the education board and the University of New Zealand senate. He was keen on racing and rugby and was president of the New Zealand Rugby Union. His book *Who are the Maoris?* was published in 1884. At the time of his death his parliamentary colleagues paid tribute to his wisdom, vigour and high principles and to his initiative in promoting the campaign for a national park.

Alfred Burton's canoe trip up the Wanganui River in company with railway surveyor John Rochfort in 1885 yielded a fine portfolio of photographs. Burton admired the 'glorious bush, with which Nature, with so lavish a hand, has clothed the banks of the Wanganui', although, after fourteen days cramped into the canoe, with much broken weather, he was glad to reach Taumarunui and dry land. Ranana, where this photograph was taken, was the site of Major Kemp's Council Hall.

in Japan, but never before had I stood upon a glacier-crowned height in the region of perpetual snow with an active volcano, rising thousands of feet, beneath me, nor had I ever beheld so wide an expanse of lake, mountain, and rolling plain mingling together, as it were, and forming one grand and glorious picture.'

Nicholls was impressed, enraptured, lyrical. His vivid descriptions flowed on — to the conclusion, and the idea: 'Here was in reality a model Switzerland under a semi-tropical sky — a region designed, as it were, by the artistic hand of nature for a national recreation-ground, where countless generations of men might assemble to marvel at some of the grandest works of creation.

'With the Te Pakaru Plain proclaimed as a public domain, New Zealand would possess the finest and most unique park in the world. For healthfulness of climate, variety of scenery and volcanic and thermal wonders, there would be no place to equal it in the Northern or Southern Hemisphere, no spot where within so small a radius could be seen natural phenomena so varied and so remarkable. It would embrace within its boundaries the hot springs of Tongariro and those of Tokaanu, and would stretch from the waters of Lake Taupo to the shores of Rotoaira. The surrounding table-land, with its millions of acres of open plains covered with rich volcanic soil, should eventually become the granary of the North Island; while the Kaimanawa Mountains and the Tuhua should give forth their mineral treasures on either side.'

Nicholls's account of his travels was popular; another influence on the climate of opinion was made by the paintings of Blomfield and Barraud, the works of the influential William Fox and a general interest in the volcanic, which had the recent cataclysmic endorsement of nature herself. In 1882 Dr Alfred Newman, Member of Parliament for Thorndon, asked the Minister of Lands, 'If the Government will reserve Ruapehu, Ngauruhoe, Tongariro, Rotoaira, Tokaanu, and the hot-springs in the district as a national park? The Thermal-Springs Act took in the districts of East Tauranga and East Taupo, but did not take in the area referred to in this question; and, as the Government had already agreed to reserve Mount Cook, it would be as well if they reserved these lands as well. As the Northern Trunk Railway was likely to pass up that way, it would be much better for the Government to acquire the district than to allow it to fall into the hands of speculators.'

John Ballance replied: 'There was no power in the hands of the Government to reserve these places, for they did not come within the Thermal-Springs Act. The Government would, however, take steps to prevent their falling into private hands.'

In winter of the following year, Alfred Burton, the outdoors specialist of the now famous Burton brothers, photographers of Dunedin, arrived in Wanganui. His record added a pictorial dimension to the poetic prose of Kerry-Nicholls. In the Maniapoto lands of the King Country he took portraits of the chief Wahanui. Later in the year, when in the Tongariro area he made a portrait of Te Heuheu Tukino, paramount chief of Ngati Tuwharetoa.

It was not the beauty and distinction of the Tongariro mountains and the thermal springs district alone that were capturing the interest of explorer-writers, artists, nascent tourism and early photographers. The impressive qualities of some South Island districts were being similarly described and communicated.

In 1874 Alfred Burton made the first of twenty trips to the sounds of the south-west. The small settlement of Jamestown in Martins Bay had resulted from Otago enthusiasm to counter trade and population losses to the West Coast gold rush. Tourism in the Sounds began in 1877 with a special excursion from Port Chalmers run by the Union Steam Ship Company. The company's travel booklet, *Maoriland*, of 1884 wrote warmly of an 'extended picnic' which attracted travellers even from Europe and America. While sportsmen would find plenty to occupy their attention, the tameness of the birds was a problem. Kakapo, wood pigeon, orange-wattled crow, weka, kiwi, and penguin were all to be met. The Sounds were a paradise for fishermen, the history fascinating, the scenery superb, and Milford Sound of 'a character of solemnity and grandeur which description can barely realise'.

'Yet even in this solitude,' said the booklet, 'men have made a home. On

Caswell Sound was visited each summer on the annual Union Steamship Company cruises to Fiordland. This particular area was rich in marble and of great interest to amateur geologists, although it was never commercially exploited.

The cruises — leisurely eight- or nine-day saunters — began in 1877, giving access to this otherwise isolated region. The combination of mountains and sea was very popular, sometimes being described as 'an alpine excursion by steamer'.

'Milford Sound' — Charles Barraud, 1880.

The sounds of Fiordland, especially Milford, were billed as one of New Zealand's scenic wonders. The sheer rock cliffs embraced by luxuriant vegetation, the shimmering waterfalls and narrow sounds combined to inspire in the tourist a feeling of awe and admiration.

a small strip of level land, just past the Bowen Falls, we can distinguish three huts.' This was Donald Sutherland's 'City of Milford'.

In 1870 the surveyor Edward Sealy climbed far up the Tasman Glacier to record in a wealth of detail the huge scale and forces of the mountain environment. It was a determined and laborious effort considering the equipment the early photographer had to carry — a 'darkroom' tent, chemicals, trays and glass plates, as well as a heavy camera and tripod.

Even without such a load, few penetrated as far for a decade. It was early photographs of Mount Cook, displayed in York, England, in 1881 that attracted a clergyman of truly formidable initiative. William Spotswood Green had climbed in the European Alps during several seasons after an initiation in 1869. Convinced that 'Mount Cook was a splendid peak', he set about its conquest, and hired Emil Boss, hotelier, and Ulrich Kaufmann, Oberland guide, to accompany him. Early in 1882 he entered Milford Sound on board the steamer *Te Anau* to 'the grandest combination of scenery upon which my eyes had ever rested'.

DONALD SUTHERLAND (1839–1919)

Donald Sutherland was a dashing character — a loner who had enlisted in his youth in Garibaldi's Thousand in Italy, fought in the New Zealand Land Wars and later became a gold prospector on the West Coast. Late in 1877 he sailed from Thompson Sound to Milford Sound ('a bully run for one man in an open boat') to found 'The City' at Milford — a bustling metropolis of three huts amidst the magnificent scenery of Fiordland. With several other prospectors, he begun to explore the sounds, discovering Lake Ada and the Sutherland Falls. Further work was done at the urging of the Lake Wakatipu County Council to find an easy route to the West Coast from Queenstown. None was found, and a century later such a road is still under discussion.

Sutherland's isolation did not last long. Cruises to Milford and other Sounds ran from the late 1870s, and within a decade the cutting of the Milford Track was under way. In 1889 the track opened for its first season. Two years later Sutherland and his wife established a hotel at Milford that would serve tourists for nearly thirty years.

Donald Sutherland founded 'The City'
at the head of Milford Sound,
photographed by the Burton brothers.
Sutherland married and his wife
began to develop tourist facilities
by building a twelve-roomed hotel that
welcomed walkers for the next
twenty-five years.

In Christchurch, Green called on von Haast, whose account of the Mount Cook area he had studied, and closely examined photographs by Sealy. Then it was off to the mountains. The first of New Zealand's true mountaineers endured all that has been the lot of climbers since. Crossing the Hooker River was dangerous. One of the horses had a delicious roll, regrettably with the pack containing the flour, tea, sugar and Green's extra clothes still on his back, and wekas stole anything that was not nailed down. Green noted that it had been customary to send a mob of about two thousand sheep across the Hooker for the summer months. The climbers could see fires circling the peaks of the Liebig Range, lit by shepherds to drive sheep down. Green and his companions enjoyed roast blue duck and kea soup.

Two weeks after leaving Fairlie they were standing on a ridge far above the Hooker Glacier — 'beyond, the glacier-seamed crags of Mount Sefton towered skywards. It was a wonderful sight, those lovely peaks standing up out of the purple haze, and then to think that not one had been climbed! Here was work not for a short holiday ramble merely, not to be accomplished even in a life-time, but work for a whole company of climbers, which would occupy them for half a century of summers, and still there would remain many a new route to be tried.'

By the evening of 2 March 1882 they were near, but not quite on, the peak, in a chilling gale. There followed a dreadful night, and a perilous descent. The climbing fraternity of Europe realised that New Zealand had opposite seasons and virgin peaks, and the stage was set for development.

In October 1884 Mr Sutter rose in Parliament to ask the Minister of Lands to set aside a sufficient quantity of land for public purposes around the foot of Mount Cook and the Mueller Glacier. His attention had been drawn to a telegram in the morning's paper claiming, 'The up-country hotelkeepers and coach-proprietors around the Mount Cook glaciers are laying out considerable sums in anticipation of the visits of tourists; and an accommodation house will soon be opened at the foot of Mount Cook.' This was the first Hermitage, a modest building situated at the foot of the Mueller Glacier. The two-day journey from Fairlie by horse and coach, with numerous stream crossings, was always long and tiring, and sometimes dangerous. Alfred Newman's plea for the reservation of the Tongariro area followed within days.

There were reasons other than tourism that justified reservation. Over-grazing and repeated burning were already causing major shingle slides. Native vegetation, such as the Mount Cook lily, was being eaten out. In 1885 the Hooker Valley was reserved for recreation purposes. The Tasman Valley was added in 1887, largely on the plea of John Baker, explorer and Commissioner of Crown Lands. The Government should, he said, 'conserve for all time a place whose beauties it would not be easy to exaggerate, which will undoubtedly be one of the attractions of the globe'.

Like Baker, other surveyors could be called explorers in a period in which their triangulation surveys carried them into remote districts. In 1884 the chief surveyor for the Lands and Survey Department, Gerhard Mueller, was writing of the Mount Aspiring region: 'I have seen magnificent Alpine scenery in my travels, but I have never seen anything to approach in awe-inspiring effect the view from Mount Ionia . . . Mount Aspiring, pure white from base to top, rising to a height well nigh 10,000 feet; the intense blue sky overhead, and the deadly stillness, broken only now and then by the sound and roar as of heavy thunder in the distance, caused by the falling avalanches and mighty landslips, is a scene which cannot be surpassed.'

It would be well over half a century before Mueller's assessment was recognised by the declaration of Mount Aspiring National Park, but the lakes that lie to the south and east were already busy. We have the evidence of the indefatigable Reverend William Green for that: 'The number of tourist annually visiting Queenstown is considerable, the steam service from Kingston being kept up daily; and from Queenstown coaches run to Cromwell, within easy reach of Lake Wanaka, on which there now plies a screw steamer.'

In 1879 the annual report of the Department of Lands and Survey commented on a less-than-desirable prospect: 'The rabbit pest had so over-run the pastoral country as in some districts to have seriously curtailed the carrying capacity of the runs . . .' Acclimatisation of the rabbit, as an achievement, had been fading for more than a decade. It was all too evident that, given suitable soil conditions and climate, burning and overgrazing produced favourable conditions. Hillsides were alive, pastures devastated, flocks starved and sheep farmers ruined.

'They would hang him now, if they could find him,' said Mark Twain of whoever introduced the rabbit. Rabbit Nuisance Acts were passed in 1876 and 1882, and in 1883 stoats and weasels began to arrive to assist, it was thought, in control. By 1886 the importations numbered many thousands, to be added to hedgehogs in 1870 and sambar deer and parma wallabies in 1875.

In retrospect, it seems to have been no more possible to check the importation of unsuitable animals than to control the destruction of forest. The implications of both were recognised and pointed out. A British scientific journal of 1872 noted 'the silly mania for acclimatisation . . . so warmly fostered by many well-meaning though ill-advised persons and nowhere more so than in New Zealand. In a reckless way animals of extremely small advantage have been transported to the Antipodes, and, unaccompanied by any of those checks which keep natural balances, the importations will inevitably

In what was described in the *London Graphic* as a 'perilous night watch', Green and his companions spent a dreadful night on a ledge near the summit of Mount Cook.

become the greatest of nuisances.' They soon did.

Green hoped that immigrants might be sought from the alpine countries, 'who are accustomed to preserve the forests as the most precious gift of nature'. In 1887 Mr Monk asked in the House if the Government was aware that 'during last summer throughout a great portion of the North Island there had been an immense destruction of forest by fire'.

The odds against survival of native bird life were still rising. The forests were in decline. Stoats, weasels and ferrets had been added to the rat menace, which had already had disastrous effects. The first deer had been imported. Dogs, cats, pigs and explorer's pots had long exacted a toll. Collectors were shooting and exporting the interesting and unusual specimens, which were to be seen nowhere else. The *New Zealand Herald* records that in March 1886 one Hori Ropiha and his friends met the Native Minister, John Ballance, to protest, amongst other things, at the rapid extinction of native forests, and as a consequence, the disappearance of native birds. What had already happened was but a prelude to the destruction to come.

Chapter 9

The Gift

Ko Tongariro te maunga;
Ko Taupo te moana;
Ko Tuwharetoa te iwi;
Ko Te Heuheu te tangata.

Tongariro is the mountain;
Taupo is the sea;
Tuwharetoa are the people;
Te Heuheu is the Man.

— Proverb of Ngati Tuwharetoa

Lake Taupo, the sea of the Tuwharetoa proverb, lies near the centre of the North Island of New Zealand. It is central also to an area of landscape and history important to New Zealand and known worldwide. Taupo's township, for much of the year, is a busy place of some fifteen thousand people. Numbers almost double in summer as a holiday throng converges from afar to enjoy the clean air, the panoramic views of lake, hills and mountains and the wondrous changing moods of the lake.

The modern houses that cram the south-facing slopes falling to the lake seem to jostle for the view. Tauhara mountain stands just behind. A few kilometres to the north and across the river rise steam clouds from the geothermal field of Wairakei.

A bridge with control gates carries the state highway north across the Waikato near its outlet from the lake. Taupo's waters now provide the energy for half New Zealand. South of the town the highway curves through small suburbs and past tourist hotels and signs offering lake-side sections before engaging in a fifty-kilometre conversation of hill country with blue sparkling water, now touching a beach, or sidling high above, now swinging away to a pine-massed plateau, to return again to Taupo Moana down a long defile in the hills.

On a fine summer's day, or in the sharpness of winter sun, the view from the jostling houses has the scale and compass to be inferred from the proverb of Tuwharetoa. East and to the left of the lake-sea lies an upland that grows darker with time as the exotic forests of pine, mostly on Tuwharetoa land, mature towards production. The view to the west seems to be dominated by enormous craggy bluffs. Native New Zealanders, be they Maori or European,

Taupo Borough and the Tongariro mountains on a winter's day in the 1980s.

recognise intuitively that these are still covered by their native flora. Many of these features, including the valleys by which streams and rivers enter the lake, are protected within the reservation system.

It is neither forested upland nor craggy bluff that first captures the eye. High above and beyond the distant lake, hazy and dark in summer, white, sharp in outline and with a deceptive closeness in winter, tower the mountains. A lazy plume of smoke and steam drifts from the tops to become at intervals a dark, sinister torrent. The evenings draw a mist of purple across the mountains, they fade from view before the reflections of sunset go from the shimmering lake and darkness falls softly on Taupo Moana. All that is left in the still evening is the sound of tinkling waters, which can turn to pounding surf when cold southerlies from the mountains raise a confused and dangerous sea.

Tapuwaeharuru, as Taupo township was usually called in the 1880s, was a very different place from the centre of today, even if its history as a tourist resort had already begun. According to the Union Steamship Company's tourist handbook *Maoriland* in 1884, 'There is little that is absolutely beautiful in the landscape, the pervading colour of which is a dull barren brown, mellowed, however, in the distance where the soft outline of the hills meets the sky. The object which the eye is ever seeking and on which it always rests with delight, is the green crest of Tauhara, an isolated, wood-covered mountain that stands about four miles from the township. Then there is the loveli-

TE HEUHEU IV, HORONUKU
(1821–1888)

This chief was the son of the great chief Te Heuheu Tukino II (Mananui) and nephew of Iwikau, Te Heuheu III. After his father was killed in a landslide in 1846, his uncle Iwikau became paramount chief of Ngati Tuwharetoa until he died, in 1862. Horonuku then succeeded him as chief of the tribe.

Owing to his kinship on his mother's side with the Waikato people, Horonuku felt obliged to help them in their struggle for sovereignty in the Land Wars. In 1864 he led a taua (war party) to the seige of Orakau. Unable to break through General Cameron's cordon, he returned to Taupo and stayed there peacefully. Ties with Waikato and Ngati Maniapoto then led

him to support Te Kooti Rikirangi in the 1870s, until the latter was defeated at Te Porere. While the chief's primary loyalty was to his own tribe and to their continued unity and independence, he supported the concept of Maori sovereignty and was present at many King Movement meetings, sometimes being described as 'the King's secretary'.

During the early 1880s, the situation regarding the Tuwharetoa tribal territory became very difficult and delicate. In order to protect the sacred mountains Tongariro, Ngauruhoe and Ruapehu from possible exploitation, Te Heuheu and his people presented them to the Government as the nucleus of a national park in September 1887. He died shortly after, in July 1888, and was succeeded by his son Tureiti.

ness of the green river, the ever-changing face of the lake, and away beyond, where the water of the lake vanishes from sight, the majesty of the snow-crested Tongariro and Ruapehu . . .'

The bedrooms of the two hotels were comfortable, according to the handbook, but there was much else to be desired. In addition to the hotels, the town had twenty to thirty houses, a large hall, a neat post and telegraph office, and the Armed Constabulary station. The constabulary had been garrisoned in Taupo since 1870, near the redoubt built to prevent any attempt at return by Te Kooti. With the help of local Maori people, the constabulary had built the roads connecting Taupo with Napier and Rotorua, and a bridge across the river. Some of the road-making help came, no doubt, from a small Maori

By the mid-1880s the township of Taupo was connected to Rotorua and Napier by road and began to provide accommodation and facilities for tourists. Soaking in hot pools, climbing Mount Tauhara and taking a steam cruise to Tokaanu, at the southern end of the lake, were the most popular tourist activities.

settlement on the west bank of the river. Canoes — and there were reputed to be some hundreds on the lake — maintained frequent contact with the township.

Such was the location of sittings of the Native Land Court during the 1880s to hear claims to vast areas of the central North Island, areas that included Tongariro, the sacred mountain of the proverb of Ngati Tuwharetoa. These hearings led to an order by the Court for the reservation of what would become the core of the future national park.

The events that culminated at the first of the hearings can be traced in part to the assault on Te Porere Pa and the roles played in the action by Major Kepa te Rangihiwinui on the one hand, and Te Heuheu Horonuku on the other.

In the early 1880s Kepa te Rangihiwinui laid claim to the Murimotu and Rangipo blocks, a huge area stretching inland from Wanganui to the base of Ruapehu. Kepa was not alone in his interest in Murimotu-Rangipo, which lay across the routes of future main roads and, of even greater import, the line of the Main Trunk railway. In the eyes of the Government, Murimotu-Rangipo was the key to the interior of the North Island.

Kepa's announced intention of setting up a land trust of some six hundred thousand hectares for his Wanganui people was received with something less than official enthusiasm. He left to mark out the land himself, travelling with about two hundred followers, a band and flags, one depicting the figure of Kepa standing on the summit of Tongariro. Carved poles were set up to signify possession of the land. In the Rangipo area Kepa and his party trespassed on the mana of Topia Turoa, a powerful local chief of both Tuwharetoa and Wanganui descent, and with King Movement sympathies. Other chiefs supported Topia, and Kepa withdrew.

The claims to Rangipo were heard before the Land Court in Taupo in 1881. Kepa, with his support of fifty followers, was more than fortunate to be present, having survived an attempt on his life at Tokaanu, possibly by a follower of his principal opponent, Topia Turoa. Supporting Topia in opposing

The redoubt of Te Porere, scene of the attack on Te Kooti on 3 October 1869 and now a Historic Site. Te Porere lies west of Lake Rotoaira, a short distance north of the Tokaanu–National Park road. On the opposite side of the road are the slopes of Mount Tongariro.

Kepa's claim was Te Heuheu Tukino (Horonuku).

Judge Maning presided over an event that must have fairly crackled with the tensions of recent history. It had its roots in the loss of the war and the King Movement's struggle against the subdivision and purchase of land. Horonuku's position was complicated in the extreme. He was the son of Mananui, who had refused to sign the Treaty of Waitangi, saying, 'I am King in Taupo.' His uncle, Iwikau, had followed the principle of friendship to all parties, and skilfully guided Tuwharetoa past involvement in the conflict, while giving general support to the King Movement. Loyalty to his Waikato relations had taken Horonuku to the battle of Orakau. The short, savage fight at Te Porere and the role of Major Kepa te Rangihiwinui was alive in recent memory.

In the hearing Kepa attacked again. He suggested that Horonuku had been party to rebellion and that he, Kepa, had raupata (conquest) rights by virtue of fighting on the Pakeha side as an officer of the Government. Had not his fires of occupation burned on Tuwharetoa land? Here was a question in which there was nothing complicated whatsoever. No chief of the Te Heuheu line was other than crystal clear in his total identification with his land and his people.

Major Kepa te Rangihiwinui — known to Europeans as Major Kemp.

Horonuku, son of Mananui, rose, and centuries of lineage and tradition rose with him. There, through the courtroom windows, in the distance, was Tongariro, mountain of proverb, mountain of his ancestors, smoke curling above.

'Who are you, that speak of your fires of occupation burning in my country? Where is your fire, your ahi-ka? Where is it? You cannot show me, for it does not exist. Now I shall show you mine! Look yonder! Behold my ahi-ka, my mountain Tongariro. There burns my fire, kindled by my ancestor Ngatoro-i-rangi. It was he who lit that fire and it has burned there ever since! That is my fire of occupation! Now show me yours!'

The subdivision of the Murimotu and Rangipo blocks was determined finally at a Land Court hearing in Wanganui in 1882. Topia Turoa's Ngai-Tama people, Tuwharetoa and Wanganui all received portions, the rulings being validated by legislation in that same year.

The legislation revealed some aspects of European ambition when it also awarded a long lease over three-quarters of the area to the sheep farmers Morrin and Studholme, in fulfilment of a promise made by the Government on the undertaking that Morrin and Studholme would not compete for purchase from the Maori owners. In the following year J. H. Kerry-Nicholls was travelling in the region, and 1884 saw the publication of his *The King Country*, with its vivid descriptions of the mountains. Alfred Burton was photographing in 1885, the year after Alfred Newman had asked in Parliament for the reservation of Ruapehu, Ngauruhoe, Tongariro and other areas as a park. Also sitting in the House of Representatives was Lawrence Grace, European son-in-law of Te Heuheu Horonuku. Such a proposition would not have passed his notice. He may even have discussed it with Newman.

Early in 1886 the Land Court again sat at Tapuwaeharuru, this time to hear claims on Taupo-nui-a-tia, an area embracing southern Lake Taupo and the mountains of Tongariro and Ngauruhoe. The western portion of the block extended within the 'rohepotae', the border of the King Country, an area in which no land might be sold, according to an agreement made by the Maori

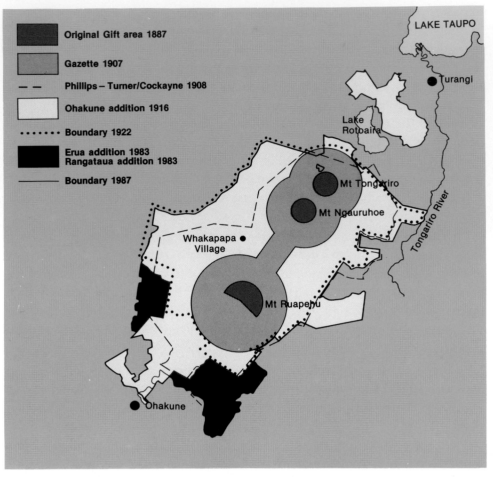

Original Gift area 1887

Gazette 1907

– –   Phillips – Turner/Cockayne 1908

Ohakune addition 1916

• • • • • • Boundary 1922

Erua addition 1983
Rangataua addition 1983

———— Boundary 1987

LAKE TAUPO

Turangi

Lake
Rotoaira

Mt Tongariro

Mt Ngauruhoe

Whakapapa ●
Village

Mt Ruapehu

Tongariro River

● Ohakune

The shaping of Tongariro National Park over time as cultural values change, land knowledge increases, and practical solutions to boundary problems are worked through.

King and the tribes. The cause of the hearing was a request from Tuwharetoa for a determination of the inter-tribal land boundary, shared with Ngati Maniapoto to the west of the lake. The Native Lands Act of 1863, however, did not provide for a simple ruling on tribal boundaries. Title to the whole block would have to be investigated. The court would grant title to a list of owners and state the size of each owner's share. Pressure to sell could then be applied by prospective buyers.

As a further complication, the hearing of title to the entire block would breach the rohepotae boundary, a prospect the Government, enthusiastic for progress with roads and the Main Trunk railway in the central North Island, viewed with hope and anticipation.

The little town in its barren brown landscape was thronged for the great hearing. Perhaps no summer before or since has seen such an event. The *New Zealand Herald* reported that up to six hundred people were in attendance. In the distant haze of summer stood the mountains.

Ngati Maniapoto dispatched a senior chief and spokesman, Taonui, to ask Te Heuheu to put only land outside the rohepotae boundary before the court. Taonui arrived four days after the hearing had begun, having been delayed (deliberately, he later claimed) by a summons to a criminal trial. By that time Judge Scannell had ruled that the time had passed for the lodging of counter-claims.

When Te Heuheu formally received Taonui on the ground outside one of the hotels, he declined to challenge the ruling. Again the paramount chief of Tuwharetoa identified totally with his land and his people. 'Your boundary splits me in two. What about the half of me that is outside?' he asked, in a question as significant as his famous statement to Kepa te Rangihiwinui four years earlier. As in 1882, Horonuku's sense of Tuwharetoa's needs and rights came first.

The threat of eventual division of land by European title loomed over the whole hearing — the sacred ancestor mountain was exposed to possible sale. European interest in the mountains was well known. They could be divided and purchased. Apparently it was Lawrence Grace who suggested the possibility of presenting the mountains to the Crown as a national park, thus placing them under the mana of Queen Victoria: 'Why not make them a tapu place of the Crown, a sacred place under the mana of the Queen. The only possible way to preserve them forever is to give them to the Government as a reserve and park, to be the property of all the people of New Zealand, in memory of Te Heuheu and his tribe.'

Te Heuheu formally offered the summits of Tongariro, Ngauruhoe and part of Ruapehu to the Crown in September of 1887. The Ngati Tuwharetoa gift lands, comprising two thousand four hundred hectares, formed a nucleus for the proposed national park at Tongariro.

John Ballance introduced the Tongariro National Park Bill in 1887 and paid tribute to Te Heuheu's generous action. The sole condition of the gift was that the paramount chief of Ngati Tuwharetoa would be one of the three trustees, the others to be the Native Minister and an appointee of the Governor. The land was particularly suitable for a national park — it had been described by a great many travellers as being worthy of a place among the grandest scenery in the world. The park was easily accessible, being only eleven kilometres from the line of the railway. Ballance believed that in the course of time it would be one of the most famous parks in existence. To a certain extent it might be made self-supporting by charging a reasonable fee to tourists.

The gifted peaks were to be held under the Domains Act until enough surrounding land had been acquired by the Crown to form a national park. It is evident that the Crown considered a larger area of twenty-five thousand hectares to be worthy of description as a national park and did not intend the Bill to become law until it had acquired the whole of the land sought.

To accomplish this aim, much time was spent establishing ownership and negotiating settlement. Many difficulties were encountered. Delay was caused by a Commission of Inquiry into a claim against the siting of the boundary between Ngati Tuwharetoa and Maniapoto lands, although the Commission's decision of 1889 confirmed the legality of the 1887 land settlement. Many owners sought what were regarded as outrageous prices, or refused sale outright. Three years after the introduction of the Bill more than five thousand hectares were still under investigation, while more than three thousand were still in Maori hands. It was not until 1907 that enough land was in Crown title for the Tongariro National Park to be gazetted.

Few national parks in a hundred years have emerged from the mainstream of a country's history in the manner of Tongariro. Behind the decision of Te Heuheu Tukino lay all feeling for the land that had grown over a thousand years of Maori settlement in Aotearoa. One of the most feared and revered of all the sacred mountains of the Maori passed into the guardianship of all the people of New Zealand. This was one of the earliest national parks in the world. The paramount chief of Ngati Tuwharetoa still belongs to the boards associated with the park. The trusteeship continues.

Tongariro National Park in 1987

By Bruce Jefferies, Chief Ranger of the Park, 1982–1987

Sir Hepi Te Heuheu — a direct descendant of the donor of the park — represents to me at least, a link with the mythical beginnings of Tongariro, the account of its origins, which adds a very special dimension to the park. A gift increases with importance as we learn more about each other as people.

On some days the overwhelming bulk of Ruapehu almost seems to filter into the horizon as the foreground designs, shapes and vegetation have an ability to draw my eye down from the snow-covered peaks to the myriad of patterns that make up the foreground.

People often ask during the summer nature programme how many times I have been over Tongariro or up Ngauruhoe. To be honest, I have got no idea. There is certainly no better way to get to know park visitors than on the long summer days, taking a trip from the Mangatepopo Valley over Tongariro or up to the summit of Ngauruhoe. It simply doesn't matter how many times you visit these places, because every time you return, it is always different and that to me is more important than counting trips.

The macro world of Tongariro is well known. The dominant forms of Tongariro, Ngauruhoe and Ruapehu rise above the surrounding landscape. However, to see the park as simply a silhouette of volcanic peaks would be the equivalent of visiting New Zealand and not leaving Auckland. Tongariro is volcanoes and people and Maori myths and legends, but it is also what is happening with shapes, threads and forms. To me, a spiderweb or lichen are just as symbolic and important as the mountains.

Without doubt, the question I get asked more often than any other is 'How do you feel about the ski-fields?' It seems almost a paradox that winter sports activity on Whakapapa or Turoa is just as important to me as the wilderness, solitude and special qualities of the summit area of Ruapehu. The natural contrasts of weather, vegetation and land forms are always readily accepted as something quite valid. The contrast of people's experiences is equally valid, and I suppose it is for this reason that I feel comfortable knowing that a wide range of expectations can be met, provided an understanding of these can be communicated between various user groups.

Tongariro's wilderness qualities are incredibly fragile. The ring of major highway systems and the focus of visitor use, both internationally and nationally, place demands on the park that are unprecedented throughout New Zealand. There are inherent dangers in trying to quantify the benefits of wilderness and this is something I have always tried to avoid. What I do believe, however, is that we need wilderness, and that each individual will choose a level of experience that suits their particular requirements. Perhaps that doesn't need park managers; perhaps it just requires someone who is aware of the values that exist out there and ensures that they are still going to be there tomorrow and the day after tomorrow.

Destroying the Forests: Saving the Birds 1888–1900

In 1887, not long after John Ballance introduced the Tongariro National Park Bill, growing economic depression brought on a general election and a change of Government. In July of the following year Alfred Newman asked the new Minister of Native Affairs what was being done to complete the formation of the Tongariro National Park. Mr Mitchelson replied that no action was currently being taken because the 'block of land in which these mountains were situated was at present the subject of an action in the Supreme Court'.

Newman's question was the beginning of a parliamentary crusade to ensure that the Tongariro National Park Bill was carried through. A year later he asked the Minister of Lands a very similar question to that of Thomas Potts in 1868: 'What steps does the Minister propose to take towards effective conservation of the forests of the colony?' The examples Newman quoted were not far from the Tongariro area: 'In the Manawatu and Rangitikei districts the forests were fast disappearing, and in five or six years' time there would be very little forest to sell.'

Then it was back to Tongariro itself. The Minister of Native Affairs was asked about completion of the Crown's title to the proposed national park. Mr Mitchelson replied that the Government had a complete title to six thousand four hundred acres, but the disputes would have to be settled before further additions could be obtained. A few days later a debate on the Trunk Railway Bill permitted Newman to discuss the fine forests on the route of the Main Trunk Railway, mentioning particularly black maire forest opposite Ruapehu. The Waimarino area would be taken up the moment it was thrown open for settlement.

In the 1890 session the two Ministers were again responding: 'Would the Minister of Lands reserve from sale all natural curiosities in the shape of hot or mineral springs, and reserve all forests along river banks in order to preserve the beautiful scenery of such rivers as the Wanganui and Rangitikei?' The Minister for Native Affairs was asked whether the Government would, during the recess, buy the balance of the land necessary to form the national park. Newman understood that some owners were prepared to sell the land cheaply. The Minister replied that some declined to sell while others asked prohibitive prices. (The Government's top price was one shilling and sixpence per acre.)

The general election at the end of 1890 saw the now-famous Liberal Government take office, with John Ballance as Premier, and John McKenzie as Minister of Lands. Richard Seddon was Minister of Public Works. Newman's questions continued. A discussion about grazing runs became a request to withdraw forest near the national park area from sale, just as a debate on tourism provided an opportunity to expand on the wonderful scenery around the mountains.

Ballance did not live to see the passing of his Tongariro National Park Bill. He had been dead three months when McKenzie rose to move the second reading in July 1893. He was utterly convinced of the importance of the measure: 'I can hardly find adequate language to describe the benefits of setting apart this portion of the country as a national park. At the present time the people of this colony have, no doubt, any amount of room to spread themselves out into the country and get the advantages of all the fine scenery for which the colony is so famous. But we should look to the future in these cases, and provide a national park, such as this Bill will provide, which at some future date will be a credit to this Parliament that passed it, as I hope it would do now.' He went on to explain how the sixty-two thousand three hundred acres (twenty-five thousand hectares) would be constituted.

Tongariro National Park as constituted in the Bill of 1893

Land given by Maori people	23,510 acres (9514 hectares)
Crown lands	15,380 acres (6224 hectares)
Land under negotiation	14,510 acres (5872 hectares)
Maori land	8,900 acres (3602 hectares)

If the House agreed to a second reading, the Bill was to go before the Waste Lands Committee: 'I will merely say that the greater portion of the land is of no great value for the purpose of producing anything, although there are places where the soil was good. When the Main Trunk Railway is taken through the North Island this park will be within a distance of six or seven miles of that railway.'

It would not have surprised the House by this time that the first speaker was Alfred Newman, any more than his opening statement that he 'would like to say a word or two in support [as] it was an exceedingly wise provision . . . A national park had been set aside in Canada, and another in the Yosemite Valley, in the United States; and there could be no question that such fine natural scenery should not be allowed to get into the hands of private persons.' He felt that the Minister who succeeded in setting aside as a national park such 'a fine country and playground' as this would be 'deserving well of the country'.

William Rolleston 'entirely approved of this Bill. There is only one point I wish to draw the Minister's attention to . . . They had been making forest reserves from time to time, and, as fast as they were made, whenever any political pressure was brought to bear they had been alienated. I would like the Minister to consider the wisdom of putting a clause in the Bill making this territory inalienable except by Act of both Houses of Assembly.'

Another predictable contribution was in the offing. Thomas Mackenzie, the Member for Clutha, saw the opportunity to raise the banner of the Sounds of the south-west, which he had himself explored. He was 'glad the Minister has at last recognised that it is important to the country that we should preserve its natural beauties'. Then heigh-ho for the south-west. 'This Bill, if extended in its provisions, might be made to apply to the country, which I have been anxious to bring under the control of the Government . . . if clause 4 of the Bill, which provided for the appointment of trustees for this national park, were extended it might provide for the appointment of trustees for the south-west portion of the Middle Island, to which I have called attention . . . a large portion of the south-west of the Middle Island and of the interior of Otago should be made into a national park.' The House, by this time, would have been quite clear on that point.

The appeal for the south-west had no attraction for Mr Buckland, who spoke next, saying he did not think its provisions should be extended so as to include 'those wretched Sounds' in the South Island!

It is plain that all the issues that have fuelled one hundred years of national parks debate were alive and well in 1893. The debate had already traversed tourism, the future, forest destruction and protection from political pressures. Now Buckland sailed into another contention. He objected to the charging of tolls and fees, and thought that provision ought to be struck out. One Member asked how the park was to be kept up and received the reply: 'Why, how did the Government keep up co-operative works? If this was to be a national park it should be free . . . otherwise it would not be a national park.'

With attention thus directed to questions of privilege and accessibility, a selection of issues, which in 1987 can be recognised as old friends, was filling out. The social concerns that were a priority of the first Liberal Government became evident. Mr Taylor asked about facilities for ordinary people to get to the park and view the fine scenery. There should be cheap travel tickets or some other means to enable poor people to visit. He supported Thomas Mackenzie, whose ideas about the south-west 'would be far more satisfactory to the country, from the tourist point of view, than this Tongariro Park'.

Mr Hogg agreed: 'I do not see why an extensive park of this description should be created in the North Island and no attention be devoted to the

THOMAS MACKENZIE
(1854–1930)

Thomas Mackenzie was at various times a surveyor, businessman, explorer, politician and conservationist. His early life as a surveyor awakened an interest in the outdoors. In the 1880s and 1890s he made a number of exploring trips to Fiordland, and afterwards he never lost an opportunity in Parliament to speak in favour of this area.

The Tongariro National Park Bill debate in 1893 gave him a chance to suggest a national park for the 'West Coast Sounds', an ambition finally achieved in 1905. Mackenzie saw clearly the economic potential of New Zealand scenery and was keen for the

Government to open up the Southern Lakes area with walking tracks.

His duties as a Member of Parliament, Cabinet Minister and as Prime Minister in 1912 occupied much of his middle life. In 1909 he became the Minister of Tourist and Health Resorts, and was able to play an important role in developing tourist services in Fiordland.

After retiring from politics, he became the first president of the new Native Bird Protection Society in 1923, a position he held until his death in 1930. He was an important link between the early days of the conservation movement in the 1890s and the modern era of public interest groups.

South Island. Nor do I see why large areas of land like this of 62,000 acres should be converted into pleasure-grounds, unless smaller areas are provided near to the centres of population for a similar purpose . . . certainly the scenery which still remains in portions of the Forty-Mile Bush is of the most beautiful character and ought to be most carefully preserved. I am exceedingly sorry that the Government seems to be taking no steps in that direction. The whole of that bush is going down rapidly year by year, and in the course of a short time the whole of this splendid scenery will be totally destroyed.' (The majestic Forty-Mile Bush between Masterton and Woodville, an object of scenic wonder even to settlers used to forest, *was* destroyed. The fifty-five hectare Mount Bruce Reserve is all that remains.)

The Tongariro National Park Bill continued its second reading in an atmosphere of general support. James Carroll reminded the House that, 'The chiefs round about the district referred to had in a noble, unostentatious, and worthy spirit made a concession to the Government, for this very purpose, of 33,000 acres, without any parade whatever.'

The reading was not completed until October 1894, being interrupted by the end of the 1893 session. There was no time lost when it completed its second reading on 11 October, or when introduced for its third reading four days later. Perhaps the prospect of further questions from Alfred Newman encouraged the House. He was merely obliged to thank the Minister and to 'hope that it would go successfully through the other chamber'. It did — at practically the speed of light, being read for the third time in the Legislative Council Chamber on 17 October 1894. The Tongariro National Park Bill had arrived.

John McKenzie was a giant Scot whose Land Act of 1892 promoted closer settlement, providing a stake in the rapidly growing dairy industry for the small man with little capital. The successful application of refrigeration gave the industry overseas markets. People moved north to the dairy-suited areas from the more populous South Island. Forest clearing for farms accelerated, particularly in Taranaki.

The 1892 Land Act also advanced the cause of conservation. The Governor could reserve from sale temporarily Crown lands required for the

The first successful shipment of frozen meat from New Zealand to Britain in 1882 gave the economy a major boost. Meat and dairy products could be produced in far larger quantities once markets extended beyond New Zealand's shores.

In the 1890s the Liberal Government's land policies spread dairy farms across the North Island in the wake of massive forest clearance. Dairy factories like this one were set up.

'Let us keep a few spots in Westland uncontaminated by the ordinary tourist, the picnicker and the photographic fiend, some almost impassable place where what is inside can be left to the imagination . . . keep them for those who care to risk there [*sic*] necks and enjoy scenery in a state of nature.'

This plea was voiced by Charlie Douglas, who spent much of his life exploring South Westland. Douglas had his 'first splendid view of Mount Aspiring and Glacier' on 26 February 1891.

growth and preservation of natural timber or the preservation of the natural fauna, or containing thermal springs or 'whereon natural curiosities or scenery may exist of a character to the national interest'.

At the same time, the two branches of the Crown Lands Department — the Survey Department and the Crown Lands Office — were brought into closer connection to form the Department of Lands and Survey. The reports of the early years of this department provide a commentary on developing New Zealand and also on what could be called the last phase of exploration. The department even had its own official explorer, Charles Douglas. Appendices to the departmental reports were often the personal observations of Douglas and the other remarkable men engaged in remote and arduous work. Thus, Laurence Cussen, District Surveyor (Auckland), in a report on a topographical survey of the Tongariro Mountains: 'I scarcely think there is in nature a scene more lovely than that to be viewed from the summit of Tongariro, looking north-east across Roto-Aira and the extinct cones of Pihanga and Kakaramea . . . It is very beautiful to watch the effects of the setting or rising sun amongst these mountains.'

CHARLES DOUGLAS (1840–1916)

If Thomas Brunner was Westland's greatest explorer, then Charlie Douglas was a very close second. For more than thirty years he systematically explored and mapped much of South Westland, first as a prospector and then as an official explorer for the Lands Department.

In the 1880s Douglas and Gerhard Mueller, the District Surveyor for Westland, made many trips into the isolated Arawhata and Landsborough Valleys. Douglas was fascinated by the Arawhata country (some of which is now in Mount Aspiring National Park) and had explored it in detail by 1891. The following year he was in the Copland Valley, attempting to find a pass to the Hermitage in the east. The Copland Pass remains an important alpine pass today.

Douglas's reports to the Lands Department record the effect of new predators (especially rats and cats) on the bird life of Westland. Nevertheless he and other West Coast explorers relied on birds for food. He gives a classic description of cooked kiwi being 'like an old bit of pork boiled in a second-hand coffin'.

In 1893 Douglas was joined by the young climber A. P. Harper, and together they worked in the Franz Josef, Fox, Cook and Karangarua Valley areas before Douglas's rheumatism forced him to undertake only short journeys. His work had taken him from the coast right up to the main divide over a large area of South Westland. Harper describes him as a 'courteous gentleman of the old school'. He was a fine explorer but not a climber, and he referred to those who went above the snow line as 'alpine lunatics'.

Douglas reported the status of bird life: 'Years ago the Karangarua and the other rivers in southern Westland were celebrated for their ground and other birds. No prospector required to carry meat with him — even a gun was unnecessary. Nothing was wanted but a hardy dog. But now all this is altered. The digger, with his dogs, cats, rats and ferrets, has nearly exterminated the birds in the lower valleys. The cry of the kiwi is seldom heard, and a weka is a rarity. The blue duck, once so tame, is now as careful of himself as the grey duck and throughout whole districts robins and other birds are extinct.' A year later, having explored the valley of the upper Waiho River in the company of Arthur P. Harper, he reported sadly that that area was no exception. 'Ferrets and stoats are now up in the Waiho Forks, and will soon be over the northern districts . . . I fear that the kiwi and kakapo are doomed. There is talk of putting some on islands in the Sounds or elsewhere; if so, the Government had better be quick about it, as it is quite possible that a few years will see the last of them.'

Douglas's observations confirmed concerns that had grown through the 1880s. Indeed, students of bird life in particular districts were noting a decline in the 1870s. Not long after the Austrian collector Andreas Reischek's visits to Little Barrier Island in the early 1880s, and his accounts of abundant bird life, the Auckland Institute urged purchase of the island as a sanctuary. Otago supported Auckland and later advocated a similar role for Resolution Island. The 1891 meeting of the Australian and New Zealand Association for the Advancement of Science resolved that 'in the interests of science it is most desirable that some steps should be taken to establish one or more reserves where the natural fauna and flora of New Zealand may be preserved from destruction'. The resolution was supported by some exceedingly eminent figures, including Leonard Cockayne, Walter Buller, and Thomas Kirk. Thomas Mackenzie was among those who pressed the issue strongly in Parliament.

LEONARD COCKAYNE
(1855-1934)

Although he had little formal training in biology, Leonard Cockayne became a world pioneer in the new science of ecology early this century. Ecology focuses on relationships between plants and animals and their surroundings. Cockayne divided the country into botanical districts, describing different vegetation types and how, after disturbance, one kind follows another.

Employed as a consultant by the Lands Department, he made a series of important botanical surveys, including Kapiti Island (1907), Waipoua Kauri Forest (1908), Tongariro National Park (1908), Stewart Island (1909), and Sand Dunes (1909 and 1911). He had previously visited some of the outlying islands — the Chathams, Campbell, Auckland, Antipodes and Bounty Islands.

His Tongariro survey recommended major additions to the park, which was virtually all above the bush-line. Cockayne was also associated with the Arthur's Pass area. He began the first account of plant succession in the park in 1898 and campaigned for the creation of the two reserves that were set aside in 1901.

Always active, Cockayne was a member of both the New Zealand Institute and the Royal Commission on Forestry in 1913. He established the Otari Open Air Native Plant Museum in Wellington and published nearly two hundred articles, both academic and popular. His major work, *The Vegetation of New Zealand*, consists primarily of accounts of native plant communities and vegetation types.

Above: Lassie, Richard Henry's dog, muzzled and belled in preparation for hunting kakapo and kiwi. After capture the birds were transported by boat to Resolution and other islands.

Bird hunting was no easy task: 'Our dog,' Henry wrote, 'often drives a bird into a crevice among rocks or stones or up a tree where he cannot get it. And, again, we cannot go near a noisy creek, though it is often the best place for birds, because we cannot hear the dog, and if he finds a bird he will not come away . . . If we do not find him he will have the poor thing nearly dead . . . Altogether, there is not much fun in hunting.'

In 1892 John McKenzie confirmed the gazettal of Resolution Island, advising at the same time that the purchase of Little Barrier should soon be completed. Richard Henry, the first caretaker for the Resolution Island sanctuary, was landed at Dusky Sound on 19 July 1894 to begin a fifteen-year struggle that has its own special place in the annals of conservation history. McKenzie introduced legislation in 1897 to make Kapiti Island 'a preserve for the flora and fauna of New Zealand'.

As to developing New Zealand, the department reported in 1892 that only thirteen miles of road construction was needed to complete a new route from Wellington to Auckland, which would 'make the central mountains of Ruapehu and Tongariro easily accessible'. The Hokitika to Christchurch road was 'a favourite route for tourists, who come from all parts of the world and cross over by coach to see the far-famed Otira Gorge'. Three five-horse coaches ran twice a week each way. In 1896 it was noted that construction of the Rotorua–Galatea–Waikaremoana road was proceeding: 'Passing, as it will, along the shores of Lake Waikaremoana for some miles, the scenery

Above left: A five-horse coach outside the Porters Pass Hotel on the Christchurch to Hokitika run.

WALTER LAWRY BULLER
(1838–1906)

Even as a boy, Buller showed a keen interest in observing the habits of birds around his home in Northland. He accompanied his father, the Reverend James Buller, on his travels and this gave him an opportunity to explore the bush and to learn much of the Maori way of life.

Brilliant, well-educated and confident, Buller made a promising beginning to his career in law, as Government Interpreter at the Magistrate's Court in Wellington. This job was followed by terms as Native Commissioner for the Southern Provinces, Resident Magistrate for Manawatu and as a judge of the Native Land Court.

These positions gave him the opportunity to travel all over New Zealand and to collect specimens and make notes for his *History of the Birds of New Zealand*. Published in 1872, this enormous and widely acclaimed work was made more valuable by the fact that J. G. Keulemans was responsible for its accurate and beautifully coloured illustrations.

In 1871 Buller qualified for the Bar and went into private practice, specialising in cases before the Maori Land Court. In 1885 he went to London to be New Zealand Commissioner at the Colonial and Indian Exhibition (earning a knighthood for his services) and to supervise the printing of a second

edition of his *History*. In 1905 he published a *Supplement*, which contained a wealth of information on rare New Zealand birds together with photographs and more of Keulemans's hand-coloured plates.

Between 1869 and 1896 he had made known to science nine new species with comprehensive Latin descriptions. Thanks to his skill with a pen and his ability as a scientific observer, Buller introduced the unique characteristics of New Zealand birds to the European world and recorded the impact of colonial settlement on bird life.

Lake Waikaremoana — J. B. C. Hoyte, 1874.

along this route should compare favourably with any in the colony.'

If the West Coast road can be called the first of the major highways to become interwoven with national park decision-making in the future, then the road through the Urewera was the second (later, the Milford Road and the Haast Highway).

Early surveyor activity of the 1880s was resisted by the independent Tuhoe people, who looked with equal disfavour at prospecting and road-making. Nonetheless, by 1891 a track from Galatea reached Te Whaiti. Tuhoe displeasure at the triangulation surveys that began after 1894 was evident. The Premier, Richard Seddon, in company with James Carroll, toured the area. The Government proposals that followed (and the sensitivity of the ethnologist Elsdon Best, who was keeper of the Government store at Te Whaiti) effected improvements in relationships, and roadmaking proceeded in a more friendly atmosphere. By the end of the decade, a Te Whaiti to Ruatahuna connection was well advanced and a Wairoa to Onepoto section was complete.

Even more significant in national park terms were the two major railway

RICHARD HENRY
(1845–1929)

In the 1880s, even in isolated Westland and Fiordland, native birds succumbed to predators such as wild cats and mustelids (stoats, weasels and ferrets, introduced after 1885 to control the rabbit plague). Richard Henry was a former farmer who settled at Lake Te Anau in 1883 and began exploring Fiordland. A keen naturalist, he was alarmed to find a rapid decline in the native bird population, especially of vulnerable ground birds such as the kakapo.

In the 1890s Resolution and Little Barrier Islands were made sanctuaries in the belief that their isolation would provide protection for the birds. In 1894 Henry became the first curator and caretaker at Resolution.

For fifteen years he led a solitary life, making expeditions to the mainland to catch kakapos, little grey kiwis and roas (spotted kiwis), which he transported to safety on Resolution Island. In the first six years he transferred over seven hundred birds. His letters and diaries contain a wealth of observation and philosophy about the abundance of wildlife.

In August 1900 he saw a weasel or stoat on Resolution Island and realized that his work was doomed. In 1909 he left the island and spent two years as caretaker of Kapiti Island before retiring. Although no kakapo are known to survive on Resolution Island today, Henry's actions will be remembered in environmental history as a determined effort to protect native fauna.

This photograph shows the road inspectors' camp at Te Whaiti in 1896, and gives an idea of the conditions experienced by the men constructing what is still one of the country's more challenging roads. Nearly a hundred kilometres of winding, metalled road climbs through the ranges, skirting high above Lake Waikaremoana. Never a major transport route, the road nevertheless made possible the opening of a government accommodation house at the lake early this century. Elsdon Best stands on the left of the group.

projects of the period: the North Island Main Trunk and the Midland Railway across the Southern Alps to the West Coast. A route for a central North Island railway had been selected by a parliamentary committee from the alternatives reported by the surveyors following their investigations (and adventures). Work started, but was halted by retrenchment decisions. Soon after the Liberal Government came to office, construction recommenced and moved quietly on through the 1890s.

In its challenge, difficulty and purpose, the Midland line had much in common with the North Island Main Trunk. According to the contract, the railway was to proceed from Springfield via Arthur's Pass to Stillwater and thence north into Nelson. In 1894, with not much more than a quarter of the distance covered and the problem of crossing the Alps unresolved, the Government took over and court proceedings replaced railway building. Engineering studies eventually confirmed a tunnel proposal in preference to

RUA KENANA TAPUNUI (HEPETIPA) (c. 1869–1937)
Tuhoe/Ngati Kahungungu

Tuhoe prophet and founder of the Tuhoe settlement of Maungapohatu. A direct descendant of Tamakaimoana, ancestor of the people of Maungapohatu in the Urewera, Rua spent most of his childhood with Ngati Kahungungu, his father's people. As a young man Rua worked on European farms labouring. By 1895, he was a well-known figure within the Ringatu faith. A series of visions beginning in 1904 convinced him that he was the successor prophesied by Te Kooti.

Believing himself to be Te Mihaia Hou, the New Messiah, Rua provided a rallying point for the Tuhoe in their struggle to retain economic control over their land, by stressing a strong, self-sufficient, communal basis to their communities.

In 1906 Rua established his New Jerusalem at Maungapohatu. By 1908 it was a thriving settlement of over a thousand people. Interpreting Rua's attempt at local autonomy as a threat, Government forces advanced on Maungapohatu in March 1916 and arrested Rua on charges of sedition.

A 'morally guilty' verdict sent him to prison, but upon the intervention of Apirana Ngata, Rua served only nine of the twelve months' sentence.

On his return, Rua continued to lead the dwindling Maungapohatu community, while allowing the introduction of education and new religions.

Work on the North Island Main Trunk Railway proceeded steadily, but without pressure, through the 1890s. This construction camp was located just north of Ohakune. At Harry Ell's insistence, the Tongariro National Park boundary was later extended to include the railway to ensure that the fine mountain and forest scenery would remain for the benefit of railway travellers.

the rack railway that was under consideration by the railway company to overcome very steep grades.

By 1897 the Midland Railway *was* involved in national park decision-making. John McKenzie was again fielding questions about a national park, in fulfilment of the important conservation role that history had thrust upon him; even if, as he observed at the time 'Honourable Members did not seem to realise it'. He was asked whether he would take steps to have the Otira Gorge and the upper valley of the Taramakau formed into a national park to prevent the destruction of scenery caused by railway construction. 'I am not prepared to say that they must not make the railway,' said the Member for Ellesmere, but he did say it should be made in such a way as to avoid the destruction of the scenery. He had also been approached by the Christchurch Beautifying Association to ask that 'the reservation should extend to the head-waters of the Waimakariri'. McKenzie agreed, but said a national park could not be made until such time as the question of the Midland Railway land area was settled.

At the reference to the Christchurch Beautifying Association, Sherlock Holmes would have made a swift and accurate deduction. Its secretary was none other than the scientist Leonard Cockayne, who made annual visits to botanise from his cottage and was well aware of the damage being done. He also lost no opportunity of advocating that the area should be made a national park. In Cockayne's view the area was 'a fine example of trans-alpine flora transition'. In *Canterbury Old and New* he wrote feelingly: '. . . the forests, the shrubs forming thickets on river terrace slopes, the great mountain daisies and other plants which fleck the upland meadows with purest whites and softest yellows are really all unique, and to be found nowhere else in the world, the remnants indeed of a far greater vegetation which spread aeons ago over the great continent . . .'

It seems that John McKenzie's sense that he was receiving something less than due credit for his efforts was justified. Not only did he have the Tongariro Bill behind him, and the Little Barrier and Resolution Island decisions, but in the previous year he had promised a Bill to form a national park that would include Mount Egmont and adjacent Crown lands. The local Member had spoken eloquently of the thousands of tourists visiting each year what '. . . was acknowledged to be the most graceful mountain in the world'.

Smaller reservations were also being made, although the record in this regard is not particularly clear. The 1904 report advised that: 'A good deal has been done in past years towards setting aside reserves for the preservation of the native fauna and flora, and to ensure the public the right to places of natural beauty, but more might be done.' The 1897 report recorded the addition of eight hundred hectares at Ship Cove in Queen Charlotte Sound: 'The reserve is nearly all forest, and is in much the same condition as when Captain Cook first anchored in the Bay.'

Towards the end of the decade the pace of departmental action appeared to quicken. The area of forest reserves was reported at intervals, notwithstanding that the Forests and Agriculture Branch, including its chief conservator, Thomas Kirk, was a casualty of retrenchment. State forest reserves began to increase from the half-million hectares to which they had fallen in 1895, in apparent confirmation of William Rolleston's remarks two years earlier.

The rising trend may well have been connected with a report by George Perrin, Conservator of State Forests of the Australian State of Victoria. As delegate for both Victoria and Tasmania Perrin attended a major timber conference in Wellington in July 1896. There he was invited by Seddon to make an inspection tour and to report on the state conservation of forests in New Zealand.

Perrin was astonished at what he saw: 'There must be something wrong when the government of a country, with eyes wide open to what is going on, stands idly by while millions of pounds worth of valuable soft woods are destroyed by this agent [fire] year after year. It is most deplorable to note the ruinous destruction by fire from one end of the colony to the other. The waste of timber in this way has been simply astounding and no country in the world could stand for any length of time such a drain on its forests. In some districts

Forest clearance today is a highly mechanised industry, with huge machines, powerful chainsaws and even helicopters. For the first century of New Zealand forest clearance (1840–1940) the muscle of men, bullocks and horses did the work. Bullock and horse teams hauled the log sections along rough and often narrow forest roads to the river or to the railhead.

Transport on the Wanganui River was revolutionised in 1892 when Alexander Hatrick began a regular steamer service from Wanganui to Pipiriki. By 1903 the service stretched to Taumarunui, and in the riverboats' heyday, twelve vessels plied the river. Steamer travel was an elegant affair, with tourists dressed formally for their special outing.

The Wanganui was widely promoted as the Rhine of New Zealand and was an important part of the route across the North Island, which from the 1890s onwards included the Tongariro volcanoes, Tokaanu, Taupo and Rotorua.

vast quantities of timber have been destroyed, chiefly by fire. In this respect the greatest sinner by far and away is the pastoralist, and the insensate destruction of birch [*sic*] forests on hilltops and about the headwaters of rivers has been carried out to an extent which is simply amazing.'

A section of the report discussed the value of the forests to the 'natural glories of the New Zealand Wonderland'. The Wanganui River was especially mentioned: 'Should this territory fall into [the hands of] the pastoralist or small grazier, aesthetic effect will speedily be sacrificed to the desire for more grass, and the forest-clad cliffs, the mossy slopes, and the fern-tree gullies of this, the Rhine of New Zealand, will soon be shorn of their natural attraction. Such a river with such a history surely deserves a better fate than to be robbed of its most striking features by the fire stick — its inevitable destiny unless the authorities step in to save these frontages, which would form the grandest national park in the Southern Hemisphere.'

Elsewhere in the report, Perrin included a suitable postscript for the decade. 'Nature is never slow to avenge herself,' he said, 'and such reckless disregard of her natural conditions results in flooded homes and ruined settlers.' After Marsh, Potts, Dobson and Vogel, the theme had more than three decades of repetition.

Chapter 11

Tourism and Scenery 1901–1920

. . . as and for an inalienable patrimony of the people of New Zealand.
— Scenery Preservation Act 1903.

The new century came in with Richard Henry continuing his now-forlorn task of transferring birds to Resolution and nearby islands. His letters appended to the annual report of the Department were packed with acute and sympathetic observation of his wild world, where the seasons ran to no predictable pattern. The crested penguins would arrive in hapus, some hundreds to each kilometre of coast. They were very noisy after laying. In fact, Henry noted that the place at times was positively orchestral with the evening concerts of the wekas, and in their breeding season, the drumming of kakapo.

The two other sanctuaries — at Little Barrier and a game farm reserve at Paraparaumu — were also reported upon. The war against wild cats on Little Barrier continued. At Paraparaumu the red deer herd was thriving. In the 1980s there is a certain irony in the idea of rearing red deer in a game

Kakapo photographed by Henry, 1900.

Henry referred to these birds as 'old New Zealanders . . . simple poor things that know nothing of enemies'. He was pessimistic about their future: 'Just now the "lords of creation" have imported ferrets and weasels that prey on all such things that sleep on the ground, and, as kakapos cannot be expected to learn in a day what their race had forgotten for thousands of years, the chapter of their history is in all likelihood coming to a close.'

A G. E. Mannering photo of Marmaduke Dixon and Tom Fyfe wearing the first sets of skis ever used on Mount Cook. In 1893 Dixon and Mannering made one more attempt to conquer Mount Cook. In crossing the Grand Plateau they decided to use home-made skis made from the blades of a reaper and binder. When Fyfe joined their party at the last minute, Dixon borrowed some old packing cases from Ball Hut to fashion a third pair. The party was then able to cross the Plateau with ease.

Skiing did not become popular at Mount Cook until the early 1920s.

sanctuary. Although the base of understanding for the needs of conservation had widened, and the effects of forest destruction were becoming more obvious, reservation was spasmodic and fragmentary. The debates on scenic beauty, tourism, native-bird loss and forest destruction may have promoted some awareness, but public opinion appeared still to be against forest protection. The reserves that did exist were established during the 'utilitarian' period of concern about flooding and erosion, and lay at the headwaters of forested catchments. Scenery reserves under John McKenzie's 1892 Land Act numbered fewer than a hundred.

Young climbers were developing their skills in various parts of the alpine chain south of Arthur's Pass, a product of the mountaineering interest promoted initially by Green's exploits on Mount Cook. Exploration went hand in hand with first crossings and first ascents. Mount Aspiring was climbed in 1909, Mitre Peak in 1910. Exploration was still a primary goal for W. G. Grave and A. Talbot in the still-unknown (to Europeans) regions west and north of Lake Te Anau.

Thomas Mackenzie returned from Britain in 1900, having been made a Fellow of the Royal Geographic Society in recognition of his Fiordland explorations, to resume his championship of the South-West. Leonard Cockayne had continued his campaign for reservation for the Arthur's Pass region. And Harry Ell, greatest of all the conservationist politicians, had entered Parliament. The creation of Egmont National Park, strongly promoted by the local bodies surrounding the mountain, was indicative of a growing interest.

The Egmont National Park Act was dated 20 October 1900. It set aside as reserve 'land comprised with a circle having a radius of six miles, and a centre on the summit of Mount Egmont', along with 'certain ranges of hills known as the Patua Ranges'. At six miles (or nine and a half kilometres) instead of the 'four and a half to five miles' (about eight kilometres) mentioned by the Provincial Superintendent, Frederic Carrington, to Julius Vogel in 1874,

HARRY ELL (1863–1934)

Perhaps the most tenacious of New Zealand's politician conservationists, Harry Ell was born near Halswell and educated at Christchurch West High School. In his free time he roamed the Port Hills. He later said, 'The wonderful beauty of the scenery of the hills has been my inspiration.'

As a restless young man, Ell tried his hand at several occupations — museum attendant, shepherd, wool scourer and surveyor. He served as a volunteer when Government action was taken against Te Whiti at Parihaka in Taranaki. His energy and strong social interest carried him then towards politics and the Liberal Party. His twenty-year parliamentary career began when in 1899 he was elected to represent Christchurch South.

With his persistent advocacy of the need to preserve native forest and

scenery, he was the major influence in the passing of the Scenery Preservation Act of 1903. Ell was also connected with much liberal social legislation. The great work and enduring passion of his life, pursued in or out of politics and in the face of any conceivable difficulty, was the Summit Road across the Port Hills, with its walks and string of reserves.

He was involved with other great figures in New Zealand's conservation history. He worked often with Leonard Cockayne, as in the campaign for Kennedy's Bush Reserve, and served briefly as a Minister in the Cabinet of Thomas Mackenzie. L. W. McCaskill, as a young man, provided slides and the lantern projector for talks about the birds and forests of Banks Peninsula by the ageing Harry Ell.

the radius was no doubt beginning to emerge towards the stark clarity with which it can be seen today.

A short businesslike document of five pages put the administration of the park in the hands of a board of ten people, seven of whom were to be appointed by the seven local authorities surrounding the mountain; recognition of the special relationship between the mountain and its surrounding land and of the unity of interest in the creation of the park that had been displayed by the counties.

The Egmont National Park Board held its first meeting in February 1901, and apparently got down to business straight away. The report of the Lands and Survey Department for 1902 mentions four meetings and work on tracks, as well as upkeep on roads and buildings. One year later the number of visitors to North Egmont had exceeded one thousand and the mountain was becoming very popular as a health resort: 'Its recuperative powers are continually being recommended by the medical profession. The high altitude, with its bracing and health-giving surroundings, coupled with the dry porous nature of the ground . . . have proved remarkably beneficial to all classes of the community.' The Tourist and Health Resorts Department agreed: Mount Egmont 'is one of the grandest pleasure-grounds of the colony, unique in its configuration and surroundings, situated as it is in the midst of a beautiful and thriving district; but it suffers at present from lack of adequate means of access and of proper accommodation for visitors'.

That criticism may have been more to the point if levelled at the older, but less accessible Tongariro National Park. There, in 1903, the first huts were being erected; one at the hot springs site of Ketetahi, to which access was said to be easier because of a bridle road, and one at the foot of Ruapehu for the convenience of climbers. The problem was not just comparative remoteness. The arbitrary circular boundaries around the peaks related to neither land form nor forest and encompassed only barren fields of ash and scoria.

The legislation for both parks put them under the Domains Act 1881. Like the United States, New Zealand had invoked the idea of national park but left its definition to the unfolding of history. 'The honourable gentleman has . . . talked about a national park, but has not explained what he meant by it,' said one of the Members in 1893. The legislators were clear that they intended to remove the land from the reach of private speculation, and to protect wildlife, vegetation and natural features. As a vehicle for administration, the Domains Act would do, and it gave a wide latitude. The board could build lodges, museums or ornamental buildings, dedicate areas for public amusement, lease for accommodation houses, make roads and adjust and control watercourses. Perhaps a national park was an over-sized urban domain.

In fact, with hindsight, and through the parliamentary debates as national park legislation developed, we can trace the evolution of a New Zealand conservation ethic; nowhere more plainly perhaps than in relation to introduced animals. The Egmont Act protected everything and forbad the shooting of birds and animals. There was still much enthusiasm for acclimatisation, loss of native wildlife, was, on the whole seen as inevitable, and the prospect of adding even larger animals to the horde of voluntary and conscripted animal colonists already in the country was being pursued with enthusiasm in the highest quarters.

In 1903 Mr Flatman, representing Geraldine, asked the Minister in charge of the Tourist and Health Resorts Department to confirm that officers had

'A person unacquainted with real alpine scenery cannot get any idea of it from a photograph. All attempts to show the gigantic size of the peaks and their distance from the camera fail hopelessly.' (A. P. Harper, 1891)

Dr Ebenezer Teichelmann, shown here, was one of the pioneer photographers who wrestled with this problem at the turn of the century. The size and cumbersome shape of the photographic equipment made alpine photography even more of a challenge.

'The overmastering love of the mountains is something which wells up from within, and will not be denied.' This was the feeling of Australian Freda du Faur, the first woman to climb Mount Cook. In 1910, aided by guides, Peter and Alex Graham, she reached the summit of New Zealand's highest mountain in record time, feeling 'very little, very lonely and much inclined to cry'.

Risking the disapproval of those 'who assured me . . . that if I went out alone with a guide I would lose my reputation', she tackled new challenges, completing in 1913 the first grand traverse of Mount Cook with Peter Graham and Darby Thomson.

made enquiries regarding moose, elk, wapiti and buffalo from America, and Caucasian and Carpathian deer, Asiatic wapiti and ibex from Europe. Sir Joseph Ward confirmed. The Government had already decided that elk and buffalo should be obtained from North America: 'There are large areas of land unsuitable for any other purpose, but if stocked with big game would be a very valuable asset to the colony.'

In the first annual report of the new department in the previous year, much more had been said. Moose as well as wapiti were obtainable from North America: 'These splendid members of the deer family should be well adapted for acclimatisation in this country. A small herd of moose have already been established on the West Coast. They and wapiti are of the same hardy nature as the Scotch red deer, and should afford magnificent sport on our forest-clad ranges, and provide the very best training in the use of rifle and camp life for our future military defenders. The above-mentioned animals successfully acclimatised would undoubtedly be the means of attracting wealthy sportsmen not only to visit, but to reside permanently in this country.'

The report moved on to a revealing comment on the status of bird life: 'Owing to the decimation of pheasants, quail and native birds by stoats, weasels, poisoned grain and bush fires, I do not recommend that the importation of birds other than water-fowl should be attempted. New Zealand being a magnificently watered country, its lakes, lagoons, and rivers afford most favourable conditions for the breeding of water-fowl.' It also advised that six red deer had been liberated near Lake Waikaremoana 'in the same locality as the previous lots'. National parks and other future national park areas became recipients of the imported game animals. The 1907 report recorded the liberation of eighteen elk in Fiordland National Park, ten of which were presented by none other than President Roosevelt. Five red deer had been released in Tongariro National Park, and eight chamois, given by the Emperor of Austria, had been released at Mount Cook.

The arrival of the chamois gave particular pleasure to T. E. Donne, Super-

Turning New Zealand into a sportsman's paradise was a major goal of the first general manager of the Tourist and Health Resorts Department, Thomas Donne. At his request, chamois were obtained from Austria — the unfortunate animals suffered a nine-month journey, beginning with their train being snowed up and then catching fire. In London their boat was first delayed by fog and then by a collision — all before their main journey.

intendent of the Department, whose personal collections of New Zealand red deer heads, birds and mounted trout adorned the head office. In 1905, with the Austrian warship *Panther* in Wellington, he had discussed with the rear admiral in command the possibility of giving live birds to Austria. Keas, wekas, kiwis, paradise ducks, grey ducks and six tuatara lizards were provided. In exchange he had asked for some chamois. The idea of exchanging tuataras for chamois has less appeal in the 1980s. Early in 1908, Peter Graham, the chief guide at Mount Cook, was able to report chamois with young. Eight thar were released in the same area in the following year to add to the half-dozen liberated earlier.

The Tourist and Health Resorts Department had become responsible, among other things, for the Mount Cook reservation and the bird sanctuaries. The 1903 report contained a feeling lament for the forests: 'No reasonable objection can be offered to the clearing of forest lands well fitted for settlement . . . But our forests have been and are still being destroyed in a wholesale ruthless manner, without a thought being given to the future . . . It is pitiful to travel through such districts in New Zealand, made bare and desolate by the destruction of these grand growths of untold centuries . . . The beauty of the Mamaku Forest, through which the Auckland–Rotorua Railway passes, has been grievously marred by the operations of the timber millers . . . I would most strongly recommend the Government to immediately proceed to resume the control of specially interesting and attractive forest lands of the principal routes of travel, and to rigidly conserve scenic forests now in the hands of the Crown where the preservation of such timbered areas would not interfere with the progress of settlement . . . The vanishing native-bird life also has sympathetic claims upon the people of the colony. Many of these otherwise useless forests [would] not only agreeably adorn the routes of travel, but also serve as a last home for the rarer New Zealand birds.' It was the parks and reserves that would (eventually) do this.

In equally forthright terms, the report drew attention to the heritage of history: 'Local history and romance have a value which very closely approaches that of scenery, and in this colony we have all the elements which should make it one of the most interesting countries on the traveller's world route . . . A deplorable indifference to such considerations has prevailed in most parts of New Zealand in the past . . . Redoubts and pas have been deliberately razed long after the cessation of Maori troubles . . . it is advisable that the principal localities should be inspected, in order to prevent any further vandalism and to obtain data on which to frame suggestions for their permanent upkeep in as nearly as possible their original form. The sites of the old pas of Ohaeawai and Ruapekapeka in Heke's war in the North; the scenes of such engagements as Rangiriri, Orakau, Ngatapa, Porere; the more important positions attacked in the Taranaki campaign; the ancient fortifications, etc., on Banks Peninsula and elsewhere in the South should all receive attention.'

The status of the 'Te Anau and Milford Sound Tour', or the Milford Track, was reported: 'The trip is destined to be one of the most popular in the colony. It is rapidly becoming recognised that in no part of the world is there anything approaching Milford Sound for grand and magnificent scenery.' But the track was not being well maintained and the Government was urged to take steps towards control by purchasing Glade House at the head of Lake Te

A track party poses for the Burton brothers' camera outside the original Beech Hut at Quintin on the Milford Track in 1890. The area was named after Quintin McKinnon, the surveyor/explorer who cut the original track on the Te Anau side to connect with the track being cut by Donald Sutherland from the Milford side.

Anau. The steamer on the lake should also be purchased, and the Government should appoint its own guides. The report finished with a recommendation entirely consonant with the views of Thomas Mackenzie.

'Between Milford Sound and Dusky Sound, and west of Lakes Wakatipu, Te Anau, and Manapouri, there is a large block of country, including the famous Clinton Valley through which the Milford Sound overland route passes, which for scenic grandeur is unrivalled. This area is interspersed with lakes, fiords, and mountains of great beauty, and is destined, if carefully preserved, to become one of the colony's foremost attractions, and in time one of its greatest assets. In addition to its value as a scenic resort, it would prove a home for a number of native birds which are too rapidly disappearing. As a big-game forest it would also be invaluable. I strongly recommend that the whole area should be reserved, and that no further private interests be allowed to grow up therein.'

In the same year, John Hay, the Commissioner of Crown lands for Southland, made similar recommendations. In August, Thomas Mackenzie asked the Hon. Mr Duncan, Minister of Lands, if 'the Land Department has yet come to a decision regarding the important question of dedicating a large portion of Fiord county for the purpose of forming a national park?' Mr Duncan replied that the department was favourable to the setting aside and conservation of the district in question, but more information was needed about this comparatively unknown country.

If reservation of Fiordland was still to be deferred, Leonard Cockayne's campaign for protection of areas in Arthur's Pass had been successful. In September 1901, almost seven thousand hectares in and near the Otira Valley, and sixty thousand hectares in the headwaters of the Waimakariri River were reserved for national park purposes. A year later the reserves of Mount Cook were extended by seven thousand hectares near the Hermitage to preserve alpine flowers. Mackenzie's reward came in the *New Zealand Gazette* early in 1905. Nearly a million hectares were proclaimed reserve to become known as 'The Sounds' National Park.

At this time, Cockayne's friend and fellow enthusiast Harry George Ell had entered the lists of Parliament in a championship of reservation that would support and extend the advocacy of Alfred Newman and Thomas Mackenzie. In Harry Ell, Parliament acquired perhaps the most persistent, tenacious and far-sighted of all the politician conservationists.

From the outset, Ell was concerned with systematic reservation — to make scenic corridors along roads, railways and rivers or to protect a percentage of an area of forest land being opened up for settlement. In 1901 his questions were directed at scenery and bush preservation along the Cheviot–Kaikoura road. In 1902 he wanted to know what reservation was being made from the Kawhia Block. His persistence was successful — over five thousand hectares was protected. The state of the kauri forests also claimed his attention: 'It has been calculated that in the course of a few years all our kauri forests will have been cut out. Our white pine forests will soon disappear altogether. We are now tapping the only forests that remain . . .' An area of kauri forest should be reserved as a means of attracting tourists. The Government replied that this was in hand. Ell believed that forests should be preserved for scenery, for recreation, for land protection, to conserve timber supplies and for their potential value for tourism.

By 1903 New Zealand's first statute on the provision of reserves for nature conservation was in Parliament. Premier Seddon complimented Ell on his persistence. The Hon. Sir Joseph Ward went further: 'For the last two or three years it is beyond all question . . . that the Honourable Member for Christchurch City [Ell] has been persistent in his representations concerning this important work . . . I believe this is one of the finest things we could do — to preserve for all time the scenery of the colony . . . One of the finest assets that we have in this colony is our natural scenery, and it is the duty of the people of the present generation to preserve it for all time.'

Eighty years later the *Hansard* record of the debate on the Scenery Preservation Bill can stir the same regret so clearly felt in the House. Ell had not been a lonely voice. Members knew what was happening, but an air of fatalism pervaded the discussion. Feeling, even poetic feeling, emerged. Seddon's remarks

The first Hermitage Hotel opened at Mount Cook in 1884. It became part of the government tourist network and was used as a base by climbers and tourists. In 1913 it was abandoned in favour of a new building on the site of the present hotel. The first hotel was near the terminal face of the Mueller Glacier, which has since retreated considerably.

echoed the vision of Julius Vogel thirty years earlier, and contained a poetry of their own: '. . . you see your beauty spots being destroyed and they can never be restored . . . nothing has been done to stop it . . . We are only in our infancy now. As time rolls on and population increases greater interest will be taken in our history, and unless we preserve these spots we will be wanting in our duty not only to ourselves, but also to future generations . . . There are our beautiful gorges and bush scenery, with the light and dark shades of green interwoven with the purple flowers of the rata, and the white flowers of the kumara, and of the other flowering trees in our forests . . . People from far-off lands, when they see the grandeur and beauty of our scenery, are much impressed by it. They go back to their homes and speak of the beauties they have witnessed. In the meantime we are letting our scenery be destroyed; we are doing nothing for its preservation . . . the time has arrived . . . when our scenery should be preserved, when the historic and beautiful places should be for all time conserved . . . the great majority of Members will regret with me that a measure like this was not put upon our statute book many years sooner.'

As with Vogel's great speech on his Forests Bill of 1874, Seddon's contained enduring insights. He would not permit a Minister to have power over the reserves. Only an Act of Parliament would allow them to be interfered with. Forests around the lakes, 'the heritage of the people', ought to be reserved for a distance.

Like Seddon, other Members regretted that the legislation had not come sooner. Each could refer to a place of beauty or particular interest in his district; the route of the Main Trunk Railway, limestone rocks at Hikurangi, kauri forest near Auckland, the history of Stewart Island, and Tuturau, the last great Maori battlefield in the south. Mr Jennings of Egmont stated that there were scenery preservation societies throughout the whole of New Zealand, and referred particularly to the good work of his own Taranaki group: 'There is no river in the whole of New Zealand which preserves so much of its old native surroundings and scenery as the River Mokau . . . it ought to receive immediate attention, so that its beautiful scenery should be maintained . . . I will say the Mokau River excels, in my opinion, the far-famed Wanganui River.' The Member for Bruce spoke of the absolute necessity of conserving the banks on either side of the Wanganui. The late John Ballance's action in securing a mile on each side of the river as scenic reserve was applauded. Mr Heke, of the Northern Maori District, pointed out that the Auckland Land Board had offered for sale very fine kauri reserves in the Whangaroa, Bay of Islands, Hokianga and Wairoa North. In winding up the debate, the Premier could express pleasure at the strong support the Bill had received.

Simple and very much to the point, the Bill appointed a commission to inspect lands of scenic or historic interest or on which there were thermal springs and to recommend to the Governor whether the land should be permanently reserved. The Governor having declared a reserve, 'no person shall cut or remove timber' or interfere in any way, and the land was to be conserved intact 'as and for an inalienable patrimony of the people of New Zealand'.

One special aspect of Ell's remarkable vision has emerged in its full significance only in the 1980s. In 1903 he had asked the Minister of Lands whether he will 'have enclosures made of small areas so as to preserve the remarkable plant life typical of various districts of the colony'. The request was agreed to by Mr Duncan and passed to the Scenery Preservation Commission.

Did conversations with Cockayne about the scientific value of preserving representative examples of typical plant associations lie behind the request? Or did Ell's vision and sense of landscape foresee the day when it would be only the remnant that could identify the landscape as New Zealand at all? Eighty years later the Protected Natural Areas programme is endeavouring to fulfil Ell's objective.

The first Scenery Preservation Commission, which could be described as a 'well-rounded' body, commenced its two-year term in March 1904. Few of the five members had more background than S. Percy Smith, former Surveyor-General, friend of Elsdon Best and founding member of the Polynesian Society with a particular interest in the Maori history of Taranaki. By March 1906 the commission had toured extensively. Six thousand hectares had been reserved, and a further one hundred and forty thousand hectares recommended for reservation. The reserves made included the Wairua Falls in North Auckland, three large areas on the shores of Lake Taupo, some scenic forest areas and several river-bank reserves. Several famous pa sites of Taranaki included Te Kawau and Pukerangiora, reflecting perhaps the knowledge and interest of Percy Smith.

A continuing and strong parliamentary interest in the work was evidenced in the discussions on expenditure and priorities and in the reshaping of the legislation, which went on for more than a decade. In 1905, Members of Parliament questioned the need to reserve land in beautiful but inaccessible places. There was 'no occasion for the Scenery Commissioners to go to Mount Cook or Milford Sound [a revealing selection!] but to confine their operations to those beauty spots near the centres of population where numbers could go and enjoy the beauties of nature'. The trouble seemed to be, in the words of another member, that 'scenery in accessible places which had not been reserved was being destroyed, whilst scenery was being reserved in the back country which could be useless for scenery purposes — in this generation, at any rate'. Parliament, public and the commission itself all agreed that land suited to settlement could not be considered for scenery reservation.

The first amendment arrived in 1906 after it became apparent that the original machinery was too cumbersome. The commission was replaced by a Scenery Preservation Board comprising the Surveyor-General, the general manager of the Tourist and Health Resorts Department and the Commissioner of Crown Lands for the relevant district. Consolidation of the legislation followed in 1908 and further amendment in 1910 and 1915.

The Tongariro National Park claimed the attention of the new Superintendent of Scenic Reserves almost as soon as he was appointed in June 1907. E. Phillips Turner was requested by Order in Council to undertake in company with Leonard Cockayne a topographical and botanical survey of the park and its adjacent lands and to recommend additions. Their survey occupied nine weeks early in 1908 and their report was read to the first meeting of the Board of Trustees in the following May.

This first botanical survey of a large tract in New Zealand attracted worldwide scientific interest. Thoroughly supported by maps and photographs, the comprehensive report was to become a benchmark and standard in park planning. Large additions that would bring the park's area to fifty-five thousand hectares were recommended, on the basis of three guiding principles. First, representations of the special plant associations of the region. 'No area gives an accurate picture of the district of which it forms a portion,' said Cockayne 'if it does not contain typical examples of all plant associations.' There was a complementary value: 'Thus our national parks become havens of refuge where the vegetation, and also those indigenous animals whose presence depends upon forest or meadow, may exist unmolested and remain intact.' The second principle was the retention of catchment headwater forests for soil and water conservation; and the third, avoidance of land suited to settlement.

The trustees recommended legislation for the extensions, and this the Government proceeded to do. By 1908, however, the Liberal Government, which had created the whole basis of New Zealand reservation, was losing power. Concern developed about 'locking up' resources, a myopia of those unable to grasp the significance and purpose of reservation. Three years later William Massey's Reform Party, essentially representative of the concerns of the small farmer, won most of the North Island's rural seats. In 1912 the Reform Party became the Government and official support for the extensions evaporated. Massey sought to delay a decision and put the matter to the Forestry Commission. The commission supported the extension, as did the New Zealand Institute. In 1914 the Reserves and Other Lands Disposal Bill gave authority for the extensions and transferred park administration to the Tourist Department. Still further lobbying failed to influence the Prime Minister's reluctance to act. World war brought other priorities and the extension proposals disappeared from view for almost a decade.

In that decade yet another unlikely but influential strand was to be woven into the extraordinary history of Tongariro. The key figure was John Cullen, the honorary park warden appointed by the Tourist Department. As Police Commissioner, Cullen had commanded an expedition into Maungapohatu in the Urewera in 1916. While it seems probable that he was not appointed warden until his retirement from police duties in 1916, his contribution to the future shaping of national park legislation, and to the problems of Tongariro, may have begun as early as 1913. With the support of the Prime Minister,

The North Island Main Trunk Railway was completed in 1908, not far from the Hapuawhenua Viaduct, which now lies within the Tongariro National Park.

Cullen sought to establish a grouse-shooting paradise on a vast scale by replacing tussock with Scottish heather. With seed and plants obtained from localities ranging from France and Britain to the Campbell Islands, he pursued his objective of covering eight thousand hectares. Objections by the New Zealand Institute, Harry Ell and others were to no avail. By 1919 about three thousand hectares had been planted.

The 1907 report of the new Scenery Preservation Board stated its priorities: scenery along the North Island Main Trunk Railway, in the Marlborough Sounds and on the West Coast, native lands in the Rotorua District to preserve and develop thermal attractions, and the Wanganui River to Taumarunui. The river proposals, as did those on the railway, echoed Ell's 'scenic' corridor ideas. Indeed, in 1903 he had asked the Minister of Lands whether he was 'making reserves of native bush at short intervals along the North Island Main Trunk and on other railway lines?' As well, the discussion about reserves along the Main Trunk reflected the public attention focused on its long-delayed completion. The first train, carrying a parliamentary delegation to meet the American Fleet in Auckland, almost literally scraped through in August 1908.

The reserves proposed in 1907 lay between Marton and Taumarunui. 'The hundred-odd miles of scenery traversed from Makohine to Mananui,' said the board, 'forms a national asset that, in our opinion, should be most jealously conserved and protected . . . The varieties of timber, the natural beauty of the forest, its magnificent situation amongst numerous deep ravines and gorges through which run rapid mountain streams, together with the background of frowning hills and lofty ranges, and in the distance the grand snowcapped peaks of the Ruapehu, Ngauruhoe, and Tongariro mountains, all unite in proclaiming this portion of New Zealand as one of the principal attractions of the colony.'

The board's survey of Wanganui River banks was reported in 1910: 'As far as possible, only the land actually between the river itself and the top of the ridge forming the skyline, as seen from the passing steamers and boats, has been taken.' Hatrick and Company's river service at its peak ran twelve steam and motor vessels and three motorised canoes. In 1903 the service was extended right to Taumarunui. It was realised that there were practical as well as scenic benefits in securing the river banks against erosion.

The eight thousand hectares of Westland scenery reserved by 1911 included a selection of the province's most beautiful lakes: Kanieri, Ianthe, Wahapo and Mapourika. The Franz Joseph reservation of almost twenty thousand hectares, which followed in 1914, was an acknowledgement of values already well known — the explorers Charlie Douglas and A. P. Harper had provided eloquent descriptions. 'The magnificent Franz Joseph Glacier and surrounding land . . .' said the board in 1915. When the Graham family, whose climbing and guiding fame in the region was legendary, took over the small Franz Joseph Hotel in 1911, they had been guiding parties across the Copland Pass from the Hermitage since the early 1900s.

By the outbreak of the First World War in 1914, a total of one hundred thousand hectares was in scenic reserve. Twenty-four thousand hectares were added in the following year, but whether or not because of the debilitating effect of the war, the rate of acquisition then slowed. The record shows that a further fifty thousand hectares was protected through to 1920.

This remarkable photograph shows the construction of a viewing platform opposite the terminal face of the Franz Josef Glacier. The platform was built by the Graham brothers. Soon after its construction the glacier began a rapid advance and in 1909 the platform was swept away. It was not rebuilt.

As with the national parks, management of the scenic reserves involved a learning process. E. Phillips Turner continued as superintendent until becoming chief officer of the Forestry Branch of the Lands and Survey Department in 1918. In the first few years he was much involved in the North Island Main Trunk and Wanganui River surveys, and, of course, with Leonard Cockayne on the ecological survey of the Tongariro National Park. His reports dealt in detail with threats that are little different decades later: fire, noxious plants and animals, stock, timber cutting, vandalism. His workload grew as the estate enlarged and spread. The appointment of honorary rangers was the solution he recommended.

From an historical perspective, the period 1901 to 1920 was truly remarkable. A dawning consciousness of scenic values, the urging of the preservation societies, sadness, even revulsion at mindless forest destruction, and the imperious driving force of Harry Ell combined to invent the mechanism represented in the Scenery Preservation Board. By 1920 the scenery reservations had laid the groundwork and established the nuclei of the national parks system: Egmont in 1900, the Arthur's Pass Reserves in 1901, large reserves 'for national park purposes' in Fiordland in 1905, the Tongariro extensions debates, a large reserve in the Routeburn Valley (part of the future Mount Aspiring National Park) in 1911, reserves at Lakes Rotoiti and Rotoroa in the future Nelson Lakes National Park in 1912, the addition of the Murchison Valley to the Mount Cook reserves in 1917 and a hundred-hectare nucleus of Abel Tasman National Park in 1918.

Elsewhere there existed a large proportion of today's scenic reserve system. In the Marlborough Sounds were many of the areas that have been brought together in the Marlborough Sounds Maritime Park. Without the reserves of the Wanganui River there could have been no proposal for a Whanganui National Park in 1985. The basis for a future Paparoa National Park was laid by the Scenery Preservation Board in 1914 with the reservation of one hundred and twenty hectares at Punakaiki. All this and much more — the Waitomo Caves, the magnificent reserves of the Buller River, other 'scenic corridors' in passes and gorges, pa sites, small pieces of native bush, and waterfalls and islands — New Zealand owes to the fiery foresight of Ell and the patient surveys of the Scenery Preservation Board.

Cutting ice steps on the Tasman Glacier in the late 1890s.

Looked at from another perspective altogther, that of ideal reservation, or the reservation that could provide New Zealand with a comprehensive representation of its lone and stormy evolution, European cultural preoccupations had flung the stable door open and the horse had bolted. The focus (understandably) had been on scenery, not science, perhaps not even to any marked degree on history. The constraints imposed by the climate of opinion within which the Preservation Board was working may be inferred from a recommendation of the Royal Commission on Forestry in 1913: 'It may be stated as a broad principle that no forest land except it be required for the special purposes of a climatic or scenic reserve and which is suitable for farmland, should be permitted to remain under forest if it can be occupied and resided upon in reasonably limited areas.' Many forest associations that were representative of regional or district ecologies had been wiped out, particularly in lowland areas, by the great drive ushered in by refrigeration. Magnificent as is the heritage, the bias towards scenery and land that was not useful for anything else shows today.

Egmont National Park in 1987

By John Clay, Chief Ranger, 1980–1987

Nowhere in New Zealand is a province so dominated by a mountain as is Taranaki. For those who have lived in its shadow, it is regarded as the Father of the Land, the home of their ancestors — in fact, the ally of all their endeavours and the source of all their wealth. It was with this thought in mind, and seeking to retain what they had already gained, that the early settlers had the mountain and its rich green forests made a provincial reserve in 1881. Nineteen years later it was to become New Zealand's second national park.

Although geologically quite young, Egmont is surrounded by its much older forefathers: the Kaitake and Pouakai Ranges. These eroded volcanic stumps, up to half a million years old, form the north-western corner of the park. Situated on the coast of Taranaki and rising from near sea level to over two thousand metres, the mountain intercepts the country's weather systems. This combination provides the variety of vegetation for which the park is renowned.

For generations the park has not only been regarded as the guardian and provider of the land, but also as a source of inspiration and recreation to the many New Zealanders and people from overseas who visit it. It offers a wide variety of activities and interests, both passive and active, to meet the needs of those seeking something from this country's magnificent outdoor heritage. A network of short foot tracks at the ends of the three major roads that enter the park offer the casual visitor a host of natural wonders within easy walking distance of their cars and in close proximity to surrounding populated countryside and towns.

Visitor and display centres at North Egmont and Dawson Falls contain a wealth of information with both natural and human history displays. Both areas also provide park accommodation, which is used extensively by the public and school groups who come to spend time in the park and use these facilities for education and recreation.

For the more enterprising visitors who are happy to carry a pack and walk for three or four days, the round-the-mountain track provides a wide variety of experiences and rewards. Mountain huts give shelter at the end of each day and a chance to meet and exchange views and information with fellow trampers, many of whom may be visitors from overseas. Perhaps it is this fellowship, set in the environment of the mountain park with its daily challenges, that are the moments best remembered once the trip is completed.

The mountain under winter conditions, with its steep and icy slopes, has long been regarded as an excellent training ground for New Zealand mountaineers. Many of the people who learnt their skills here have gone on to climb greater mountains, not only in this country but elsewhere in the world. All have learnt, however, that Egmont, with its unpredictable weather patterns, and more particularly, under winter snows, should never be taken lightly. Care, equipment and technique are all essential ingredients of survival on the mountain.

The mountain park has much to offer,
not only to the people who have always
lived around it, and with whom there is
a long-standing partnership, but to all
who visit it. The partnership is vital for
the well-being of the province and for all
the future generations who seek to live
or enjoy the experiences offered within
its shadow.

Chapter 12

Animals and Erosion 1920–1940

'We agree with your objectives — the national parks for the people . . .'
— Michael Joseph Savage

It will be apparent that the fortunes of conservation are tied much less to a rational philosophy of land use, based on observations of the characteristics of the land (which means everything related to it) than to cultural attitudes expressed through political processes. Settlers from an old and stable landscape had attempted to introduce the cultural practices and the animals and plants they knew into a country that was totally different in its geology and evolutionary history.

The learning process associated with a mis-match of land and culture can be extraordinarily harsh, particularly when the land is inherently unstable and its ecological systems vulnerable. The awakening that had generated the splendid work of the Scenery Preservation Board was not unrelated to cultural learning. The 1890s saw the emergence of the first generation of European New Zealanders born to the land (if not tangata whenua) and relating to it rather than to some fondly recalled piece of English countryside. If cultural spectacles were still distorted by inherited attitudes, some, at least, of the unique values of the country they would eventually call home were being revealed.

The year 1920 arrived with Massey's Reform Party still in power. Political strength shifted to the North Island as expansion, fertilisers, electricity, motor vehicles, road improvements and herd testing carried the dairy industry forward. The first years of the 1920s were a period of some prosperity, but by 1929 the country was drawn into the world depression. In 1935 the first Labour Government replaced the weak coalition that had preceded it. The Second World War commenced in 1939.

With these political circumstances, it was hardly to be expected that the remarkable conservation progress of the early 1900s would continue. The scenery destruction alarm had generated action and there were reserves and 'national parks', albeit undefined in concept and a total mystery in terms of management. The conservation leaders in Parliament had been removed by time or politics or were pursuing their convictions in other places.

There were, however, more cultural shocks to come, more awakenings to endure. It is tempting to see in New Zealand conservation history, cycle after cycle of cultural adjustment, related always to the falling away of cultural scales as each new generation re-appraises values and takes a hand in the shaping of politics. Argued this way, a degree of conflict is inevitable between the young, active vanguard of a further adjustment to perceived land values and the older-established representatives of earlier attitudes. The process must remain reactive and, regrettably, based more on perceived loss than on a clearly stated ethic pursued into land- and water-use decisions.

The 1920s and 1930s saw a replay of the cycle evidenced in the rise of the scenery preservation groups of the 1890s. This time the activist groups that emerged to shape the ethic eventually to be stated in national parks and reserves legislation were concerned with management of the heritage estate put in place by the Scenery Preservation Commission. The perceived problem was protection of native birds; the new cultural shock, the impact of animals on the forests, which were confirmed by repeated flood disasters in their role as protectors of the lowland production won by so much agony and effort.

The new activist groups — the New Zealand Native Bird Protection Society and the Federated Mountain Clubs — were to forge the citizen participatory component in New Zealand reserves administration that gives it world distinction and, on the historical argument, seems to be inevitable as well as indigenous.

The 1921 report of the Department of Lands and Survey summarised the achievement of the previous twenty years. More than one hundred and twenty-six thousand hectares had been added to the twenty thousand reserved before 1903. 'It may be pointed out that seven national parks comprising 2,771,202 acres [1,121,505 hectares] have also been set apart for the preservation of scenery.' These were scheduled. Almost half the area contained in 1985 in national parks and reserves had been added in twenty years.

Egmont	79,922 *Acres*	(32,344) *(Hectares)*
Tongariro	62,280	(25,205)
Hooker Glacier	38,000	(15,380)
Tasman Park (Mount Cook)	97,800	(39,580)
Arthur's Pass	150,000	(60,705)
Otira Gorge	17,000	(6,880)
Sounds	2,326,200	(941,362)

FEDERATED MOUNTAIN CLUBS

William Spotswood Green's near-successful attempt on Mount Cook in 1882 focused climbing interest on the Southern Alps area. Mountaineering exploration soon took place in other parts of the Alps. While the New Zealand Alpine Club was formed in 1891, the advent of skiing and tramping clubs (Ruapehu Ski Club 1913, Tararua Tramping Club 1919, Hutt Valley Tramping Club 1923) indicated a widening enjoyment of the mountains — no longer solely the realm of the Alpine Club and the guided mountaineers. The clubs played a notable part in the formative stages of the earlier national parks like Egmont and Arthur's Pass. Their track work, hut-building and map-making often meant that their knowledge of particular areas and conditions was the best available.

In 1931 the New Zealand Alpine Club, through its president, A. P. Harper, convened a meeting of the fifteen mountaineering clubs that had been established. They discussed the problems of reservation, which like Topsy had 'just growed' as Harper put it, and agreed to set up a federation to act for those whose recreation lay in the mountains and bush.

The FMC was both active and influential. Sub-committees developed knowledge and practice related to huts, mapping, reservation and mountain safety. Regional associations were formed as mountain and bush recreation expanded and more clubs were formed. The federation contributed its knowledge and experience to bodies like the Geographic Board, to overseas expeditions, which included Antarctica, and to developing legislation.

Most significant of all the work of the FMC was its contribution during the 1930s and 1940s to the shaping of policy and administration eventually expressed in the National Parks Act 1952.

In 1980 terms, the schedule embraced five national parks: Egmont, Tongariro, Mount Cook (the Hooker-Tasman combination), Arthur's Pass (the Arthur's Pass-Otira Gorge combination) and Fiordland. Tongariro and Mount Cook were administered by the Tourist and Health Resorts Department, which leased the Hermitage area and the reserves to the Mount Cook Motor Company in 1922.

Egmont had its board. The heather that had been so assiduously planted by John Cullen was now a sea of pink around Ruapehu, and a complaint had been made by the New Zealand Institute. The heather 'was in no way detrimental to the native vegetation,' said Cullen.

It was Cullen who led the effort to revive and implement the extension of Tongariro National Park. With the support of James Gunson, Mayor of Auckland, he promoted the park as a playground for the people of Auckland, and a huge game reserve for gentlemen shooters. The Tourist Department procrastinated but Cullen and Gunson, with a groundswell of support, felt confident enough to draft their own Bill adding seventy thousand hectares. This became the basis of the Tongariro National Park Act 1922. The Minister of Lands, when introducing the Bill to the House, referred to their interest: 'These gentlemen, together with many other progressive persons, have felt that a board of control modelled on the lines of the Mount Egmont Park would tend to develop and popularise the Tongariro National Park.' The board was to include the Paramount Chief of Ngati Tuwharetoa. Apirana Ngata read Te Heuheu Tukino's letter about the gift. There were generous tributes: 'His name will never be forgotten in connection with this great gift,' said the Hon. Mr Guthrie. At least two members favoured the erection of a statue to the illustrious chieftain.

Members were still quite unclear as to the objectives of a national park. The only definition provided by the debate was that the park was for the good of the people of the country and for visitors from overseas. 'And as a sanctuary for birds,' said the Minister of Lands. Confusion was evident in the continuing argument about heather planting. 'There are hundreds of acres of it,' said the Minister. Supporters claimed that it would not spread, that it would provide habitat for quail and grouse, and appeal to the large number of Scottish people

Heather in Tongariro National Park. John Cullen's confidence was misplaced — today the plant is a major problem.

THE ROYAL FOREST AND BIRD PROTECTION SOCIETY OF NEW ZEALAND

Public concern at the loss of New Zealand native bird life led to the founding in 1923 of the New Zealand Native Bird Protection Society by Thomas Mackenzie. Early executives of the society, who included Leonard Cockayne, R. A. Falla, G. M. Thomson and E. Phillips Turner, were a 'Who's Who' of conservation of the time. Another conservation leader, Captain E. V. Sanderson, was secretary and later president of the society. Its goal was '. . . to co-operate with the New Zealand Foresty League — with the object of advocating and obtaining unity of control in all matters affecting wildlife and also the advocating of a Bird Day for our schools'. The society immediately launched into a programme of lobbying and education built around three recurring themes: the problems and dangers of introduced animals, erosion, and the chaotic state of wildlife management.

In 1937 the society recommended that all remaining native forest be classified either protection or commercial, and that protection forest should be administered by a Department of Conservation, responsible for all protected areas. The society's advocacy of these recommendations and the hard-hitting editorials of the journals played a major role in the steps eventually taken to control introduced animals as well as to introduce a Soil Conservation and Rivers Control Act.

In 1948 the society became the Forest and Bird Protection Society of New Zealand and continued its role as advocate in major issues such as the setting-up of the Waipoua Kauri Sanctuary, the establishment of the Urewera National Park and the campaign to save Lake Manapouri. In recent years the society has actively lobbied for a comprehensive network of protected areas.

Construction of the Midland railway line was very much a part of the early history of Arthur's Pass National Park. Damage caused by this project inspired the first calls for the establishment of a park. Excursions from Christchurch, once the Otira Tunnel was opened in 1923, led to the setting up of a park board, and accelerated the first general national park legislation.

in New Zealand. Opponents pointed to the history of imported gorse and blackberry, and feared the worst. 'I, for one, would be very sorry to see the purity of our beautiful native vegetation in our national parks disturbed,' said Mr Field, the Member for Otaki, getting close to eventual national park objectives. With the passing of the Bill, the park area was enlarged to sixty thousand hectares. A major extension based on the recommendations of Leonard Cockayne and E. Phillips Turner had, at last, been achieved.

At Arthur's Pass the long struggle with the wet, difficult conditions of the Main Divide, which had been going on since 1907, was finished when the Otira Tunnel was opened in 1923. Alpine rail excursions commenced in 1924 and the people of Christchurch swarmed to the area. Local residents became increasingly alarmed at destruction. By 1928 it was clear to public-minded citizens that control was needed. The excursions had connected Christchurch with Arthur's Pass, as the Cullen and Gunson initiative had related Auckland

THE NEW ZEALAND INSTITUTE
THE ROYAL SOCIETY OF NEW ZEALAND

The first societies for the promotion of scientific investigation and discussion were the provincial institutes and philosophical societies, set up with their parent body, the New Zealand Institute, in 1867. In 1903 this body became the Royal Society of New Zealand.

It was the scientists who best understood the significance of losses during European settlement and who were constantly warning of coming problems or proposing correctives. The Auckland Institute's recommendation for the purchase of Little Barrier Island

as a sanctuary for endangered bird species in the 1880s was followed by the Otago Institute's advocacy of a similar step for Resolution Island. The later reservation of Kapiti Island and the protection of the Cape Kidnappers Gannetry in 1912 were other examples of initiatives towards protection of scientific values.

The Royal Society was one of the agencies that shaped the instructions of the National Parks Act from two predominant issues. One of these was the extensive planting of heather in Tongariro National Park. The other was the expansion of deer populations during the 1900–30 period. The Royal Society, the Forest and Bird Protection

Society and the Federated Mountain Clubs all drew attention to the effect of deer on the forests and to the dangers of erosion and flooding. Their warnings led to the introduction of the Soil Conservation and Rivers Control Act in 1941. The Royal Society was also behind the later establishment of the Nature Conservation Council and was deeply involved with conservation controversies preceding the setting-up of the Waipoua Kauri Forest Sanctuary, and later, the proposed raising of Lake Manapouri. Because of the scientific importance of national parks, a nominee of the Royal Society is a member of the National Parks and Reserves Authority.

to Tongariro. A large gathering in Christchurch, chaired by the mayor, was unanimously for a board of control.

The Government was sympathetic and indeed had concluded that the time had come for more general legislation. The Public Reserves, Domains and National Parks Act 1928 was debated and passed. Among its provisions for domains and reserves, the Governor-General was empowered to declare land under the Land or Forests Acts, or any public domain, or areas reserved by the Scenery Preservation Act to be 'National Park'. Much of the discussion

These two photographs of a camping trip at Arthur's Pass in 1908 show signs of a problem that was to grow as excursions to the region became popular. Visitors felt free to carry off plants or chop down trees for firewood. In the early 1920s, residents became increasingly worried at the damage that was being done to trees and shrubs by railway excursionists. The road over the gorge was at times 'strewn with ferns, branches, moss, orchids — just abandoned. People would pick far more than they could carry, or else see better things and drop what they had . . .' (Grace Adams).

Arthur Dobson

in the House was about parochial matters. The Minister of Lands was 'quite satisfied that many of the reserves all over the country are in a disgracefully neglected state'. Seddon referred to the excursions: 'There is no government body to control the excursionists in their rambles about the mountains, and their depredations in the way of taking valuable plants.' While 'National Park' remained undefined, Field could see clearly towards an objective: 'I hope that these parks will be maintained as truly national parks — that is to say, for the preservation of our native birds and flora. There should be no exotics or foreign animals or birds or plants introduced into them. If that policy is not adopted it will be a misnomer to call our parks national parks.'

It was at once appropriate and remarkable that Arthur Dudley Dobson, the engineer-discoverer of the pass, should become a member of the first Arthur's Pass National Park Board. The Otira Tunnel, one of New Zealand's great engineering projects, had shaped events in the area he had originally explored. Another feat of engineering was about to influence the future of Fiordland. Deepening economic depression brought unemployment, and with it the need for created work on projects high in labour content. A decision was made to extend road-formation work in the Eglinton Valley. In the middle of 1933, with road works approaching the head of the valley, a survey and estimate were made for a complete link to Milford. Two years later a wheelbarrow gang of five men, ten kilometres in advance of the road, began to dig away at an approach to a tunnel. Rarely has work in New Zealand gone ahead in such bleak, pitiless conditions. They were attacking a circle of mountains, rearing more than a thousand metres above. Storm, flood and avalanche, and the sparkling grandeur of alpine days were their lot. The Homer Tunnel contract began at the end of 1937 and was holed through in 1940.

Scenery reservation continued on into the years of depression. On the one hand the estate was enlarging rapidly, while on the other, a miniscule flow of money dwindled and virtually ceased. With these divergent trends the inevitable and predictable happened — major problems of management emerged.

By 1940 the area reserved had grown to three hundred and forty thousand hectares in a thousand sites. There had been additions in the Marlborough Sounds. Island reserves included the Poor Knights. Hen Island (Taranga) became a bird sanctuary. Trounson Kauri Park was reserved in 1929, in the same year as some nine thousand hectares at Lake Rotoroa. History in the north was acknowledged with the protection of Marsden Cross in 1930 and the flagstaff site at Russell in 1932. Further reserves on the banks of the Wanganui River, and large reservations on the Reefton–Maruia Springs road (1936) and along the Lewis Pass in 1937 signalled that the concept of scenic corridors was still alive and well. There were reserves in the Buller Gorge. 'The growth of motor transport had greatly increased the attention paid by the public to scenic areas,' said the 1932 report of the Lands and Survey Department. In the preceding year there had been two further notable Maori land gifts by sub-tribes of Te Arawa. The magnificent Lake Okataina Reserve was given by the Ngati Tarawhai people, and the bush-clad cliffs and bluffs that lend so much charm to Lake Rotoiti by Ngati Pikiao.

In 1931, in the largest reservation of the period, fifty thousand hectares in the vicinity of Fox Glacier, the Copland Valley and the Twain and Karangarua Rivers laid the foundation to Westland, sixth national park after the series reported in 1921. 'This magnificent region embraces numerous glaciers, including the Fox, and many notable peaks, and is destined from its varied attractions to become one of the principal scenic assets of our Dominion,' said the department. The previous year's report, supported by an appendix on 'The Glacial Scenic reserves of Westland' by Cockayne and Tiechelman, had advised that some five thousand hectares had been put under protection at Fox Glacier. When in 1936 thirteen thousand hectares in the Travers Valley were added to the earlier reservation at Lake Rotoroa, the foundations of a future Nelson Lakes National Park were laid.

The origins of the eighth national park, in the North Island, and contrasting with the essentially alpine character of the previous seven, lay in the Urewera highlands. While surveys for hydro-electricity and the Urewera Lands Act of 1921–22 'to facilitate the settlement of the Lands in the Urewera District' appeared to suggest development intentions, press and public opinion was changing. Perhaps the only large tract of native forest left in the North Island should be valued for its natural beauty. By 1924 there had been severe floods in Marlborough, Northland, Mid-Canterbury and Otago. The Lands and Survey Department advised that it did 'not intend to develop all for settlement, rather the rougher portions could be permanently reserved to prevent denudation of higher slopes, with the aim of regulating run-off and preventing flooding'. A year later the Commissioner of Crown Lands gave the first official support to the notion of a national park.

The Tourist Department commented on the popularity of Lake Waikaremoana. The 1927 report noted that the Tourist League was pressing for completion of the road from Ruatahuna to the lake. The road and a hydro-electric station were both opened in 1930.

In the same year Bernard Teague, the future advocate for an Urewera National Park, (as had Alfred Newman for Tongariro and Thomas Mackenzie for Fiordland) moved to Wairoa. The Depression had brought some pressure for examination of the milling and farming potential of the Urewera, but community resistance was strong. In 1932 nature provided a reminder of the facts

Flooding in the Wairarapa-Manawatu,
1932.

of forest protection with severe flooding on the East Coast. In November 1936 Frank Langstone, Commissioner of State Forests and Minister of Lands, announced that the whole of the Crown's interest, some one hundred and twenty thousand hectares, was to be declared a reserve, mainly as a protection for the native bush and bird life. 'I say definitely that if we allowed the bush to be cut out in the high country here, the rich areas of the Rangitaiki Plains would be washed out to sea,' said the Minister. He went on with a lament for the forests, not unlike some of earlier years: 'It is unfortunate that most of the bush-clad country has been felled and denuded of forest in the interests of settlements, many of which have been absolute failures, and settlers have lost their money in loans and so on. There has been disaster after disaster, after thousands of pounds have been spent in roads, bridges and other facilities.'

The common factors of national park activity during the period were increasing numbers of visitors, track-making (which was often much assisted by mountain clubs) and the introduction of skiing. Arthur's Pass was the most heavily visited — the thousand people brought in by a single weekend excursion could equal the total of visitors for a year at Tongariro. Here, the board's efforts to provide accommodation had led in 1928 to a lease and loan to the Tongariro Park Tourist Company. The Chateau was opened on 1 August 1929 and used for winter sports. A continuous stream of visitors was reported but success was transitory. Unable to sustain running costs, the company was wound up in 1931 and the board took possession, noting gloomily that, with the financial depression and falling-off of tourist traffic, it would have difficulty carrying on.

In 1923 the new, exciting sport of skiing had kept the Hermitage at Mount Cook open for the first time during winter. It was already in vogue on the Whakapapa slopes of Ruapehu. By the end of the decade the growing band of enthusiasts had sought out suitable slopes and snow at Arthur's Pass and Egmont. The first New Zealand ski championships were held at Mount Cook, near Ball Hut, in 1935.

By the early 1930s, board and departmental reports were registering

Skiing first became popular at Arthur's Pass in the early 1930s when one-day railway passes offered excursionists from Christchurch the opportunity to try the new glamour sport. A record crowd of 1200 people visited the park during the weekend in August 1930 when this photo was taken.

increasing concern at animal damage on the one hand, and with financial problems on the other. The two issues were often related, as the shooting of deer and goats required both manpower and money. Concern turned to alarm as the decade wore on. Goat eradication in Egmont National Park was essential to the protection of the farming lowlands. Chamois were part of the problem for the Arthur's Pass Board, which reported each year on animal damage and lack of finance. A menace of the most serious kind had grown through much of New Zealand's mountainland, as the warden for Tongariro National Park noted. The deer, he said, were coming from the Kakaramea and Pihanga Ranges to the north and the Kaimanawa Ranges to the east.

In fact the glow of promise radiating from big game, which was in 1903 to be such a valuable asset to the colony, had dimmed by the early 1920s. Some culling had been needed to suppress damage to farms and 'maintain the quality' of the herds. Better judgement had, fortunately, negated a proposal to add vicuna, alpaca and llama to the enrichment of the waste lands. 'Deer were a serious pest of little value,' said E. Phillips Turner, Director of Forestry, in a report on the state forests in 1918. It was, in some areas 'a matter of deer or forests' said A. N. Perham in a major report on deer damage in 1922. He estimated that there were more than three hundred thousand of the animals, mostly in the South Island.

The forests and their values were being examined from a number of aspects. A Rivers Commission looked into flood problems of South Island rivers, and in 1921 Leonard Cockayne published his *Vegetation of New Zealand*. The link between deer, forest degradation, flooding and erosion was becoming plain.

In some areas, goats, including chamois and thar, were as much a menace as deer. Dr Arthur Hill, Director of the Royal Botanical Gardens at Kew, invited to New Zealand in 1927 to report on a possible National Botanical Gardens, was horrified alike at the depredations of goats in Egmont National Park and at the spread of heather in Tongariro National Park.

Growing public concern was evidenced by the foundation of the New

This photograph of the forest floor in an area heavily browsed by deer illustrates the severity of damage. Without understorey plants, draught enters the forest, and without young trees the forest cannot regenerate.

NATURE'S REVENGE

Forest and Bird, August 1937

Zealand Native Bird Protection Society in 1923. The society's attack focused initially on erosion and plant-eating animals, and later, on the disunity of administration. Editorials, cartoons and lectures hammered away at the issues. 'It took our forests thousands and thousands of years to produce the soil on our hills,' stated an editorial in 1927. 'Are we living on our capital and calling it profit, and will there be a day of reckoning when budgets refuse to balance and our eroded and insect-infested lands refuse to yield a sufficiency?' 'A greater menace to New Zealand than any German or Russian menace is that of the presence of plant-eating animals in our forests,' said Captain Sanderson in 1929. The opossum was also indicted, even if the nature of the destructive partnership between deer and opossum was still not understood.

By 1930 the component elements of the essential land character of New Zealand and some of its implications had been identified. Some relationships, like that of plant-eating animals, forests and erosion, were established and were being driven home by bodies like the New Zealand Native Bird Protection Society. Scenery, or wonder at scenic New Zealand, had been a favourite preoccupation dating from European explorer days (as it is a hundred years later). It surfaced in the scenery debates of the 1890s and reached one of its periodic climaxes with the passing of the Scenery Preservation Act. The 'why' of scenery remained unidentified, although scientists since Ernst Dieffenbach had been pointing to it for almost one hundred years. The intuition that informed the wonder sensed a connection with forest, so forest preservation and scenery were related. The society's concern to protect distinctive bird life was getting further towards fundamentals, as was the insistence of Field, that a national park must be representative of the original nature of New Zealand — no exotics, no foreign animals, birds or plants — unalloyed. But the ultimate reason for scenic wonder, forests, and rare birds, as for geological instability and sensitivity to exotic plants and animals, remained (and remains) largely uncomprehended — unique evolution. Perhaps the inherited instincts of a people who have developed their culture by manipulating nature cannot cope with an evolutionary 'nature without humanity' situation.

An extraordinary array of talent, applied over a short period, had informed the observation — Mackenzie, Ell and Cockayne, to mention a few of those whose perceptions had built on the insights of Von Haast, Dieffenbach and other naturalists.

But the perceptions were not related together. Scenery, forest, scientific values, the losses of whole species of bird life and the need to defend against exotic plant and animal invasion were the separate concerns of different groups. Fragmentation of departmental responsibility mirrored the situation. 'There are officers in the Lands Department looking after scenic reserves; officers in the Tourist Department looking after wildlife sanctuaries; officers in the Forest Service Department looking after forestry; officers of the Agricultural Department looking after rabbits, stoats, and weasels, etc . . . to say nothing of officers employed by other bodies outside government departments — all supposed to be looking after wildlife, including forests and all they contain; yet with all this energy, or rather this dissipation of energy, because of the divided control — what is being done?' asked the *Journal of the New Zealand Native Bird Protection Society* in 1932.

The first recorded proposal for co-ordination of control was made by the

Forest and Bird, November 1938

Director of Kew Gardens in 1927. Dr Hill suggested that the director of the proposed botanical gardens should be chairman of a board having some direct control over the management of the national parks and reserves. Jane Thomson, in *Origins of the 1952 National Parks Act*, remarks that the proposal was treated with traditional New Zealand disrespect for expert opinion. Perhaps it was not made clear that there were cogent reasons for taking note of the views of the Director of Kew Gardens about the significance of New Zealand plants. The herbarium at Kew contained the extensive collections of Menzies, the Cunningham brothers, J. D. Hooker, Colenso and others. Hooker, a former director of the gardens, had written the first New Zealand botanical handbook.

Even if Hill's views were ignored, the real driving force for a unified administration had been triggered — in one of the 'national parks'. Late in 1926 three Egmont-trained climbers, W. G. Mace, F. Allan and R. Syme, arrived at Mount Cook for a climbing holiday. 'This is *our* place,' said the manager of the Hermitage, suggesting that they could camp two miles back. Ignoring the advice, the party went on up the Tasman Valley to find sheep 'camping' at the first suitable site. Mace, Allan and Syme decided to challenge their own exclusion, and to work for the exclusion of sheep from a national reserve. As members of the New Zealand Alpine Club they had the ear of its eminent and widely respected president. Arthur P. Harper had been already lobbying against the renewal of the lease of the Tasman Reserve to the Mount Cook Motor Company.

The New Zealand Alpine Club agreed to sponsor a meeting of mountain clubs. It was decided that a federation of mountain clubs be formed so that the recreation users of the mountains could speak with one voice. The idea that the parks should be 'of the people' was stated by F. W. Vosseler, the presi-

ARTHUR PAUL HARPER
(1865–1955)

Arthur Harper, or 'A.P.' as he was known, is remembered for his long association with New Zealand's mountains, both as an explorer and later as an advocate for mountain recreation and national parks.

In 1893, after legal studies in England and climbing in Switzerland and New Zealand, Harper became an assistant to Charlie Douglas, South Westland's greatest explorer. His abilities as a mountaineer complemented Douglas's exploring skills, and for the next three years they explored many of the areas now in Westland National Park, including the Franz Josef and Fox Glaciers.

Harper had a life-long connection with outdoor groups. He co-founded the New Zealand Alpine Club in 1891, and was its president from 1914 to 1932 and again in 1941. He was the driving force behind the formation in 1931 of the Federated Mountain Clubs

Explorers Charlie Douglas and Arthur P. Harper with Douglas's dog, Betsey Jane, in the valley of the Cook River in 1894.

of New Zealand, and was also president of the Royal Forest and Bird Protection Society of New Zealand from 1948 to 1955.

The creation of major scenic reserves in Westland in the 1920s and 1930s owes much to Harper's persistence. He was also instrumental in the formation of the FMC's national park policy and in subsequent efforts to have national park management centralised, but with local and central representation for groups such as the federation. In 1952 the National Parks Act was passed, and at the grand age of 87 Harper became a member of the first National Parks Authority.

dent of the federation at its first annual general meeting in 1932. 'We must guard closely the welfare of our national parks and reserves. These latter we should not regard as the property of our Ministers and our government departments, but that they belong to the people of today and tomorrow.'

Investigations into administration were reported to the federation in 1934 by L. O. Hooker. 'I have now realised,' he said, 'that the work we are doing . . . is one of Dominion-wide importance, not only to the present generation but for posterity.' It was, however, a complex problem and the best way to proceed would be to bring representatives of several departments onto a committee to collect information. This did not eventuate. Instead, a Federated Mountain Club's sub-committee, consisting of Hooker, Vosseler, and Harper, was formed to investigate and confer with the Government. Having confirmed that New Zealand's national parks had neither policy nor uniform control, the sub-committee decided to advance proposals based on 'the successful and businesslike examples of the United States and Canada'. Their first proposition was strongly orientated to recreation. There should be free right of access and facilities for camping. Established clubs should be able to erect huts. The policy of leasing large areas to commercial interests should be abandoned.

Quite independently of the mountain clubs, there had been some public discussion of unified administration. An address given by E. Phillips Turner focused on a number of weaknesses. The legislation did not define the purpose of reservation, and the introduction of exotic plants and animals was not prohibited. Management by boards was not, in his opinion, satisfactory: 'There is no consistent policy, and members generally have little interest in and no knowledge of the measures necessary to ensure the maintenance of the vegetation of the park and its strictly natural condition: indeed, there are some members who hold the opinion that the maintenance of natural conditions is not desirable, but that it is desirable to introduce foreign animals, birds and plants.'

Perhaps Phillips Turner had in mind the sea of pink heather in Tongariro National Park. By this time conservation objectives were incorporated in the reform proposals being considered by the Federated Mountain Clubs' sub-committee. There had been discussions with representatives of the New Zealand Native Bird Protection Society. A profound learning process, derived directly from the mountains and forests of New Zealand itself, was shaping the recommendations.

The 1935 annual meeting of the federation was told that large trees in Egmont National Park were being felled for sale as posts and firewood. The meeting decided that a deputation must wait on the Government. The 1935 general election intervened. It was early in 1936, and with a new Government in power, when L. O. Hooker, A. P. Harper, S. A. Wiren and F. W. Vosseler met the Prime Minister, Michael Joseph Savage, together with the Minister of Lands, F. Langstone, and the Minister of Internal Affairs, W. E. Parry. Conservation was the essence of some of the prevailing problems quoted by the deputation. Timber was being cut at Tongariro as well as Egmont. The Mount Cook lily in the Tasman Reserve had been virtually eaten out by chamois. Although their reception was sympathetic, it was clear that money could not be instantly provided, even for animal control. The central principle was acknowledged. 'We agree with your objectives — the national parks for the people . . .' said the Prime Minister.

Arthur's Pass National Park in 1987

By Peter Simpson, Senior Ranger
Arthur's Pass National Park, 1984–1987

To me the elements of Arthur's Pass National Park are the mountains (and mountain weather), the rivers,
the interesting and beautiful plants of the area, the people who come, and all
their various ways of discovery and enjoyment.

As in the days of Maori trade in greenstone, the pass itself is the reason for human presence. It is the route for the railway and for electricity transmission, as well as for the road. In this rugged country the only experience of the park many people have is what they take in from their car.

There are many roadside camping areas for those who can pause but wish to remain close to the road. Klondyke Corner, with its recently constructed public shelter, is an example. This area was the site of a short-lived settlement before the turn of the century.

Those who want to get away from roads and congested cities can shoulder a pack and head into the wide open spaces, like those of the Waimakariri Valley. This will inevitably involve contact with water, possibly the need to ford streams, as the party in this photograph is about to do.

As people are never isolated from the weather in a mountain environment like this one, contact with another aspect of water is inescapable. If it is not raining now it soon will be — as in the case of this photograph of a north-west storm heading down the Waimakariri Valley. With a rainfall of up to five thousand millimetres a year on the western side, down to fifteen hundred millimetres on the east, it is not hard to see how the climate has such an effect on the park's environment.

Winter brings snow — sometimes very heavy — and snow brings skiers to the small field at Temple Basin where skiing began in 1929. Those prepared to tackle the one-hour walk to the ski-field will be rewarded with excellent sport and magnificent views of the mountains, including Mount Rolleston (a popular climbing area), on the other side of the pass.

The mountain environment may seem quiet, even timeless, but in fact it is very much in a state of constant change. Erosion is a relentless process, with other events imposed on it. Several large landslides have been recorded at Arthur's Pass, and this mountain (called, appropriately enough, Falling Mountain) literally collapsed in half following an earthquake in 1929.

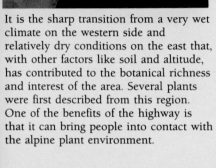

It is the sharp transition from a very wet climate on the western side and relatively dry conditions on the east that, with other factors like soil and altitude, has contributed to the botanical richness and interest of the area. Several plants were first described from this region. One of the benefits of the highway is that it can bring people into contact with the alpine plant environment.

As this party on the Dobson Nature Walk is finding, the natural world of Arthur's Pass is completely fascinating.

One of the most engaging denizens of a fascinating natural world is this intelligent and mischievous comedian. Keas, being very inquisitive, will turn their beaks to many things, including the quite unskilled mechanical work being carried out on this park vehicle.

Chapter 13

Aims and Allies
1940–1952

There had been no further formal discussion about national park administration between 1936 and 1940, when the Federated Mountain Clubs
sought the support of the Royal Society of New Zealand and leading botanists.
With the world at war, the Minister of Lands told the FMC that there could
be no possibility of major changes in policy during the conflict.

Nonetheless, official thinking was shifting towards that of the FMC. Their
views had been revised and restated in a letter to the Minister in 1938. There
should be a national authority for control of general policy and distribution
of finance. A board in each park should include persons able and willing to
visit the park frequently. The central principles of administration should be
free access, the right to camp and build huts, the preservation of native plant
and animal life and the extermination of exotic plants and animals. Departmental officers referred to the letter when reform was debated. With the
passage of time its arguments were accepted.

The Department of Lands and Survey's 1940 annual report advised the
proclamation of well over two hundred thousand hectares of permanent State
Forest, some of which would one day become national park. Years of concern,
advocacy and investigation into erosion, flooding and forest destruction were
shaping public policy towards the passing of the Soil Conservation and Rivers
Control Act in 1941. The department reported another six thousand hectares
of reservation under the Land Act. In the Sounds National Park a patrolman
had been appointed to supervise campsites in anticipation of the completion
of the Homer Tunnel. A year later the Tongariro Mountain road had been
constructed.

As New Zealand became increasingly preoccupied with the war, activity
connected with reservation slowed except for one important event connected
tenuously with the conflict — the establishment of the Abel Tasman National
Park.

It could be said that the formation of the park began when Perrine
Moncrieff and her husband arrived from the United Kingdom to live in
Nelson. They visited the Astrolabe Roadstead area on the western side of
Tasman Bay, site of d'Urville's studies and first anchorage for the ships of the
New Zealand Company's Nelson investigation. Captivated by coves of golden
sand, the crystal water, lagoons and waterfalls, the Moncrieffs first leased and
then purchased a large holding. In 1939 they had the land declared a private
scenic reserve.

Interest in nature, particularly in native bird life, led Mrs Moncrieff to establish a branch of the New Zealand Native Bird Protection Society in Nelson. She was leader of a group actively concerned with the protection of forest remnants in the district.

When the prospect of timber milling on the coastline north of the Moncrieffs Astrolabe Reserve became evident, Moncrieff sought financial assistance to purchase areas that could be logged. She had all but despaired of success when a suggestion was made that 'the best way to save the bush' was to work for the formation of a national park. Once again, as with Tongariro, Egmont and Arthur's Pass, the national park idea was invoked as a reactive-protective device.

Mrs Moncrieff acted as spokesperson for her group. The potential area and boundaries for a park were deduced from a map obtained from the Department of Lands and Survey. Scenery, botany, birdlife and administration were all described, and a case set out. The *Nelson Mail* of 28 June 1941 reported that the Nelson City Council had been asked to nominate one of its members to join in a request to the government.

Her proposal 'appears to be arousing no little interest in the district,' said the Commissioner of Crown Lands to the Under-Secretary for Lands. It had indeed. A councillor appointed by Nelson City Council to investigate, reported that: 'The wider aspects to the country as a whole should be evident to all and the setting-apart of this area, which is unique in its varied appeal, would give this part of the Nelson province a distinction having far-reaching effects.' The council heartily supported the concept. So did the other local authorities — for various reasons. Nelson City's main interest had been recre-

---

PERRINE MONCRIEFF

Perrine Moncrieff devoted much of her time and energy to ensuring that the bush and coastline around Nelson were preserved. She was a foundation member and vice-president of the Royal Forest and Bird Protection Society, and in 1928 she set up the Nelson branch. A noted amateur ornithologist, she wrote a book called *New Zealand Birds and How to Identify Them*.

In 1936 she and her husband, Captain M. M. Moncrieff, bought a two-hundred-hectare section at Astrolabe. In 1939 she had the whole section gazetted as a private scenic reserve. She then purchased a litho from the Lands Department Office indicating all the vacant Crown land, forestry areas and reserves from Marahau on the south to Totaranui on the north. She tramped through some parts, noting the area's interesting historical and natural features.

In 1941 the *Nelson Evening Mail* reported that Mrs P. Moncrieff had written to the city council seeking its support for a request to the Government to declare a block of Crown lands and state forest as a national park. The time was most appropriate, as Nelson would celebrate its centenary in the following year. The name suggested was the Tasman National Park. It was proposed that all the scenic reserves along the coast should be included. Moncrieff made every effort to stir up public enthusiasm for the idea and was ultimately successful.

Moncrieff was appointed to the Abel Tasman National Park Board in 1942. Five years later she donated nearly one hundred and fifty hectares of hardwood-podocarp forest at Okiwi Bay for a reserve. In 1974 the decoration of the Order of Orange Nassau was conferred on her by Queen Juliana of the Netherlands. She retired from the park board in 1974 and was awarded the C.B.E. in 1975. She died four years later.

ation and access. The rural counties also discussed bush and watershed protection, prevention of fire and the desirability of a sanctuary for native birds.

By the end of the year the proposition had the official sponsorship of all the local governments of the region and the Automobile Association, and a petition had been placed before the Government. 'The people of Nelson province are wholeheartedly behind the proposal,' advised the local member of Parliament. In the petition the local bodies stated that should the Government accede to their request, they would do their utmost to maintain a scenic asset that would be of value, not only to Nelson, but also to the whole Dominion.

Central government was pondering related issues. The land was useless for settlement. Reports were sought from both the Lands and Forest Departments as to whether the area was worthy of national park reservation. They were 'happy to associate themselves with the people of Nelson,' said the departments. Whether in history, geology, botany or scenic beauty, the area was qualified. Botanically, it had the special interest of South Island rainforest mixed with North Island species. According to the geological report, the area had, in the last ice age, been a refuge for flora and fauna unable to exist in the colder south. The scenic beauty of the country had long been recognised, particularly the beautiful rivers, the rugged coastline and the golden beaches with their background of bush-clad ranges.

There were, in addition, special political circumstances relating to the war. In November 1941, Europe had been under German domination for more than a year. The Battle of Britain had been fought out. General Wavell had chased the Italian Army westward across North Africa, but Rommel and the Afrika Corps had retrieved the position and were advancing towards Alexandria. In June 1941, Germany had attacked Russia. The war was the total preoccupation of all.

The Nelson group, having already drawn the Council's attention to 1942 as the centennial of the city, now pointed out that the same year was the tercentennial of the visit of Abel Tasman. The park could be called the Abel Tasman National Park, and the Queen of the Netherlands requested to become its patron. 'Thereafter,' said Mrs Moncrieff in her book *People Came Later*, 'all went smoothly, for the great government fish had risen to the beautiful Netherland fly and was safe in the landing-net.'

The fish really rose, of course, to a felicitous idea, appropriate at any time, and particularly so in the context of the war. The Minister of Internal Affairs said: 'The question of a small monument, probably at Pohara Beach, is being considered. If the petition for constitution of a national park can also be given favourable consideration, the tercentennial would undoubtedly be marked in a manner befitting the occasion, and under present circumstances in a manner that would be particularly pleasing to our ally in the present war, the Netherlands.'

Such sentiments gave additional energy to a proposition that must, in its accumulated support, have been well-nigh irresistible. The Department of Lands and Survey's very brief report of 1942 made one reference only to additional reservation: 'Proposals have been approved for the reservation as national park of approximately thirty-six thousand acres [fifteen thousand hectares] in Tasman Bay, Nelson.'

The opening of the park at Kaiteriteri on the afternoon of 19 December 1942, three hundred years to the day after Tasman came to anchor in Wainui

Bay, made history of its own. For the first time on New Zealand soil, two representatives of monarchs came together — the Governor-General of New Zealand and the representative of the Queen of the Netherlands. Dr Charles O. van der Plas confirmed that Queen Wilhelmina had consented to become patroness of the park.

In January 1944, a key figure in the evolution of administrative policy addressed the Tararua Tramping Club on national parks and other 'closely related subjects'. As chief clerk of the Department of Lands and Survey, Ron Cooper was not a senior official. He had, however, been responsible for national parks and reserves since the late 1930s. The invitation from the tramping club was significant. Cooper's interest and authority were acknowledged by the clubs, as within his own department. It was he who dealt directly with the Federated Mountain Clubs and with other advocates of reform such as L. W. McCaskill. His speech was a fascinating survey of the status of the parks and a penetrating appreciation of the balance of administration between government and citizen. He considered that New Zealand's parks were in the nature of 'wilderness area set apart for preservation in as near as possible its natural state, but made available for and accessible to the general public, who were allowed and encouraged to visit the reserve. In such an area the recreation and enjoyment of the public is a main purpose, but at the same time the natural scenery, flora and fauna are interfered with as little as possible.' Without mentioning reform, Cooper discussed the anomalies that had grown from an accumulation of legislation. At no stage was there even a hint of the possibility of defining the objectives of a national park in law, but the philosophy stated (and even the words used) revealed the draftsman of the legislation to come. 'Such a reserve should contain scenery of distinctive quality, or some natural features so extraordinary or unique as to be of national interest and importance,' said Cooper. He concluded with philosophy: 'Our national parks and scenic reserves are not properties in any commercial sense, but natural preserves for the rest, recreation and education of the people. So much natural beauty has been destroyed that it is imperative that what remains should be jealously preserved.'

If confirmation was needed that Cooper was presenting a departmental viewpoint, it was provided four years later by the Director-General, D. M. Greig, in a paper to the New Zealand National Tourist Conference. Greig imported most of Cooper's address without change, adding only some comments about the value of the parks and their appeal to the general public and the tourist: 'They are of immense value not only as climatic and water-conservation reserves, but also as reservations of extensive tracts of virgin country providing for the rest, recreation, enjoyment and inspiration of the people. Their aesthetic and spiritual values cannot possibly be set down in mere words. They appeal to the adventurous spirit of the tramper and the mountaineer; but no less strongly to those who find rest and refreshment of spirit in quieter contemplation of nature's intricate pattern of mountains and glaciers, forests, lakes and rivers, and the majestic sounds of the sea . . . These great national reserves should be so administered and maintained as to be preserved . . . in their natural state. Native plant and animal life should as far as possible be preserved, and introduced plant and animal life should as far as possible be exterminated.'

This was the precise wording of the later National Parks Act, drawn, no doubt, from the legislation Cooper was drafting. The thoughts of his speech to the Tararua Tramping Club had been incorporated into a report submitted and adopted by a Tourist Development Committee in 1945. Four years later Greig agreed that its proposals could form the starting point for legislation.

Near the end of his paper Greig referred to an event of great importance that was to lead to the incorporation of special areas, or the ability to provide for strict reservation within the general public-access philosophy, which had clearly been accepted by all. In 1948 Doctor G. B. Orbell had discovered takahe in a mountain valley west of Lake Te Anau. If not quite the equivalent of finding that moa still stalked through remote districts, the rediscovery of an evolutionary relic of the 'ancient islands' nonetheless stirred both national and international interest. A special area of over one hundred and sixty thousand hectares, to which access could only be by permit, had been immediately set aside.

Nor had the Federated Mountain Clubs allowed shining hours to pass without any improvement. It was, after all, their 1938 letter that had been the yeast in the whole evolving mix. They again pressed for reform after the Tararua speech. In 1949 senior representatives were once more in the office of the Minister of Lands, advancing a detailed scheme for a National Parks Authority and boards similar to the proposals the department was itself generating.

Early in 1950 a draft of the legislation was circulated to the park boards, other government departments and special-interest groups such as the Federated Mountain Clubs. By this time debate focused on significant details — membership of the authority; the varied composition of park boards that reflected historical and regional circumstances. The relationship between the authority and the Minister was established when, at Harper's insistence, a clause empowering the Minister to give directions was withdrawn and replaced by an obligation on the authority's part to 'have regard to' representations from the Minister. Other checks and balances dealt with appointments, policy-making and responsibilities for park management. The central objective of preservations in perpetuity was, on the one hand, buffered against political interference, and, on the other, provided with an insurance that policy decisions would reflect a wide spectrum of values.

A long delay ensued. Administration of Egmont National Park and control of tourist facilities were matters that demanded extended consultation. There was a change of government, the Waterfront Dispute of 1951 and a snap general election.

It was twenty years from the formation of the Federated Mountain Clubs when the Minister of Lands, E. B. Corbett, introduced the Bill for its second reading on 5 August 1952. In an atmosphere of unanimous support the Minister was congratulated on its quality. Te Heuheu Tukino and the original gift of the Tongariro peaks were recalled with appreciation. Themes from previous debates about reservation recurred: once again loss of forest was regretted, advocates for new national parks emerged as they had done in the past — the Urewera highlands and Waipoua kauri forest. Generous tributes were paid to Ron Cooper, who had retired. 'He has written . . . [in] the spirit in which we intend this legislation to be administered,' said Corbett, 'and presented a picture of our goal in our national park administration.' Cooper's 'fine touches that are characteristic of the layman' can be read in 1987 in one of New Zealand's finest and most durable pieces of legislation.

Abel Tasman National Park in 1987

By Geoff Rennison, Chief Ranger, 1980–1987

These images reflect Abel Tasman National Park as I see it and as I think of it. They are faithful echoes of a landscape small in scale, yet rich in texture; satisfying, somehow, in its attention to detail.

It is my privilege to see the park through the ebb and flow of the seasons, to catch it in all its moods. This photograph shows the park as I like it best: in winter, with a great empty sky, a flat sea with coldness somehow implicit in its tranquillity, and with the deep shadows of headland and island celebrating the low, feeble sun.

This is the bone and sinew of the granite land, its strength revealed in the lazy, sensuous curves of the half-sunk rocks in the foreground, its sense of the eccentric displayed by the long, rectangular block above them; a misplaced sarcen from Stonehenge, perhaps, or a caprock from some neolithic tomb. Now it is the home of seal and seagull, and a discovery for visitors.

The past is never far away from the present along the park coast. Benign ghosts are quickly conjured, never more readily than at Tonga Quarry, where the sawn, square granite blocks lie painted with lichen under a young forest. This was once an industrial area, but over the years it has sunk quietly into the landscape. So have the many other endeavours that once flourished along its coast.

I relish my visits to the Canaan area, for I am constantly impressed by this ancient marble landscape. Consider the intricate fluting, the miniature watersheds on these rocks, with their peaks, valleys and saddles — the astonishing result of a bitter rain, tinged with acid, which has tunnelled this plateau to its heart.

The shapes and curves of the land are echoed in these forests, with columnar beech accompanied riotously by pineapple trees. I enjoy the high forests of the park because they experience the seasons' march to the full, enduring in turn, deep winter snow and sapping summer drought. There is a pattern to their lives that is somehow lost, or at least diluted, in the sea-level life their cousins lead.

It is thought that the tangata whenua of pre-European times lit the fires that bared these hills. D'Urville in 1827 called the Torrent Bay shrublands 'a gloomy, sterile desert' and in some weathers his pessimistic comment is still apt. The seasonal migration of the early tribes is gone, replaced by a modern tide of people, peaking in the hot days of summer and ebbing to a trickle six months on.

Chapter 14

Unified Administration
1953–1964

Hindsight can identify 1953 as a year, like 1903, in which creative legislation again gave forward impulse to the national parks saga. Was it also a year of significant omens? A memorial bust of Te Heuheu Tukino was unveiled at Tongariro. The work of Alex R. Fraser, a Wellington artist, the sculpture had been cast in England and exhibited at the Royal Academy, where, according to reports, it had been praised by the judges. Did the chief approve of what had been done? Did his mana still cover the expanding enterprise he had started? Progress in the next decade would suggest, perhaps, that it did. Today the bust resides in the park visitor centre, still in the shadow of the mountains.

The nine members of New Zealand's first National Parks Authority, which met on 15 April 1953, were not strangers meeting for the first time to discuss an unfamiliar assignment. David Greig, the chairman, as Director-General of Lands had worked closely with the Minister in drafting the legislation. Arthur Harper (explorer-companion of Charlie Douglas in the 1890s) and Lance McCaskill were reformers who had spent years shaping many of the ideas now in the Act. McCaskill had studied national parks administration in the United States. Harper, with Dr W. R. B. Oliver (a nominee of the Royal Society of New Zealand) and N. M. Thomson (of the Federated Mountain Clubs) were a triumvirate of non-ministerial appointments. As nominees of their respective bodies they added greatly to the general store of personal knowledge of the park areas, guaranteed the continued input and interest of their societies and rounded out the corporate ability of the authority in one of its fundamental tasks — the long-term assessment of values. As well, they introduced a balance to the political and developmental pressures that inevitably surround the administration of large areas of great value.

McCaskill was appointed by the Minister to represent the national parks boards. L. Avann, the deputy chairman, was Assistant Director-General of Lands. The Department of Internal Affairs, responsible at the time for control of introduced animals, was represented by its Secretary, A. G. Harper. The remaining members were Alex Entrican (Director-General of Forests) and R. W. Marshall (General Manager of the Department of Tourism and Publicity), both departments having major commitments in and around the parks.

The mission of the new body was to control administration in the national interest. Thirteen hundred scenic reserves, totalling some three hundred and eighty thousand hectares, remained under the Department of Lands and Survey, although the distinction between national parks and some of the larger reserves was a fine one. In carrying out its mission, the authority was to be an advocate for the protection and development of the parks, to recommend enlargement of existing ones and the setting aside of new parks, to advise how money budgeted by Parliament should be spent, and to administer the national parks boards.

Of these there were four — Tongariro, Egmont, Abel Tasman and Arthur Pass (Arthur Pass became Arthur's Pass in 1956). The former Peel Forest National Park, a spectacular and varied reserve by the Rangitata River, was excluded from the Act on account of its small size.

The authority became in effect the board for the other national park at the time — Sounds (thereafter called Fiordland), which was administered by the Commissioner of Crown Lands at Invercargill. Within a year the responsibility extended to three, as Urewera and Mount Cook National Parks had been constituted, the basis of the latter being Tasman Park and Aorangi Domain, the two reserves under the control of the Tourist and Publicity Department.

Corbett announced at the 1952 annual general meeting of the Forest and Bird Protection Society that the Government intended to create a national park of two hundred thousand hectares in the Urewera. Appropriately, this followed an illustrated talk on 'The Forest Land of the Tuhoe Tribes' by Bernard Teague, the chief protagonist of the park. In *Forest and Bird* a few months later, Teague concluded an article with a summary of his vision: 'Here in these halls of Tane, if we can check destroying animals and prevent fire,

LANCE McCASKILL
(1900–1985)

Naturalist, conservationist, agricultural instructor, educationalist, writer and research director, Lance McCaskill was a man of great energy, whose enthusiasm and concern for the well-being of the land and people of New Zealand led him to focus his interest on four main areas — soil conservation, nature protection, scenery preservation and agriculture education.

McCaskill taught agricultural science at both tertiary and secondary levels of education and has been called the 'father of soil conservation in New Zealand'. In the 1940s he fought to have the soil erosion problem dealt with effectively. He was a leader in the campaign that encouraged Parliament to pass the Soil Conservation and Rivers Control Act in 1941, and went on to spend long years of service in water and soil administration. He made efforts to protect indigenous flora, setting up, for example, a teaching garden of over four hundred native

species at Christchurch Teachers' College and campaigning for the establishment of a Nature Reserve to ensure the survival of the Castle Hill buttercup.

A foundation member of both the National Parks Authority and the Arthur's Pass National Park Board, he emphasised the scientific and conservation roles of the parks and tried to protect wilderness areas from overdevelopment and large-scale commercialism. He led New Zealand into membership of the International Union for the Conservation of Nature and Natural Resources.

Intolerant of bureaucratic mismanagement, McCaskill was described by Kenneth Cumberland as having terrier-like qualities — 'demolishing poorly informed criticism, or taking obstinate officialdom by the scruff of the neck [to] shake some sense into it'. A. P. Thompson says that it was McCaskill 'who more than anyone else fought for decisions on the basis of principle rather than expediency'.

On his retirement, he became a writer

and historical researcher. His distinguished work in a variety of fields was acknowledged by awards and honours including the Bledisloe Medal for service to farming, the CBE and the IUCN's Peter Scott Award for Conservation.

men and women centuries hence will still hear the dawn chorus of the birds, will still see the wood pigeon swoop across the valley, will still follow trails that were pioneered in the stone age and will find pleasure, recreation and health.' As soon as the fifty-thousand-hectare nucleus for the park was declared, however, the controversial matter of cutting rights on land owned by Maori people, but closely related to the park, became the subject of years of debate. It was acknowledged on the one hand that the owners had every right to realise on their asset, but regretted on the other that milling could take place along the highway, as well as in headwater areas.

Of the two national park issues —Waipoua and Tararua — raised during the debate on the National Parks Bill, one was still unresolved. Waipoua Kauri Forest was proclaimed a forest sanctuary in 1952, but the proposal for a Tararua National Park, promoted by a special committee, moved on to the authority. The New Zealand Forest Service developed the forest park concept as an alternative to national park and submitted proposals for the Tararua State Forest to operate as a forest park for a ten-year trial period. These were endorsed by the authority in 1954.

It must have been an exceedingly busy time, with a great deal of detail connected with the parks for which the authority was, for the time being, responsible. Nelson Lakes National Park was created in 1956. Each new park meant that a board must be set up. By the end of 1958 the authority could report that the 'organisation for the control by park boards is now complete for all parks with the exception of Urewera National Park'. Westland National Park was formed in 1960, the year of Westland's centennial, and boards for both Westland and Urewera were appointed in 1961.

Large areas added to Fiordland in 1956 brought the southern lakes into the park and established identifiable boundaries. Over one hundred and thirty thousand hectares were added to the Urewera nucleus in 1956. Fiordland and Urewera would receive still more addition, along with Mount Cook and Abel Tasman.

BERNARD TEAGUE
(1904–1982)

Born in Feilding, Bernard Teague had a varied career as a telegraph messenger, Methodist home missionary and nurseryman. In his youth he enjoyed tramping through the Rangitikei — a factor that helped increase his respect and admiration for native flora and fauna.

After moving to Wairoa in the early 1930s, Teague spent much time in the Urewera. His extensive knowledge of the land and people inspired him to write short stories and articles for some thirty publications. His love for the region encouraged his wish to have the area preserved.

Supported by Violet Briffault, he led the Royal Forest and Bird Protection Society in a campaign to have the Urewera declared a national park. This was successful and, in 1954, the new park of approximately fifty thousand hectares was officially gazetted. He maintained a keen interest in the activities of his district and was a member of the Urewera National Park Board. He was awarded the Loder Cup for work in the conservation of New Zealand flora, including the establishment of the Urewera National Park.

Teague was an outstanding member of the Royal Forest and Bird Protection Society. He was the first chairman of the Wairoa branch and a member of the council for many years. He organised the society's first family camp at Waikaremoana in 1952. In 1969 he was elected vice-president.

Periodic field inspections of the parks commenced in 1954. Those who are concerned with decisions about land must get on the ground, and those responsible for the standard of a system must see its operation for themselves. By 1964 the authority was advising its intention of visiting three parks each year.

Inevitably there were changes in the membership of this tightly knit group, which was certainly not immune to strongly contested debate but had a very clear understanding of its role. Thomson died suddenly in 1953. His replacement, Rod Syme, in no way diminished the corporate background of the authority. Deeply involved in the activities of the Federated Mountain Clubs, Syme had been one of the Mount Cook climbing party that in 1926 had decided to challenge both 'no camping' and the running of sheep on the reserve. Harper died in 1955. The retirement of Greig in 1958 removed one of an illustrious succession of departmental officers whose contribution belongs in the mainstream of national park history. He was succeeded as Director-General of Lands and chairman of the authority by D. N. R. Webb.

Policy was, of course, being made by decisions, even if the first prepared summary of policy was not issued until 1964. In later years, in a letter to McCaskill, Greig remarked, 'I have no doubt that a lot of things that I view as decisions became part of policy.' McCaskill recalled that the process began at the first meeting, and gave as examples by-laws for the guidance of park boards, rules for the style, construction and maintenance of mountain huts and the interest of the authority in the wilderness proposals in the Act. The 1964 policy statement has particular interest as a benchmark — the work of a group whose core had devoted most of two decades to defining a philosophy that became incorporated into legislation, and subsequently had spent ten years with the practicalities of its application. There were some insights into philosophy: as few restrictions as possible on the public, no exclusive rights, no single dominant activity in the use of waters in parks, and minimum direction to boards, provided they acted within the framework of the Act and general policy. Of the 1964 policy, much of which is relevant in 1987, it is only the ruling on accommodation facilities that has changed in any significant way. The permissive position of 1964 has changed now to an emphasis on location outside of park boundaries. The success of the national parks has been such that the attempt to accommodate visitors inside the parks would surely detract from the very qualities people wish to experience.

The 1964 policy statement dealt also with other major issues never far from the concern of administrators: research, visitor services, wild animal control, planning and finance.

Much scientific work on national parks can be called pure research. The parks are laboratories of nature, where scientists can study geological processes, original ecosystems and indigenous, sometimes rare, species of plants, animals and insects. In contrast to pure research, management is often in need of scientific information about cause, effect and trends, or the scientific description of a park's resources provided, for example, by botanical and zoological surveys. So the authority gave early encouragement to scientific work generally, with special emphasis on that which would help management, and soon appealed for reports from scientific expeditions. There was an excellent example of management-orientated research at the time, with wildlife officers studying the habits and habitat of the rare takahe colony. The

discovery of a live specimen of the even rarer kakapo near Milford Sound led
to searches in other areas. Five birds were found and removed for breeding
experiments, but only one survived. The initiative with botanical surveys was
taken in 1957 in Abel Tasman National Park; similar work followed in Nelson
Lakes, Mount Cook and Arthur's Pass. In the meantime, information on geological processes was accumulating from such work as the study of charred
timber on Mount Egmont, glaciological research and the siting of a climato-
logical and rainfall recording station at Mount Cook, establishment of seismic
recording equipment at Tongariro, and the publication by the Department of
Scientific and Industrial Research of a handbook on the volcanoes of Tongariro. A mustelid research programme in Fiordland National Park sought
means to control the stoat and weasel menace, while investigations into the
habits of deer, chamois and hares in Nelson Lakes National Park addressed
the control of browsing animals. Much of this research was done by or in co-
operation with the Department of Scientific and Industrial Research, the New
Zealand Forest Service and the Wildlife Division of the Department of Internal
Affairs; financial support for national parks did not come solely from the
Department of Lands and Survey.

Such projects serve to illustrate the varied nature of the scientific effort
that is an endless and necessary support to the management of large natural
areas. It is work relating to education as well as science, and work that com-
plied with the policy objectives of the first authority as soon as the developing
system drew increasing numbers of visitors. 'The authority, through the
boards, aims to see the parks used and preserved as living examples of natural
New Zealand,' said the 1962 report. Once basics like signposting of tracks and
the preparation of maps had received some attention, small gardens containing plant specimens of particular parks appeared. Illustrated talks were
first given in 1954 at Arthur's Pass National Park (we may suspect the
influence of Lance McCaskill and even perhaps the long shadow of Harry Ell,
remembering that McCaskill had once acted as lantern-slide operator for Ell),

Early stages in park interpretation with a
talk by R. L. Cleland at Arthur's Pass. It
was a time when rangers even drew their
own maps.

D. M. Greig, Director-General of Lands and chairman of the first National Parks Authority, speaking at the opening of the first Tongariro National Park visitor centre. One of the architects of the National Parks Act, Greig is a historic figure in New Zealand's national park development.

where a year later the first visitor centre was built and a park handbook published. Edited by McCaskill, this was in fact the second Arthur's Pass handbook — the first had been compiled in 1935 by R. S. Odell. Even this had been preceded by James Cowan's *The Tongariro National Park* published by the Tongariro National Park Board in 1927.

The second Tongariro handbook did not emerge until 1965, but others followed closely behind that of Arthur's Pass, as did the construction of visitor centres at Mount Cook, Tongariro and Fiordland. In 1963 the Arthur's Pass board again took an initiative — the temporary employment of a park naturalist, who arranged a two-week nature study programme made up from half-day and all-day walks and occasional illustrated evening talks. In the following year all the parks were offering summer programmes of this kind. Other kinds of natural history education were well established, going back to a series of expeditions from 1954 into Fiordland by the Southland Girls' High School. The 1962 report referred with pleasure to the 'wide use of national parks for study courses undertaken by groups interested in natural history'.

None of this progress was possible without the key figures in national park management — the rangers. In 1953 there were five, working mainly on animal control and track-making. In the words of Ray Cleland, 'It was a solo front-end job' — one ranger to a park; sometimes, as with new parks declared in the 1950s, starting completely from scratch. Cleland was appointed ranger at Arthur's Pass in 1950, and has given some impressions of 'providing essentials for public recreation and establishing living quarters [which were] something better than the corrugated iron shack provided'. Active patrolling was 'a priority because of the lack of it in previous years. Being seen anywhere in the park became good public relations, whether it was regularly meeting the midnight train from Christchurch or restraining railway surfacemen from poaching trout or using mountain beech forest near the railway line for practice for wood-chopping competitions.' Another reminder of the period comes from his report, which mentioned, 'Feed for the packhorses was not sufficient to complete and the material is at present stacked at the Hawdon forest edge.'

When Cleland was appointed Supervisor of National Parks in 1958, an important part of his work was to do with the growing service; as authority policy put it later, to 'develop a tradition of service to National Park ideals' and to establish ranger training.

The rangers' forum at Arthur's Pass, a four-day event held in November 1959, began the programme of ranger training. This spanned from conservation philosophy through interpretation to the practicalities of signs, buildings, fire control and equipment. It is no surprise to find that the speaker on park interpretation was Professor L. W. McCaskill, who talked about the needs of park visitors, communication, illustrated talks (showing colour slides was 'a new disease' in New Zealand, asserted McCaskill) and nature trails.

By 1964 the ranging staff numbered thirty-eight, if trainees and assistants were included; most selected on the Cleland criteria that 'many qualities were more important than specific professional training'. High on the list were 'a deep appreciation of natural beauty and good taste in many things'. In esprit and skill, a ranger service was in place, and the authority could report summer programmes in all the parks.

At the 1959 rangers' forum there was a serious discussion about animal control, led by G. G. Atkinson, chief ranger of Egmont National Park, who reviewed the status of the opossum in his park. Twelve thousand had been destroyed in the preceding year, eight thousand was an average, and over fifty thousand had been killed in a peak year. Some fifteen thousand goats and two hundred and thirty thousand opossum were eliminated in the decade to 1953.

Wild-animal control, the Achilles heel of the national park ethic in New Zealand, was a serious and ongoing concern for the first National Parks Authority, as it has remained for all subsequent administrations. The year 1953 was close enough still to the 1930s and 1940s for recollection that the instructions in the National Parks Act (that 'except where the authority otherwise determines . . . introduced plants and animals shall as far as possible be exterminated') were based on real-life conditions rather than on conservation theory. If any reminder was needed that animal control is vital for the preservation of the parks, there was McCaskill to do it.

Year after year annual reports, park by park, recorded comment on the status of the war against deer, goats, chamois, thar, pigs, wild cattle, cats, ferrets, stoats, weasels, rabbits, hares and rats. In 1956 the New Zealand Forest Service took over field operations from the Wildlife Division of the Department of Internal Affairs. Large numbers of animals were destroyed, the deer kill in Fiordland National Park, for example, being usually between three and six thousand animals. Reports were sometimes optimistic; a perceived improvement in vegetation being attributed to successful animal control, an abundance of bird life to stoat trapping in the preceding year. But what really emerged from the reports was the message that the war was, and is, never-ending and that the perceived improvements did not necessarily indicate that control was about to be achieved. Nine thousand opossums and fifteen hundred goats were killed in Egmont National Park in 1955. Vigorous regeneration and healthy forest were reported during the following three years. Fifteen thousand opossums and nearly three thousand goats were destroyed in 1959. A reduced animal population with a good food source has a powerful capacity to 'bounce'. To drive numbers down, it is necessary to reduce a population to below its recovery level.

As with introduced animals, so with introduced plants. Annual reports trace a similar struggle during a period that saw a shift from hand-grubbing to the extensive use of sprays. In 1957 the Botany Division of the Department of Scientific and Industrial Research gave its view that introduced heather in Tongariro National Park could be neither controlled nor eradicated. *P. Contorta*, spreading vigorously from adjacent state forest and army land, has been another serious threat to the integrity of Tongariro National Park; attempts to control it have been only partially successful.

Physical development within the parks accompanied this rapid evolution of a unified system. Track systems in the established parks at Tongariro, Egmont and Arthur's Pass were upgraded and extended. Buildings were renovated and new huts built. Track planning, with due regard to existing routes (and, on occasions, the needs of wild-animal control), closely followed the establishment of new parks. In 1958 good progress in Abel Tasman National Park was reported towards 'opening the main network of tracks approved by the National Parks Authority'. Here, as in many other parks, local tramping clubs were helping with the work. The walk around Lake Waikaremoana in Urewera National Park, under construction in 1963, was cut by volunteer parties of secondary-school pupils, 'acceptance of requests from schools to participate [being] limited only by the amount of supervision the ranging staff can undertake'.

A parallel growth of tourism kept pace with the expanding facilities. The 1954 report's expectation of 'a tremendous influx of visitors to Milford Sound' following the opening of the Homer Tunnel late in the year proved to be well founded. Passenger-launch bookings totalled almost twenty-seven thousand. An airstrip at Milford was in service. Another, at Tongariro, was in use by 1955 but was closed later. The Mount Cook Tourist Company had laid down an airstrip close to the Hermitage, but the first DC3 aircraft, heralding scheduled flights into Mount Cook, landed on an airstrip in a somewhat different location in 1961. Major expansion of skiing was under way at Mount Ruapehu by 1955 with the operation of a chairlift. Two chairlifts and a T-bar were functioning by 1956, when up to six hundred cars were parked at the road terminus in a day. Four thousand people in one day in 1961 became five thousand people in a day in 1962. The total number of visitors to all national parks increased from three hundred and fifty thousand in 1962 to four hundred and fifty thousand in 1963 and to half a million in 1964.

Inevitably, roads within and without the parks influenced expansion. In

A survey party setting out from camp below Mount Talbot for work on the Milford Sound Road. This photograph was taken in 1935, but the Homer Tunnel, key to motor access to the Sound, was not completed until 1954.

Tongariro National Park the road serving the Whakapapa ski-field was the subject of relentless upgrading as ski-field use increased. The Ohakune mountain road on the south-western flanks of the mountain was begun by local interests in 1953 and opened in 1960. It was improvements on the access road to Totaranui in Abel Tasman National Park that allowed a 1962 report to note a record number of visitors and campers. Camping grounds and picnic areas were set up in many park areas.

Late in 1960 the final obstacle was breached on the Haast Highway, last of the alpine crossings and another great road destined to be identified with a national park. A national park of the alpine region between Mount Cook and Fiordland National Parks had long been the ambition of mountain clubs, particularly those in Otago. In 1959 the authority, while agreeing that the area merited national park status, considered this to be premature. Two events conspired to change this situation. On the one hand, completion of the Haast Highway greatly improved accessibility; on the other, a public meeting in Dunedin, attended by representatives of over thirty organisations, had voted unanimously in favour of the park. The foresight of the Scenery Preservation Board and thirty years of work by Otago enthusiasts had prepared the ground.

With the gazettal of Mount Aspiring in 1964 the number of national parks reached ten, and remained so for twenty-two years. A large number of proposals were declined: Waipoua, Tararua, Wanganui River (suggested by the Lands Department in 1954), Rotorua-Tarawera, Coromandel Peninsula and a national park around Lake Taupo. It was all, no doubt, a replay of the historical situation, with the protagonists really seeking the designation of national park as, in their view, the one guarantee of land protection.

The first authority found finance no easier a problem that had the boards before it, or the administrations to come. The 1955 report invited the people of New Zealand to reflect that the national parks cost twopence farthing per head. Some £19,000 had been expended that year. In 1964 it was £100,000. It is no shock to read that 'The money available for new capital works is falling behind the needs of the park boards.'

'It is fair to say that the average New Zealander has little appreciation of what is being achieved,' said the 1960 report, before softening the comment with, 'He has little opportunity of obtaining a full knowledge because the parks are so vast.' Perhaps there was some comfort two years later when the National Parks Authority of New Zealand received a diploma of honour and a gold medal at the eighth Annual Exhibition of Flowers held in Trieste, Italy. The award — for a collection of alpine plants — took account of measures for the protection of alpine flora. New Zealand's national parks had received, albeit modest, international recognition.

Like the Milford Sound Road, the Haast Highway was begun as a means of providing work in the Depression years of the 1930s. The Fish River Bridge was under construction in 1940, but the connection through to Haast was not made until 1960.

Fiordland National Park in 1987

By Paul Green, Chief Ranger, 1982–1986

After four and a half years in Fiordland I am still amazed by its magnificence — its size, its wilderness and the dramatic influence of the weather. Water stands out as influencing all life in Fiordland. It has carved huge glaciers that can be seen today as the great lakes in the east of the park. To the west, magnificent fiords have been cut — steep in the north, while flowing and soft in the south. Fiordland is a land of many moods.

Evidence of the power of water is particularly impressive in the Darran Mountains, where cirques and hanging and U-shaped valleys are all striking evidence of the work of glaciers on a granite land.

In pre-European times the Maori used the waterways of Fiordland on food-gathering trips, frequently sheltering in caves. Food was plentiful but the life was hard.

The Fiordland coast and sounds attracted European explorers such as Captain James Cook, followed by sealers and gold miners. Cook had something to say about water: 'The almost continual rains may be reckoned another evil attending this bay, though, perhaps, this may only happen at this season of the year; nevertheless, the situation of the country, the vast height, and nearness of the mountains, seem to subject it to much rain at all times.' Richard Henry, caretaker of Resolution Island in the 1890s, was much more terse: 'This is fine country for the waterproof explorer.'

Captain Cook's comment was, of course, about Dusky Bay and not about the sort of weather these tourists enjoyed in Milford Sound.

The waterfalls of Fiordland are one of its great features and a source of interest and pleasure to visitors in 1987 as they were in the 1880s when the Union Steam Ship Company's travel booklet *Maoriland* described their character well: 'On every side are seen waterfalls making their way down the mountain slopes — some, rushing torrents leaping and bounding over the rocks and carrying before them all that seek to bar their progress; others, winding like a silver thread in and out of the bush, here hidden from sight, and there reappearing where their course is open; while others again spread out in "great sheets of gossamer that become dissipated in mist before they reach the bottom".'

What is less apparent than the waterfalls is the effect under the surface of the high volumes of fresh water pouring into the fiords. A unique ecosystem under water matches that on the land. The overlay of fresh water enables black coral to live in as little as five metres. It is a reminder that we still have much to learn in these libraries of the past and of nature — sources of study, education, research and inspiration.

The impact of water can be devastating. Floods are frequent. Heavy snow followed by a torrent of rain causes avalanches on the Milford Track and Milford Road. Pompolora Hut was destroyed in September 1983 but Tourist Hotel Corporation staff contractors and park staff worked collectively to ensure the hut was replaced in six weeks. Today up to ten thousand walkers enjoy the Milford Track each year.

National Park, and the greatest of New Zealand's environmental controversies, seemed to have touched a national nerve: an intuitive sense of unique New Zealand.

Discussion about Fiordland's water resources has a long history. A detailed report, in 1904, on the potential of hydro-electric resources generally, by P. S. Hay, Superintending Engineer of the Public Works Department, concluded that: 'It is not likely, for scenic reasons, that a high dam would be built at Manapouri — the present beauty of the lake is worth preserving to the fullest extent.' The first major controversy, in the 1920s, focused on the Bowen Falls in Milford Sound. A Wellington business syndicate acquired a provisional licence to use the Bowen Falls for hydro-electricity to process nitrate fertiliser from the air, using a process already proven and operating in Norwegian fiords.

Response was instant once a letter from the Minister of Works was made public, advising that, 'The proposal to authorise the syndicate to commence its new and important industry has been approved, but so far no licence has been issued.' G. M. Thomson, an eminent and respected scientist and politician, led the opposition. 'Sir, there is only one Milford Sound in the world . . .' said Thomson in his opening salvo. A general controversy ensued. 'All honourable men,' said an anonymous Auckland correspondent of the syndicate, 'as honourable as any made famous by the eulogy of one Mark Anthony; yet such as they have been known to carry daggers and to plunge them a little too freely into a vesture loved of the people.' There were discussions in Parliament, much official advice, the provisional licence was withdrawn and the syndicate invited to select another source of power for their purpose. It chose Manapouri and was granted a licence to generate power. New Zealand Sounds Hydro-Electric Concessions Limited met in 1926 and set about raising capital. In spite of an encouraging prospectus, which included a photograph of 'a site suitable for Munition Factory' in Hall's Arm, the scheme eventually collapsed.

In 1960 the New Zealand Government gave the Consolidated Zinc Proprietary Limited of Australia an exclusive right to generate power from the waters of Lakes Te Anau and Manapouri for ninety-nine years. Manapouri was in Fiordland National Park. The agreement was made just eight years after

---

THE NATIVE FORESTS ACTION COUNCIL

The council was formed in 1975 when action groups that had successfully opposed the West Coast beech clearance scheme came together to broaden their goals and form a national campaign organisation.

NFAC's founding charter, the six-point Maruia Declaration, was later launched as a nationwide petition. When presented to Parliament in July 1976 with 341,160 signatures, it was New Zealand's largest petition to that date. The declaration called for legal protection for most native forests, except for a small area that could be managed for a sustained yield of high-quality decorative woods. The declaration also called for the creation of a Nature Conservancy with an undivided responsibility for safeguarding New Zealand's natural heritage. The declaration's goals were achieved in respect of publicly owned forest by 1987.

The council's first major victory was in 1978 when logging of Pureora Forest was halted following a dramatic tree-top protest. Indigenous timber production declined rapidly over the next few years as public campaigns led to successive state forests being set aside from logging.

NFAC has been a strong advocate of broadening the national park concept to give proper recognition to natural ecosystem concepts, scientific values and the intrinsic values of nature; concerns included in the revised National Parks Act of 1980. The application of these concepts to the justification of lowland additions to the predominantly montane national park system was taken up by NFAC in a series of major published reports on Okarito, Whirinaki, Paparoa and Waitutu.

Since 1980 the council has acted as the driving force in the Joint Campaign on Native Forests, a coalition of NFAC, the Royal Forest and Bird Protection Society and Federated Mountain Clubs.

The 1960s proposal to raise the level of Lake Manapouri in Fiordland National Park, to submerge some of its islands and clear forest around its perimeter, aroused the greatest environmental controversy in New Zealand's history to date.

legislation 'preserving in perpetuity as national parks for the benefit and enjoyment of the public, [areas] so beautiful or unique that their preservation is in the national interest'. There had been no consultation with the National Parks Authority.

The Government was obliged 'to advise the company of its requirements for the preservation of the scenic features of the area', and in April 1961 instructed tree felling and vegetation clearance in relation to bank slopes and water levels. In 1963, after advice from the company that it was unlikely to be able to proceed, the New Zealand Government became responsible for building the electricity supply. Extensive studies of engineering, economic, and aesthetic factors led to an announcement by the Minister of Electricity in July 1966 that the operating level of Manapouri was to be lowered.

Whereas the 1960 agreement permitted Consolidated Zinc to raise Lake Manapouri some thirty metres to the same level as Lake Te Anau, the new scheme proposed the raising of Manapouri about ten metres and provided for the same order of lake rise and fall during operation.

Public concern about impacts on Lakes Manapouri and Te Anau mounted steadily through the 1960s, reaching the dimensions of a major political storm by the end of the decade. At the outset, in 1960, the Royal Forest and Bird Protection Society submitted a petition with some twenty-five thousand signatures to Parliament. Another petition, organised jointly with the Scenery Preservation Society, followed in 1965. In 1970 the Government set up a Commission of Enquiry, which reported in October on the Crown's contractual obligations. In an atmosphere of intense public agitation, and with 'Save Manapouri' committees all over the country, a third and very large petition, signed by over two hundred and sixty thousand New Zealanders, was presented to the House of Representatives in June 1971. In September 1971 the Government announced that the high dam planned for Manapouri was to be deferred.

The future of Manapouri became an issue of the 1972 election, with the incumbent National Government opting for a dam which would maintain existing levels, but provide an option for future raising, and the opposing Labour Party promising to preserve the shorelines of both lakes. Labour victory which followed was widely attributed to this policy. New Zealand had been presented with the hypothesis that it is neither governments, nor legislation, but the people, who preserve the parks.

'The prompt decision of the new Government to ensure that Lakes Manapouri and Te Anau be held at their natural levels was appreciated by the board,' said the 1972/73 report of the Fiordland National Park Board, who, like the authority and the Nature Conservation Council, had opposed lake raising. The 1964–80 period might be called 'the reign of the boards' and the Fiordland Board, like others, was wholly responsible for the administration of its park under the general control and oversight of the authority. Generally, the boards consisted of eight members appointed by the Minister on the recommendation of the authority — a check against political patronage. In the case of an alpine park, two of these members could be nominees of the Federated Mountain Clubs and the New Zealand Ski Association. Harking back to Horonuku's letter, the National Parks Act provided that the Paramount Chief of Ngati Tuwharetoa should be a member of the Tongariro Board. These citizen boards were chaired by the Commissioner of Crown Lands for the relevant land district, an arrangement that established a virtual partnership with the Department of Lands and Survey.

In selecting nominations, the authority was concerned to secure a range of complementary skills, backed by demonstrated knowledge and interest, related to the needs of park management. These included expertise in business, law, recreation, conservation, planning and science. Although boards met formally four or five times a year, committees, inspections and personal interest meant that members were very often to be found in their parks, and a diverse range of skills meant that someone always had detailed knowledge of a track, how a concession was faring, the aspirations of a local group for a hut, relationships on the park boundary, progress with park interpretation or the needs of planning.

A board was effectively the directorship of a park. Its executive officers, employed by the board, were the rangers. The working relationship was close: it was not uncommon for a board member with a specific area of interest to assist and support a ranger in representative situations. But if relationships between boards and the authority were geographically distant, there appeared at times to be a gap of understanding greater than the distance. 'An unresolved gap seemed to exist,' said Lance McCaskill, the identified representative of the boards. It was notable that one of the duties of the first Supervisor of National Parks was 'to foster close relations between the authority and the boards', and also that a second board representative was appointed to the authority in 1969.

It seems probable that the cause of distant relationships and occasional friction was simply insufficient liaison. The task was more than one representative, even of McCaskill's energy, could do. At best, a board would meet the authority once in two, or more likely, three years. Nonetheless, visiting experts were able to remark, with surprise, at the common understanding of goals and policy extending from the authority meeting room to field management in the parks.

Common understanding of goals and policy was greatly needed in the pressures of the 1964–80 period. Visiting numbers climbed steadily: the half-million of 1964 doubled within two years and doubled again to two million in the following six years. At no stage did funding keep pace with the

THE PARK RANGERS

A small band numbering just over one hundred rangers are the public representatives of parks and reserves, advising on routes and weather, interpreting the parks in summer programmes and ensuring that tracks and huts are maintained. They are also the 'on the spot' land managers, the representatives of authority, the guardians of nature and people in the parks, and they take a leading role in rescue operations. It is the rangers who know the parks best, who see them in the full year's round from wild winter storm to summer sunshine.

The first and perhaps most famous was Richard Henry, appointed 'curator and caretaker' at Resolution Island in 1894. He moved to the sanctuary at Kapiti Island in 1909, twelve years after the appointment of its first caretaker, Malcolm McLean, in 1897. The first 'curator' of Little Barrier Island was R. H. Shakespear. The main tasks of these men were protecting and establishing native birds and eradicating introduced predators. There were few in this role in the following thirty years. A warden might be appointed on an honorary basis, as was ex-Police Commissioner John Cullen, honorary park warden at Tongariro from 1916 to 1924, promoter and organiser of heather planting.

It finally became apparent that there was a need to employ full-time rangers in the national parks. The plans of park boards to appoint them were hindered by a shortage of income and were dependent on government funding. In 1929 a ranger was appointed at

Arthur's Pass on a part-time basis; he received the princely sum of £25 a year. In 1930 the Egmont National Park Board employed two men to control goat extermination, but in 1935 the board complained that absence of government finance would not allow the programme to continue. In the following year increased funding enabled the board to appoint a permanent ranger. His main responsibility was eradication of pests, especially goats, and protection of native flora and fauna. It was noted that the control of eighty thousand acres (thirty-six thousand hectares) was a heavy job for just one man!

In the 1940s and 1950s most parks were supervised by just one ranger. One of these dedicated individuals who gave sterling service is Ray Cleland, ranger at Arthur's Pass in the 1950s. A man of versatility, energy and enthusiasm, Cleland furthered the extermination programme of noxious animals and weeds, developed building projects within the alpine village, established walking tracks and gave informative talks to the public to increase their awareness and enjoyment of the park. Active patrolling was a necessity, whether 'it was regularly meeting the midnight train from Christchurch or restraining railway surfacemen from poaching trout or using mountain beech forest near the railway line for practice for wood-chopping competitions'.

So impressed was the Director-General of Lands, D. N. R. Webb, that in 1958 Cleland was appointed Supervisor of National Parks, with

overall responsibility for the work of rangers. A ranger training scheme was set up, the first trainee appointed to Arthur's Pass in 1959, and the first chief rangers' forum was held. A strong desire emerged from this 'to do everything possible for the preservation of the parks as near as possible in a natural state'. Experiences were exchanged and it became apparent that more funds, equipment and labour were required, and that rangers needed to possess diverse talents from an extensive knowledge of flora and fauna to fluency in public speaking.

By the late 1960s the days of the 'lone ranger' were numbered. Park rangers were employees of individual national park boards and reserve rangers were department staff, so no unified career service existed. Legislation transferred park ranger employment to the public service and a new occupational group was established in the Department of Lands and Survey. The way was clear to develop education programmes for existing rangers and to attract men and women to a ranger service equipped to meet future management challenges.

Cleland had returned to the field as his first love, and Gordon Nicholls came from Westland National Park to Wellington to lay the foundations of the career service, later consolidated by John Mazey, who had served with distinction at Tongariro.

They and their pioneer colleagues leave a legacy of commitment and high standards of service reflected in the work of today's rangers and their support staff.

increased numbers, as authority reports pointed out year by year. Samuel Weems, a US National Park Service officer of long experience who visited New Zealand in 1969, forecast steeply rising overseas tourism: 'Sooner than you realise your magnificent parks will be heavily visited . . . you will be hard pressed indeed to prepare your parks in time.'

At that time special committees were studying problems at Mount Cook and the phenomenal growth of skiing at the Whakapapa ski-field on Mount Ruapehu. In 1971 similar studies into growth at Milford Sound commenced. Events drove planning. Tongariro National Park Board took an early initiative with the preparation of a master plan. Other boards followed. A broad classification of national park land into wilderness, natural environment, development and scientific areas was adopted as an aid to methodical planning. On Weems's recommendations a team approach was attempted. The authority convened a general conference on planning in 1970. The preparation, approval and implementation of management plans proceeded through the 1970s, as did detailed planning for the areas of great tourist pressure — Mount Cook, Milford and Tongariro. Special financial grants permitted a start on major development at Mount Cook.

All this might be described as a penalty of success. Administration as well as planning was being driven forward. In 1965 a working party of three senior officials began a review, seeking information on national parks administration in the United States, Canada and Australia, as well as in New Zealand. Their report in 1966 attracted public interest and additional submissions. In 1967 the first New Zealander of several over the next few years left to study park management in the United States. An assistant director (parks and reserves) was appointed in the Department of Lands and Survey — one outcome of the administrative review. A great deal of thought was given to the ranger service, recognised as the key to the future. 'A unified career service for park rangers is generally recognised as having many advantages over the present situation where the Supervisor and Assistant Supervisor of National Parks are officers of the department and park rangers are employed directly by each of the ten park boards on a salary scale determined by the authority,' said the 1968 report. The establishment of a career service was the main topic of a two-day conference with the boards convened by the authority. Both reserves and national park rangers transferred to the Public Service in April 1969. The appointment of P. H. C. Lucas as the first Director of National Parks followed in the next year. High among his priorities was formal training courses for the rangers. In-service training courses commenced in 1970. The first block diploma courses for in-service rangers began at Lincoln College in 1975, followed shortly by the first three-year, full-time diploma course intake.

Inevitably, the ceaseless struggle with introduced animals continued, but with increasing sophistication. Wild-animal control plans, based on scientific assessment of animal density, were formulated and supervised by the New Zealand Forest Service, and approved by the park boards. The rise of venison prices in the 1950s brought reinforcements to the battle; the successful application of helicopter shooting in the 1960s introduced a new army. Venison recoveries climbed steeply through the 1970s, with an export of one hundred and thirty thousand carcasses in 1971. After 1973 commercial recovery began to fall. For the first time some measure of control had been achieved.

But to this general control policy, focused primarily on the most success-

P. H. C. Lucas (left), J. W. M. Mazey (centre) and G. Nicholls (right) were key figures in the development of national park management expertise in the Department of Lands and Survey. Lucas was the first Director of National Parks. Mazey and Nicholls were both, at different times, chief rangers of parks and supervisors of national parks. All three studied national park management in the USA.

ful colonist — the red deer — there was one exception. The larger American elk or wapiti, greatly prized by hunters, is located in a region of Fiordland National Park that includes the habitat of the rare takahe. Deer control in Fiordland has for twenty years been punctuated by debate arising from the incompatibility of national park extermination policies, and concern to ensure the survival of the takahe, with the aspirations of the hunters for the survival of wapiti. Selective shooting of red deer as a priority in suppression of the total deer population has represented an uneasy compromise.

Conservation concerns in the North Island in the early 1960s were of a very different character from those of Fiordland. In a period of increasing affluence and mobility the beaches of a distinguished coastline were being sold. The hub of the problem was the major urban centre — Auckland. Mobility, for Aucklanders, extends to the sea and the cruising waters of the Hauraki Gulf. Several islands in the north had been purchased or were under threat of purchase by overseas interests; others sold for restrictive purposes or destined for subdivision. Senior officials in the Auckland office of the Department of Lands were much involved, the focus of enquiries about purchase on the one hand; on the other of vigorous expressions of concern from conservation interests, as well as Auckland's yachting fraternity. The Commissioner of Crown Lands, Jack Sinclair, saw the potential of Motutapu Island as an endowment, providing income for a park assembled from the island reserves of the Gulf. Motutapu, formerly a fort on the approaches to Auckland, was farmed by the department.

Te Paki Station, in the far northern district properly called Muriwhenua, had been offered to the Crown several times, but a gap between asking price and valuation prevented a purchase agreement. Sinclair was confident that, firstly, the gap would remain, secondly, that values would rise, and thirdly that the heritage values of Te Paki were outstanding. He bought the station, intending initially that it could be subdivided into separate reserve and land settlement areas. Accumulated knowledge has shown that Te Paki's farmland should be managed as a unit. It has indicated even more the over-riding importance of the heritage values represented in Muriwhenua's Maori cultural values, historic places, rare plants, and the scenery of its great sandhills and spectacular coastline.

In 1967 the Hauraki Gulf Maritime Park Bill received the support of both sides of the House of Representatives. The potential of the same idea for the reserves of the Marlborough Sounds, controlled at the time by four scenic boards and sharing the services of a single permanent ranger, was plain. Over the next four years there was a great deal of discussion in the Marlborough region, and much doubt on the part of farming and fishing interests. Support gathered. On 1 October 1972 the Marlborough Sounds Maritime Park Board assumed control of twenty-eight thousand hectares, an area large enough to be a national park, including ninety-five reserves, over six hundred kilometres of foreshore reserve, and Ship Cove, one of New Zealand's most historic places. Let us hope that somewhere in the Elysian Fields there was a word of approval in a broad Yorkshire accent. It was but a step to the application of the same concept, with a particular emphasis on history, in the Bay of Islands, cradle of European settlement. There too, the same Yorkshire accent had discussed a 'very uncommon and romantic' prospect.

By 1974, in the prevailing climate of land interest, it was clear that the

To ensure that the conservation option would be considered in land-use decisions, the National Parks Authority and the Department of Lands and Survey launched an investigation in the 1970s to identify land worthy of detailed study as potential national park. Stewart Island was one of the areas examined.

reservation option would go by default unless a national investigation was undertaken into the conservation values of uncommitted land. Out of concern that the remaining native forest in the Kaimai Ranges would be compromised by proposals to plant exotics, public interest groups in the Bay of Plenty pressed for a national park. The battered Kaimai forests did not meet the requisite standard, but the investigation resulted in an improved definition as to the criteria for size and representation for the selection of new or additional national park areas. All district offices of the Department of Lands and Survey were asked to indicate land that, on the basis of existing knowledge, would justify investigation.

Among the most interesting of the areas identified were the Lewis Pass, upper Wanganui River, the Punakaiki region of the West Coast, Stewart Island, the Red Hills west of Mount Aspiring and land adjacent to Westland National Park. The most controversial were the Dart and Whirinaki State Forests. Most of the candidates, however, were alpine or forest landscape. A meeting with eminent scientists and conservationists added Te Paki in the far north, the Cape Palliser district, and the Old Man and Remarkable Ranges of Central Otago.

Investigations have continued into 1987, formalised public consultation procedures being provided by the revised National Parks Act of 1980. By 1981 it was plain that further investigation of the Wanganui River was justified, and that it was probable that southern Stewart Island and parts of the Chatham Islands would technically meet national park criteria. Whirinaki State Forest would be acceptable as national park but the authority stated clearly that neither social consequences nor other conservation options were considered. recommendations were made for addition of Waikukupa and Okarito Forests to Westland National Park, of the Haast Range to Mount Aspiring National Park, and for an extension to the south of Nelson Lakes National Park, along with adjustments and the declaration of a national reserve still further south in the Lewis Pass area. National park status in the Cape Palliser district and on the south-east Otago coast had been declined. The most difficult issue of all proved to be that of the Punakaiki-Paparoa region. After long discussion the authority had to report that it was unable to reach agreement and recommended a combination of national reserve status and protective management.

The Punakaiki-Paparoa prospect, change of status for Whirinaki State Forest, and any consideration of extension of Nelson Lakes National Park as far south as the Lewis Pass were strongly opposed by the New Zealand Forest Service. Any move likely to change future management options for production forest was rejected, a position that also delayed additions to Westland, Fiordland, and Mount Aspiring National Parks. Willing support, in contrast, was given to proposals for change of status for protection forest.

In 1977 a silver jubilee conference of park users, tourist and mining interests, and conservation groups reviewed the twenty-five years since the 1952 Act. A number of policy changes were recommended, but those dealing with the composition of the authority and boards were overtaken by the decision of the Minister of Lands in March 1979 to appoint a Caucus Committee to investigate national park and reserves administration. The committee reported four months later, proposing that the system of an authority and separate board control of each national park should be replaced with a national parks and reserves authority and a structure of regional boards. The Department of Lands and Survey (including now the ranger service) would manage both parks and reserves, but the policy and the management plans that guided management would remain the responsibility of the authority and the boards. In spite of a declaration by the Minister of Lands, Venn Young, that 'the basic philosophies and spirit of the National Parks Act 1952 have been brought forward unchanged', the Bill implementing these changes received a stormy reception in the House of Representatives. At issue were justification for change, time allowed for public consideration, abrogation of authority powers and an apparent diminution of the role of the boards.

Public reception was, likewise, stormy. Some hundreds of submissions to the Select Committee considering the legislation argued strongly against the proposed changes.

In moving the second reading of a substantially amended proposal, the Minister reaffirmed his view of the need for change, stating that the authority and the boards had become remote from the people while use was escalating. The previous Act made no provision for public participation in policy and management. The Bill separated responsibility for policy from administration. Boards needed no longer to become submerged in trivia but could devote themselves to the formulation of policy, the involvement of the public and the assessment of additions to parks and new park proposals.

The authority and the boards would become wholly citizen in their constitution — there would no longer be departmental representatives. In most cases ministerial powers could only be exercised in accordance with management plans. The authority's relationship with the Government was established by its obligation to 'have regard to' Government policy. (The Bill as introduced had required the authority to 'give effect to' Government policy. The amended Bill reverted to the position defined in 1952.)

Opposition members were able to agree that the Bill was improved but claimed that significant defects remained: the balance of responsibility between department and the boards lacked clarity; the boards had lost their central function of controlling and managing the parks; the boards had not had an opportunity of defending their administrations; appointment by the Minister after consultation with the authority should revert to the original — on the recommendation of the authority; that delegation by the Minister was an inadequate means of defining board and authority responsibilities for reserves. The Bill passed into law without further amendment. In a series of controversial debates both sides had referred to the parks of the people. 'They remain the people's parks,' said Young in moving the Bill's third reading.

The National Parks Act 1980 required more adjustment on the part of the boards than on the part of the authority. From total executive responsibility for a single national park, boards moved to a region-wide concern for management plans, and general oversight. In some regions the previous direct relationship with the rangers was no longer possible. The statutory procedures for public involvement in policy making, management planning and national park investigations represented a step forward, but the perceived benefits of a clear distinction between policy making and its management implementation by the department had a serious impediment. If resources of money and skill were not available to the department the combined machinery of the system could not function as intended. Boards in particular, accustomed in the past to taking decisions about priorities and resources, could find their new role frustrating. Nonetheless, boards set about the task of getting to know the reserves of their regions, of creating public contact and establishing relationships with local government.

For the authority it was plain that one of the first main tasks would be revision of policy to reflect changes made by the new legislation. Among these were two of particular significance — the preservation of ecological systems and the scientific importance of areas were included for the first time as fundamental objectives of national park status. More than two hundred years after the commencement of European scientific study in New Zealand the significance of unique evolution had arrived in the law! The two-year process of publishing draft policy, analysing submissions, holding public hearings and preparing amended final policy was completed late in 1983.

With new policy available, boards and the department were able to proceed with management planning aimed at creating varied and interesting opportunities for park visitors, while ensuring that the quality of the park was protected. Management planning is thus the essential mechanism for balancing preservation and use. As visitor numbers continued to rise towards an annual three million, progress was necessary, but, with scarce resources, difficult. A rising proportion of overseas visitors placed particular stress on Milford Sound and Mount Cook, historic locations of tourist interest. Successive economic studies gave indications that the national parks were major contributors to tourist income. Milford Sound and Mount Cook, visited by one in every four tourists from abroad, were among the most important drawcards for tourism.

The capital demands of development of tourism infrastructure at Mount Cook Village distorted all national park funding for several years and reduced funds available to other national parks. The refrain sounded by the authority's continued reporting of funding shortage was remarkably similar to that of the first authority in the 1950s.

The greatest benefit of the new legislation lay in the extended responsibility into reserves administration. Against the background of the proposal for

The lunchtime rush hour at Milford Sound. In the peak of the season up to one hundred and eighty buses make the spectacular journey from Te Anau.

Mount Cook is one of New Zealand's greatest attractions for visitors from overseas. The planning, funding and construction of tourist facilities in the Hermitage area has been a major concern of national parks administration.

The National Parks and Reserves
Authority of 1987 in the field during
investigations of the Red Hills area. A
national park investigation, involving the
assembly of a great deal of information,
as well as extensive public consultation,
may take many months or even years.

Paparoa National Park, built on a less
majestic scale than Mount Cook or
Fiordland, nonetheless offers exquisite
beauty.

a New Zealand Conservation Strategy prepared by the Nature Conservation Council, and informed by the national park investigations carried out by the department for the previous authority, an assessment of reservation in New Zealand could be made. Attendance of a strong delegation at the third World Congress on National Parks in 1982 permitted a confirmatory external view. New Zealand's national parks and their administration commanded international respect. The instructions of the Reserves Act inferred a complementary goal as important as the parks: 'Ensuring, as far as possible, the survival of all indigenous species of flora and fauna, both rare and commonplace, in their natural communities and habitats, and the preservation of representative samples of all classes of natural ecosystems and landscape which in the aggregate originally gave New Zealand its own recognisable character.'

The first step towards representative reservation was taken in 1981 when a meeting of scientists was convened by the authority and the Department of Lands and Survey to explore the possibility of defining ecological regions and districts. Early in the following year the Biological Resources Centre produced provisional maps, and a scientific working party convened by the centre examined methodology and resources. Field parties were engaged in pilot programmes during the following summer. Regrettably, in the years that have followed it has become clear that the rate of survey and implementation of the Protected Natural Areas programme, as it has come to be known, is unlikely to exceed the rate of loss. New Zealand, one of few countries with an opportunity to do so, may not reach the goal of a truly representative reservation system.

In extending the national parks system towards its completion, the foresight of the previous National Parks Authority has fostered notable progress. Additions were made to Westland National Park in 1982, to Tongariro, Nelson Lakes and Mount Aspiring National Parks in 1983, and a further addition of the Haast Range to Mount Aspiring National Park in 1987. Recommendations for a high level of protection for the Kaimai Ranges were made in 1984, and for World Heritage status for Fiordland, Mount Cook and Westland National Parks in 1975. Recommendations for additions to Arthur's Pass National Park

Charles Mariekura performing the wero (challenge) to guests, including the Governor-General, the Very Reverend Sir Paul Reeves, at the entry to the marae at Pipiriki on the occasion of the opening of the Whanganui National Park in February 1987.

have been made, while investigations into the values of the Waitutu State Forest adjacent to Fiordland National Park and for the the Red Hills west of Mount Aspiring continue.

Two new national parks have been created. Incorporation of ecological and scientific values in the criteria for national park selection allowed further investigations of the Paparoa region of the West Coast, probably the most intensive and public of those carried out. The ecological and scientific as well as the recreational and scenic values of an area strikingly different from any other within national park protection well justified national park protection.

On 7 February 1987, on the marae at Pipiriki, the Governor-General, the Very Reverend Sir Paul Reeves (of Te Atiawa tribe of Taranaki), declared the opening of the Whanganui National Park. Almost one hundred years from the Gift, the great forests of the Wanganui Basin and a heritage of centuries of Maori history passed into the safekeeping of all the people of New Zealand. Tongariro, 'the Gift'; Egmont, gifted for the purposes of a national park to the people of New Zealand by the Taranaki Trust Board in 1978; Urewera, of the Tuhoe people. The Maori people of the Wanganui River had pondered long about their land but now, the ceremony and generous welcome on the marae, signified their agreement to their taonga (treasured possession) joining the other great heritage areas of Maori people.

Hauraki Gulf Maritime Park in 1987

By Rex Mossman, Chief Ranger, 1981–1987

This essay describes the diverse values of just seven of the nearly fifty islands in the park — truly a treasure at Auckland's doorstep.

The Hauraki Gulf Maritime Park is as diverse as it is widespread, covering all levels of protected lands and stretching from Auckland city's doorstep out to the distant offshore islands. Ronald Lockley has described the gulf much better than I could: 'This was the splendid Hauraki Gulf, large enough, it is boasted, to hold the navies of all the world, but, more importantly for us, haunted by innumerable seabirds, by whales and dolphins, by marlin, mako shark, and other remarkable giant ocean fish, and by many subtropical marine creatures — a marine biologist's, a yachtsman's dream of perfection.' Rangitoto is one of Auckland's most prominent and well-known landmarks.

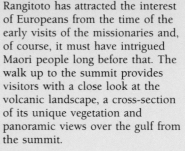

Rangitoto has attracted the interest of Europeans from the time of the early visits of the missionaries and, of course, it must have intrigued Maori people long before that. The walk up to the summit provides visitors with a close look at the volcanic landscape, a cross-section of its unique vegetation and panoramic views over the gulf from the summit.

A short trip down the harbour lies this grassy little island, which is closely associated with Auckland's history. The remains of old ferry boats, scuttled in the early 1900s, lie in the mud. John Logan Campbell, the 'father' of Auckland, bought Motukorea (Brown's Island) and described it in this passage from his book *Poenamo*, which recalls the first time he entered the Waitemata in 1840: 'Behind us basking peacefully in the morning sun lay the little island . . . in all its beauty, with its crater hill, and through the broken lip we could get a peep into the crater itself. How silent and peaceful were Waitemata's lovely sloping shores as we explored them on that now long long ago morning . . . On that morning the open country stretched away in vast fields of fern and Nature reigned supreme.'

In this scattered and widespread maritime park a boat is indispensable; management is impossible without it. *Hauturu*, the park's service vessel, runs a regular service trip every fortnight, delivering mail and supplies for staff, and building materials, equipment, fuel and stores for park operations. Often carrying researchers, staff and other personnel necessary for the running of the park, the boat provides a vital link to and around the islands.

The trip out to Little Barrier Island (Hauturu) always has an air of excitement about it as we steam out early in the morning to catch the dawn calm for unloading. A nature reserve and a sanctuary for many species of birds, the island has very special qualities. In 1880 Andreas Reischek, the Austrian bird collector, described it as a 'precipitous and overgrown [island] with luxurious bush consisting principally of giant kauri trees . . . reaching skywards like mighty cathedral towers, while below the dark green arches of manuka and nikau palms, and the tender soft green veil of broad fern-tree fronds, were richly contrasted'.

Tiritiri Matangi Island, well known for its powerful lighthouse, is recognised amongst conservationists for its current revegetation project. Many have helped in the planting which will one day recreate the native forest suited to the warm climate of the Hauraki Gulf and provide a sanctuary for the rarer bird species. Saddleback have been released already and are of particular interest to visitors.

Northernmost of the park islands are the Poor Knights, renowned among scuba divers for the marine reserve that surrounds them. Access to the islands is especially restricted on account of their fragile and important ecosystem, which supports a large seabird population.

Contrasting with the precious natural values of the Poor Knights is Kawau Island, known to most people as a yachting haven and as the home of Sir George Grey. The island is also fascinating for its remnants of an early industry. After the discovery of copper and manganese, this bay housed an active and thriving community of miners during the mid-1880s. The enginehouse and chimney were built in 1854 and the chimney was restored in 1981.

Marlborough Sounds Maritime Park in 1987

By Kerry Johnson, Chief Ranger, 1976–1987

New Zealand's history is one of colonisation, first by the people and animals of Polynesian islands to the north and later by their European counterparts. Although gradual from the beginning, changes in the quality of our landscape and in the whole ecological process brought about by our need for adequate living space and the means to maintain an existence were dramatic, to say the least.

The Marlborough Sounds shared this phenomenon with many of the more accessible parts of the country, where resources were utilised to the full as this new land shed its isolation from other parts of the globe and made way for increasing numbers of people.

Policy of the day meant that land must be cleared for the benefit of communities and the country as a whole, little thought being given to the need to conserve intact some of the unique qualities of our local environment.

Two world wars, changing economics and a growing awareness of environmental values are factors that eventually fostered a change of attitude towards land use.

Local settlers were instrumental in setting up an organisation, supported by government departments, that brought about greater control of fires — one of the most positive moves in the process of refining land-management practices the area has ever seen. The growing awareness of this part of New Zealand as a recreation resort gave impetus to the development of seaside cottages and new small communities in choice localities and, in addition, created greater demand for the provision of more and better public facilities. The development of forestry in a limited capacity is another ingredient in this process of change.

What can readily be appreciated today is a clearer definition between land uses; with farming now more confined to the better-quality land in the central and outer coastal regions, forestry situated on steeper or less suitable farm land and much of the remainder reverting to bush cover.

The retention in public ownership of a coastal area as a farm park, as shown in this photograph, provides an opportunity to carry out traditional farming, while, at the same time, encouraging recreational and educational use. Significant areas of public land, much in near-original state, have been expanded by further purchases and substantial gifts from individuals.

Representing something over a third of the land mass, key components of this collection of reserves have been provided with additional protection to foster the recovery of important biological elements in the district.

The management of previously farmed islands, such as Maud Island, as highly important conservation units now provides protection for rare, indigenous and introduced wildlife.

Lush secondary growth on Motuara Island supports a healthy population of native birds and other fauna. Further encouragement for rationalised land use comes from a number of privately owned bush areas.

The result that is emerging today is a clearer definition of land uses, bringing about a greater balance, maintaining the particular character and improving the quality of the area for the benefit of all.

For example, historic sites are preserved to retain their interest and charm, and to cater for education and recreation demands.

Old tracks, formed to give access to most parts of the Sounds in the days of early settlement, now serve as popular walks for visitors as part of the walkway system. Planning processes continue to emphasise the need to manage this resource in a complementary manner.

As this photograph indicates, sites originally cleared of bush and farmed are now important recreation and conservation areas. The Marlborough Sounds Maritime Park has a big role to play in this process of rationalised land use. There will always be room for improvement, but the path being followed shows great promise in providing for the needs of both the local and the wider community.

The Bay of Islands Maritime and Historic Park in 1987

By Shaughan Anderson, Park Naturalist and Interpreter, 1982–1987

The Bay of Islands Maritime and Historic Park might well be one of the most recent and just a mere speck on the map, but there is more to it than first meets the eye. Early Maori and European explorers made their first landings in other parts of the country, yet it was the Bay of Islands they chose to settle. Captain Cook named it 'on account of the Great Number [of islands] which line its shores and these help to form several safe and commodius [*sic*] Harbours . . .' This was a tremendous advantage in a time when water transport dominated and, for a short time, the bay was very prosperous.

When you are small you have to aim high to make the best of the resources you have — bigger is not necessarily better. The Bay of Islands Maritime and Historic Park is fortunate to be used today much as it has been for centuries. People still migrate to the coast to collect kaimoana (food from the sea) and enjoy the bay. Our aim is to ensure that future generations may also have this opportunity to appreciate the Bay of Islands.

Numerous cultural and historical relics from this early period of Maori and European settlement remained relatively unmodified as a result of limited development. The fortuitous preservation of New Zealand's birthplace lasted over a century, but this could not be guaranteed to continue. Formal conservation measures were taken to ensure that this part of our heritage remains for future generations to appreciate. Much has been achieved since the park was created in 1978, but more remains to be done. Progress has been largely due to the support of local communities and a highly motivated staff.

While situations, conditions and equipment have often been less than ideal,
what better motivation can there be than the environment one works in?
A striking example of this would be shearing at Kahuwhera Pa.

Traditionally, the Bay of Islands has been a playground for New Zealanders. Neither today nor in the foreseeable future is this likely to differ, although overseas visitors are increasing in numbers. Summer becomes a time of incredible activity on, in, under and around the bay. Whatever their age or interest, if the weather is hot and sunny, this island paradise lures people from afar.

The active involve themselves in tramping or waterskiing, while others repair to the many secluded, sandy beaches for pure relaxation. Most visitors are escaping the urban scene and everything it stands for. To help them appreciate the area and absorb as much of the outdoors as possible, we organise summer nature programmes. Staff actively participate in the interpretation of the environment to the public. Demonstrating the feeding action of barnacles is an example of the interpretation of our cultural, biological or historical heritage, which is probably one of the most rewarding and important aspects of park work. The rather surprising thing about this park is the variety it has to offer. At one moment the sea might provide a titbit of information; the next, a tasty morsel. The value of the park and its many uses are dependent on the visitor's perspective.

Even in autumn the weather is relatively warm and although visitors may be less evident, work pressure remains constant. Staff effort at this time tends to be diverted from the service of the public to focus on the resource itself. Although a few jobs are the result of an all-too-busy summer, many are seasonally dependent. Keeping grass growth in check is one of the first matters requiring attention. Several of the reserves are stocked in order to minimise the fire risk that rank grass can present, and to maintain open areas suitable for recreation. Prior to the arrival of holidaymakers, the animals are removed again.

Trees are planted as part of a programme to enhance the beauty of the park. An especially satisfying aspect of this work is planting a tree like a kauri, which could well be providing shade, shelter, and habitat eight hundred years hence. Indeed, how can we place a value on the work we do now when it may still be appreciated in the year 3000? Often, simple tasks, such as shifting stock or planting trees, are complicated by the very character of a maritime park: the sea. But however difficult the access or the job, the personal satisfaction is correspondingly of more value when successfully completed.

Climate plays a strong role in the park's use and management. In rough or wet weather the park may not attract the public, but the facilities and machinery still require maintenance. The marine environment is very hard on equipment and items such as the watering buoy demand considerable attention. Winter is not the park's 'on' season, but its demand for management attention does not diminish. Patches of bad weather interrupt the flow of work, yet efforts continue largely unabated.

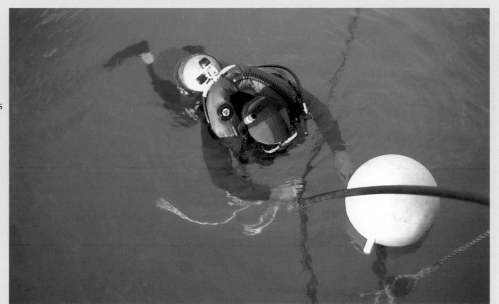

Much of the visible work in the park is channelled toward facilities and people, but our role as protector of the natural environment goes on. Our wildlife may not have as high a profile as the black robins of the Chathams, but it is not overlooked. This aspect of park operations is ever-changing, much like nature itself. Recently attention has concentrated on endangered flax snails. With the assistance of outside agencies, we hope to gather sufficient data on which to base management decisions that will improve the snails' chance of survival.

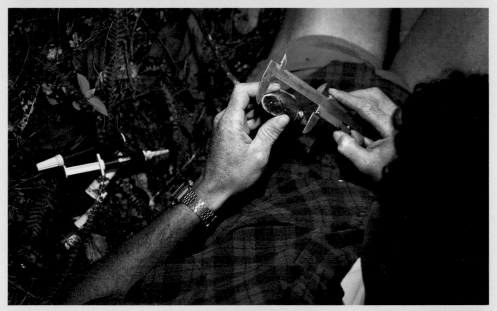

Spring is heralded by the blooming of the kowhai and clematis in July and August. The subtropical climate of the Bay of Islands is never more evident than at this time. It can be warm but the rain is unpredictable. This weather is superb for plant growth and very frustrating for staff, especially those attempting to control noxious weeds. To prevent a take-over by aggressive plant species, some highly toxic poisons are used. Spacesuited staff may look humorous, but the noxious plant problem would be serious if these measures were not taken.

In spring we usually aim higher than our resources can achieve by programming everything we would like completed by summer. Much of the work directly relates to the impending invasion of people or their use of the environment. Fish stocks are monitored at Mimiwhangata and favourite island picnic areas are cleared of long coarse grass.

Whanganui National Park in 1987

By John Lythgoe, Senior Ranger, 1984–1987

According to Maori legend, the valley of the Wanganui River was created after a family dispute between the mountain gods in the centre of the North Island, when Taranaki (Mount Egmont) left Tongariro, Ngauruhoe, Ruapehu and Pihanga and made his way to the coast. A great channel was carved out of the land by the moving mountain. This was filled with fresh water by Tongariro and became the Wanganui River.

On a fine day, from the Matemateaonga Walkway, trampers can look across the forests of the Wanganui basin to see Mount Ruapehu and the legendary home of Taranaki. However, the view is often blocked by mist. Water is a vital component in the ecosystem of this park and mists are experienced throughout the year.

The Whanganui National Park contains one of the largest remaining tracts of lowland forest in New Zealand, almost half of which is below three hundred metres and in a generally mild climate. These forests were 'farmed' by the early Maori, who learnt to utilise the trees for shelter. There are a great variety of birds to be found here, not only because of the size of the park but also owing to its lower altitude compared with its neighbours, Tongariro and Egmont National Parks.

At the entrance to the tributary Mangaio Stream, in the Te Wahi Pari (the place of cliffs), it is easy to recall stories from the past when the steep-sided, bush-clad gorges provided the natural fortification for the pa of the tangata whenua. When an enemy taua (war party) approached, the vine ladders were swiftly withdrawn and boulders rolled down onto the opposing warriors and their canoes. Some of these boulders are still visible when the river is running low and clear.

'The Drop Scene' was an important feature for tourists travelling by Maori canoe or riverboat from the luxuriously appointed accommodation at the Houseboat or Pipiriki House. Nowadays many people view this much-publicised scene from jet boats or canoes.

The source of the title has been lost in the last hundred years, and several versions are given by the commercial operators, including a story relating it to the theatrical backdrop for Victorian stage shows.

In the romantic style of writing common at the turn of this century, one author described the Wanganui River as 'a river of pictures and of peace'. Unfortunately, not all visitors are able to enjoy such perfect reflections.

For visitors it can be confusing to find farmland within the wider boundaries of a national park. These farms date back to the riverboat era, and, in the Mangapurua and similar areas, to the rehabilitation of soldiers following the First World War. The evocatively named 'Bridge to Nowhere' has become a focal point for walks in the park; the Mangapurua track follows the disused road between Whakahoro and the Mangapurua Landing. Whichever way this valley is approached, the heartbreak of the early settlers in this isolated valley can be easily appreciated. This concrete bridge now remains as a memorial to all who served their time in these settlements.

Because it has fewer rapids than the 'whitewater' rivers, the Wanganui offers an ideal opportunity for the novice and the less adventurous to enjoy an outdoor holiday with a difference. Increasing numbers visit the area for a river trip, but not all realise that they pass through national park and privately owned areas, including Maori Incorporation land.

When travelling through the beautiful gorges, with the distinctive lowland forest cover and the abundance of bird life, tourists can appreciate the traditional Maori harmony with nature. The lifestyle is simple, the pace leisurely. It is easy to imagine oneself in the past, or what it was like when travellers used steamers or Maori canoes. Unlike the old canoes, which were made from massive totara trees, modern craft are constructed from synthetics. The extra stability of the Canadian canoe not only offers more security for the inexperienced, but also greater capacity for stowing extra supplies for passengers.

Although many commercial operators now use Canadian canoes, the single and, less commonly, the double kayak are still seen on the river in commercial and private groups. In fact, the typical do-it-yourself Kiwi is found here too!

An 1894 guidebook told travellers that at Pipiriki, 'Rioni, an elderly Maori, has a paddock and looks well after horses left in his charge', and the accompanying map showed the house as next to Huddle's Temperance hotel. This house is now the information centre and museum for visitors to the park. Although the headquarters are in Wanganui, the majority of tourists come to Pipiriki and that is where the main visitors centre is based, with ancillary services at the northern entrance to the park, in Taumarunui.

Whether they approach it by river or road, most people arrive at Pipiriki experiencing a sense of going back in time to when life was free from the pressure of modern society. One of the main attractions is that there is no artificiality and a lack of even normal facilities associated with a modern resort. The romance of the past lingers around the old deciduous trees that dominate the village landscape; it is claimed that the linden trees were a present from Kaiser Wilhelm to Alexander Hatrick, pioneer of the riverboat service and mayor of Wanganui, to plant beside his 'Rhine of New Zealand'.

Paparoa National Park in 1987

By Grahame Champness, Reserves Ranger, 1973–1987

I predict that although it is the youngest of our national parks, Paparoa will rapidly become one of the most popular. The park's relatively small size is no indication of the variety or uniqueness found in such a small package. The closer one looks, the more exciting the area becomes.

The park's major geographic features are related to the geosyncline. Sedimentary rocks from the seafloor, which were uplifted by the folding of the earth's crust, now dominate the west side of the Paparoa Range in the form of cliffs and plateaux.

The limestone beds have developed into a karst landscape under ideal conditions. Hard, pure limestone, low altitude, warm climate, a rich forest cover and an ample supply of rain have all combined to create these conditions.

Curiously fluted rocks, together with potholes, dolines, closed depressions, natural arches, disappearing streams, springs, underground drainage and caves are all distinctive formations found in karst landscapes.

Young caves and cave systems exist where flood waters and ground water still shape their interiors. Some undiscovered caves must still lie hidden under the cover of rich vegetation.

This mantle of vegetation forms a mosaic as plant species follow the soil types and geology of the area. Climate or micro-climates also add to the conditions under which species or communities contrast with each other.

The most popular and well-known part of
the park is Dolomite Point, where many
thousands of visitors come each year to see
the spectacle of the Pancake Rocks and the
blowholes.

Sea-bottom sediments, layer upon layer,
laminated together by time, calcium,
weights and pressures, have been uplifted to
stand above the present sea level. The acid
waters from flax bogs exploited the cracks,
melting and sculpturing the blocks of
limestone into columns of pancakes.

Dolomite Point provides a grandstand
from which the Tasman Sea and its
many moods may be experienced.
The awesome power of the sea is evident
when the blowholes are working at
their best.

From Okariko Point in the south to Needle Point in the north, the coastline is constantly being buffeted by westerly seas. The geology of each area shows its individual character as it weathers against the storms.

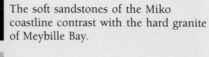

The soft sandstones of the Miko coastline contrast with the hard granite of Meybille Bay.

One unique feature of the park is the location of the nesting colony of the Westland black petrel. These large ocean-going birds visit land each winter to breed. They build their nests in large burrows dug out of the hillsides.

Chapter 16

International Connections

In 1939, with the world emerging from depression but at the brink of war, New Zealand resumed its connections with the stream of ideas about national parks flowing from the United States. Much had happened in the sixty-five years since the original information about Yellowstone had come to New Zealand through the travels, writing and painting of William Fox.

The United States had set aside a number of famous parks, including Yosemite (the scene of Fox's paintings), Sequoia, Mount Rainier, Crater Lake, Glacier, Hawaii, Grand Canyon, Zion, Grand Teton, Carlsbad Caverns, and Olympic. The US National Park Service, twenty-three years in evolution, was already of notable reputation. Nearly fifty historical sites had been transferred to the care of the service by Franklin D. Roosevelt, a conservation-conscious President who was committed to the concept of a Civilian Conservation Corps. Three hundred thousand young men in a thousand camps had been at work, mostly in national forests and parks, catching up with the backlog of projects: campgrounds, buildings, trails and bridges. Yellowstone had survived one of the periodic exploitatory threats that is the lot of great national parks, when a proposal to construct dams and flood huge areas in order to supply Idaho potato farmers with water eventually failed.

New Zealand was far behind. There were three national parks constituted:

Mount Everest in morning mist; to the Nepalese, Sagarmatha — 'Mother of the Universe'.

Tongariro, Egmont, and Arthur's Pass. All were under separate local administrations. There was neither co-ordinated policy nor a field service.

Lance McCaskill, lecturing in biology at Christchurch Teachers' Training College, had been a regular visitor to Arthur's Pass National Park, with and without students, since 1932. He had developed a philosophy that the theory and practice of conservation was a core around which his teaching would centre. Some of his non-student visits were for the discharge of a typically selfless commitment to maintain two gardens of native plants of the district, the Railways Department having terminated its maintenance of one of the gardens at the Arthur's Pass station.

McCaskill sought, and was awarded, a Carnegie Traveller's Grant to visit the United States, Canada, Great Britain and Scandinavia to study the teaching of biology in schools and teachers' colleges, with special reference to the use of the field trip. What was of more direct relevance to the future of national parks in New Zealand was his intention to see if the policy on national parks proposed by L. O. Hooker, F. M. Vosseler, and A. P. Harper of the committee of the Federated Mountain Clubs was supported by what was being done in the United States.

He visited Mount Rainier, Yosemite and Grand Canyon National Parks, as well as several 'national monuments' (historic landmarks, historic and prehistoric structures and other objects of historic and scientific interest), discussing education schemes and their relation to nature conservation. In May 1939, at Lava Beds National Monument, a ranger gave him his personal copy of *The National Parks Portfolio*, an account of American parks published soon after the founding of the US National Park Service in 1916. This text became McCaskill's main reference in his subsequent attempts to obtain a parks service for New Zealand.

War took over when McCaskill returned. On leaving the army in 1944, he discussed his American experience with Ron Cooper, chief clerk of the Department of Lands and Survey. They agreed that an American system was the most desirable one for New Zealand. Harper had, as McCaskill discovered, become quite convinced on that score. By 1949 when Cooper had formulated a draft National Parks Bill there was a direct American input from Dr Olaus Murie, who had come to New Zealand to take part in the Pacific Science Congress. Murie expounded the American concept of 'wilderness' — country that would remain in a totally undeveloped state, without even tracks or huts, to be entered on nature's terms. What was, in fact, being fed into the New Zealand legislation, with the support of two successive Ministers of Lands (E. B. Corbett and C. F. Skinner) was argument from one of the great American public controversies, not unlike the later New Zealand controversy on proposals to raise Lake Manapouri.

Dr Murie, as president of the American Wilderness Society, had been in the thick of a great public debate over dam proposals that would have flooded canyons of the seven hundred and eighty square kilometre Dinosaur National Monument on the border of Colorado and Utah states. This area of wilderness, Dr Murie had said, was essential 'for our happiness, our spiritual welfare, for our success in dealing with the confusions of a materialistic and sophisticated civilisation'. The ancestral concepts of the wilderness provisions of the 1952 National Parks Act came from a new American frontier.

McCaskill's appointment as the member representing National Park

Boards to the first National Parks Authority brought him into an official involvement with administration. He had thus an enlarged background for the study of parks made in 1955 on an overseas visit as a member of the staff of Lincoln College. A nine-page report with recommendations was the outcome. When in the same year McCaskill became an individual member of the International Union for the Conservation of Nature and Natural Resources (IUCN) he had achieved a direct personal connection with the agency that would become the mainspring of international progress in national parks. IUCN convened the first World Conference on National Parks in Seattle in 1962, New Zealand being one of the sixty-one countries represented. While McCaskill was not present, two New Zealanders were — Jack MacKenzie, of the Fiordland National Park Board, and Ray Cleland, Supervisor of National Parks. With a common interest and meeting ground in Arthur's Pass National Park, Cleland and McCaskill had often talked together. The channel for the flow of ideas into New Zealand increased, particularly as Cleland was appointed to the International Commission on National Parks.

By this time, at Arthur's Pass there was tangible evidence of McCaskill's observations abroad. He had been impressed by the fact that in the United States each park had a special headquarters as a base for staff, usually associated with a display centre with lecture room and general education facilities. The Arthur's Pass National Park Board commenced fund raising in 1958 and its visitor centre was opened in October 1959. McCaskill noted that: 'Everything possible was done to make the building fit into the surroundings and plant the area with natives.' Remembering an alpine garden he had seen at Yosemite in 1939, he had been urging the authority, with marginal success, to support the planting of native-plant gardens for their educational value.

Nor, initially, was the authority swayed by McCaskill's enthusiasm for joining IUCN. He went at his own expense as representative of the Royal Forest and Bird Protection Society to the meeting at Lucerne in 1966, subsequently serving on various committees. An amendment to the National Parks Act later permitted the authority to become a 'government agency' member of IUCN, carrying New Zealand forward to a widening and very active membership, especially after New Zealand became a 'state' member in 1974.

While McCaskill's vision and enthusiasm were laying the institutional foundation for New Zealand's international connections, the remarkable deeds of another New Zealander were creating a climate of prestige, interest and contacts that would meld into the contributory and leadership role of the 1970s and 1980s.

On 29 May 1953, Edmund Hillary and Sherpa Tenzing Norgay reached the summit of Mount Everest. Hillary's association with Nepal, and particularly the Sherpa people, continued with his establishment of the Himalayan Trust and recurring visits to build schools and hospitals in the alpine valleys on the approaches to Everest. Three and a half years after the Everest expedition Hillary led the Ross Sea party of the Commonwealth Trans-Antarctic Expedition, whose role was to establish a reception base at McMurdo Sound and to lay supporting depots toward the Pole. This work done, he led his tractor team to the Pole itself.

Hillary raised New Zealand's profile in both Nepal and the Antarctic. Thereafter, international conservation circles needed no assurance of a *raison d'être* for New Zealand interest.

In New Zealand, meantime, the foundations for another stream of American influence, and for wide-ranging international connections, was being laid. Sir Thaddeus McCarthy, first chairman of the Winston Churchill Trust, determined that an emphasis of early fellowship awards would be broadening of the expertise available for park management in New Zealand. The first recipient, in 1967, was Gordon Nicholls, then chief ranger of Westland National Park, later to become Supervisor of National Parks in New Zealand. Nicholls, like later recipients of fellowships to study park management in the United States, attended an International Short Course in administration of National Parks and Equivalent Reserves offered by a combination of United States agencies, including the US National Park Service, the University of Michigan and the Conservation Foundation.

Perhaps thirty countries would be represented in a truly international mix of Africans, Indians, Nepalese, South Americans and New Zealanders. A naturally stimulating situation was extended by travel and 'on the ground' case studies. From Yellowstone to Colorado, the group visited national parks, archaeological sites, historic places and wildlife and recreation areas. University facilities or national park auditoriums near the sites were used for lectures and case studies. Every conceivable aspect of management was presented and debated: wildlife management, park preservation and use, visitor motivation, regional tourism, recreation, preservation of archaeological resources, historic sites and research.

The reports that came back answered New Zealand problems, shaped New Zealand management, and confirmed the Yellowstone model. In 1968 Nicholls recorded that in six months he had travelled twenty-seven thousand kilometres, visiting over fifty national and state parks, eleven national monuments and thirteen national forests. He went on to discuss roads, visitor centres, nature walks, campgrounds, interpretation, marine parks and staffing.

The next two recipients of Churchill Fellowships, in 1969, were John Mazey, chief ranger of Tongariro National Park, and P. H. C. (Bing) Lucas, Assistant Director of Administration (National Parks). Lucas's report *Conserving New Zealand Heritage*, published in 1970, was the most comprehensive and influential of all the returns of information.

Mazey undertook a study tour, but Lucas, like Gordon Nicholls before him, attended an International Short Course, using a campervan to travel across the United States and into Canada, staying in and studying national parks there as well as in the United States. As Parks Canada had become a partner in the Short Course, the travelling and case studies had ranged more extensively — from Jasper to the Grand Canyon. He set out to look for 'Lessons for New Zealand'. These were recorded in a report ranging the gamut of policy, into management. The summary of the 'Lessons' is still relevant today, but unlike many potential lessons for New Zealand, most of Lucas's recommendations entered policy-making and practice. The reason was a simple one. On his return, Lucas became Director of National Parks and Reserves, a number of incipient problems were avoided and national park administration in New Zealand moved forward rapidly. Among the 'Lessons' was the observation that: 'New Zealand has a responsibility to play a more effective part in international and regional co-operation in the field of national parks and conservation, particularly in the South Pacific and in South-East Asia.'

The last two fellowships were awarded in the 1970s. Tamaroa Nikora, planning officer for Urewera National Park, visited the United States to study management of cultural areas, and George McMillan, Assistant Director of National Parks, studied marine park management in Japan, Canada and the United States.

By 1972, and the major international event in national park administration, the second World Conference, the travels of the New Zealanders, their friendships and contacts through the Short Course, and the rapid application of 'lessons' at home had promoted a growing confidence and reputation. R. J. MacLachlan, Bing Lucas and the author, attending the centenary celebration at Yellowstone National Park associated with the second World Conference, found that New Zealand's historic initiatives in national park establishment, its unique administration and the quality and scale of the parks themselves commanded both interest and respect. By this time the central figure in international contacts, the main channel of communication and the successor, in that sense, to Lance McCaskill was Lucas, who had succeeded Cleland as a member of the IUCN Commission on National Parks and Protected Areas in 1967.

In 1974 he had his first opportunity to apply one of the 'lessons' abroad. With the encouragement of Sir Edmund Hillary, the Nepalese Government sought New Zealand assistance in investigating, establishing and building a management structure for the Sagarmatha National Park, which would encompass Mount Everest. Lucas went off to lead a small combined New Zealand/Nepalese team to assess the possibilities for a park and to recommend an aid programme. The mission spent three weeks in a region higher than the summit of Mount Cook, camping, trekking, giving conservation talks to Sherpa children and discussing the concept of a national park with local people and their spiritual leader, the High Lama of Tengboche Monastery.

Accompanying Lucas were Ross Hodder, of the New Zealand Forest Service, and Norman D. Hardie, of the Arthur's Pass National Park Board. While it is tempting to draw attention to a (coincidental) continuity of Arthur's Pass National Park connections with international activities, the real

The park house built for the Nepal National Park Service by Gordon and Esther Nicholls in the traditional stone, timber and slate of the Khumbu region.

Gordon and Esther Nicholls with the High Lama of Tengboche Monastery, who became a member of the Sagarmatha National Park Board.

The peak of Ama Dablam from Tengboche.

reasons for Hardie's presence were his knowledge of high Nepal and his reputation as a climber, enhanced by conquest of Kanchenjunga.

The general objective of the aid project was to establish a framework for on-going management of the Sagarmatha National Park, to be addressed first by the researching and production of a management plan; secondly, by the training of Nepalese park managers in New Zealand; thirdly, by the construction of facilities within the park.

The first New Zealand project manager to take up residence near Namche Bazar was Gordon Nicholls, accompanied by his wife, Esther. Prior experience as a chief ranger of a national park in New Zealand was less relevant than his trade as a builder, the time spent with the representatives of twenty-six countries at the International Short Course in the United States and especially the discussions there about the difficulties of establishing new national parks in foreign countries.

The Nichollses were concerned with the establishment phase, with debates about boundaries and scale, with initial designs for facilities: a trekking lodge at Tengboche, others on the main trekking route and a visitor and administrative centre near Namche Bazar. Life at Namche Bazar was strikingly, if not totally, different from life at Franz Josef in New Zealand as chief ranger of Westland National Park. The food was different — staple Sherpa diet depends on potatoes, barley and buck wheat, grown during a short season in restricted areas of relatively good soil. The language was different, and the compound of language and administrative difficulties could be frustrating. Decisions on day-to-day management were by consensus with the Nepalese park warden, and after discussion with the National Parks and Wildlife Conservation Department in distant Kathmandu.

There were many compensations — the cheerfulness, charm and humour of the tough, resilient Sherpas, the charm of the villages, with their natural stone and weathered timber blending into the mountain setting, the glory of rhododendron forest in spring and the unsurpassed alpine grandeur in which their everyday life was enfolded. Famous, towering peaks of mountaineering lore were part of the work environment. Ama Dablam was often visible from areas close to Namche, and Nuptse further away up the Khumbu Valley. Thirty kilometres away on the northern boundaries of the park lay Cho Oyu, Lhotse and Sagarmatha (Everest) itself, the Nepalese 'Mother of the Universe'.

A distinguished succession of rangers from other New Zealand parks followed the Nichollses and, supported by wives and families carried the project on until its completion in 1981: Bruce Jefferies from Tongariro, Peter Croft from Arthur's Pass, Mal Clarborough from Nelson Lakes. The visitor centre and the trekking lodges were completed and, with New Zealand forester expertise, nurseries were set up for reforestation in parts of the park.

In fact, the nurseries engaged a problem of fundamental concern in the Himalayas — loss of forest. Prior to the 1960s, a system of forest guardians appointed on a village-by-village basis had exercised control over forest use. This system had been supplanted at a time of increasing ecological pressure. On the one hand, there was an influx of refugees from Tibet, with their yaks. The demand for grazing increased. On the other hand, the increased popularity of trekking and the need for fuel introduced firewood as a cash crop into the Sherpa economy.

When Keith Garratt, Director of Planning of the Department of Lands and

The nursery at Tashing was set up, with the assistance of New Zealand Forest Service officers, to provide a practical example of what could be done to rehabilitate the forests of Sagarmatha. It was located on the main trekking route so that visitors could see the positive work being done in the region.

Survey, went to Nepal in 1979 to prepare a management plan for the national park, it was already well understood that the most urgent issue to be dealt with was degradation of forest by human use. In the longer term, other issues, such as the protection of the unique culture the Sherpas had brought from Tibet in the sixteenth century, were not less important. Sagarmatha, like most of the great national parks, had endangered plant and animal species; the musk deer, snow leopard and Himalayan wolf.

The third major component of the New Zealand aid programme was training; for local Sherpa people within the park itself, and in New Zealand at a special school set up at Turangi. A programme of four months' duration dealt with resources, visitors, interpretation, conservation education, public relations, facilities, management and operational skills. While established for the Sagarmatha project, the Lands and Survey Department's operational training courses and study tours have since 1974 trained over sixty officers from Turkey, Fiji, Malaysia, Western Samoa, Papua New Guinea, Japan, Thailand, Indonesia, Burma, United Kingdom, Hong Kong and Peru, while ranger exchanges have taken place with New South Wales, Tasmania and England.

Assistance to Peru and Western Samoa was similar in kind to the Nepal undertaking. Lucas visited Peru in 1974 as a member of an expert mission on forestry, agriculture and national parks. The national park system was in its infancy, but the variety of Peru's wildlife and the range of its landscapes, from coastal deserts to the high Andes and the tropical jungles of the Amazon Basin, offered a potential for national park formation that attracted increasing government interest. New Zealand assistance in specific parks was suggested, but after a tour (which included the famous Machu Picchu site) Lucas recommended that aid should be concentrated in the Lima region in order to benefit most people. The national parks he had seen were remote — some with great difficulties of access.

Two reserves, one north and one to the south and both within three hours' driving from Lima, attracted the efforts of the New Zealand advisors — Harold Jacobs and Pat Sheridan successively between 1975 and 1979. Much

Nepalese students Nima Sherpa, Lal Gurung and Shailendra Thakali from the Turangi training centre at the historic Waihohonu Hut in Tongariro National Park.

Peru's Huascaran National Park embraces landscape of the high Andes as well as Huascaran itself, Peru's highest mountain. The puya, a rare and endangered plant of this region, is a relative of the pineapple. After perhaps a hundred and fifty years of growth it extends its flower some ten metres and then dies. The puya is sometimes burned by graziers, who regard its spiny base as a threat to stock.

A park guard in Peru's Paracas National Reserve constructing a lookout above a seal colony, one of the facilities provided to attract the interest of the Peruvian people. Projects such as this were part of the 'learn by doing' approach used by the New Zealand advisors.

the more significant of the two reserves was the large and spectacular Paracas National Reserve in the south, an area of great archaeological and historic interest (site of the landing of liberating forces under General San Martin in 1821) and high natural values; sealions, condor, and flamingoes were among its wildlife.

Jacobs and Sheridan were formerly chief rangers of New Zealand parks. With their advice on planning and management, the two reserves were to be made model conservation units. The greatest educational need was at the 'doing' level, and Jacobs particularly concentrated his early efforts on park guards, using day-to-day situations in the reserves (for example, the planning, design and construction of facilities) as his teaching material. Sheridan, in the latter three years of the project, played a central role in training courses at La Molina University in Lima. By this time, senior Peruvian officers had returned from a study tour in New Zealand. The university courses, concentrating on senior national park management, could fulfill another New Zealand obligation: the broadening of expertise throughout the system. These courses continued beyond the termination of the project, assisted by an annual scholarship awarded by the New Zealand Government.

Western Samoa provides a specific example of the general Pacific Island situation: small and fragile ecosystems, which are vulnerable to development but which, because of their evolutionary interest, have great conservation significance. There are five reserves, each expressive of a different facet of indigenous nature and culture. The largest, O le Pupu-Pu'e National Park, approaches three thousand hectares and contains most of the tropical forest left on Upolu, one of Western Samoa's two main islands. Palolo Deep Marine Reserve, a large hole in a reef, less than two kilometres from the centre of Apia, has an excellent display of corals and tropical fish. The reserves on Mount Vaea include the tomb of Robert Louis Stevenson. Vailima Botanical Garden is a long-term project aimed at representation of the flora of the Pacific Basin, while Togitogiga Recreation Reserve is a very popular picnic area twenty-five kilometres from Apia.

Leaders of Peruvian conservation units in the classroom at La Molina University. The professor in charge of the course had been on a New Zealand study tour.

Left: The coast of the O le Pupu-pu'e (literally, 'from the hill to the sea') National Park in Western Samoa. Here a lava flow has plunged into the sea.

Below: The collapse of part of a lava tube has created the entrance to Pe'a Pe'a Cave in O le Pupu-pu'e National Park.

Above: The tomb of Robert Louis Stevenson is set in the Memorial Reserve near the summit of Mount Vaea, one of two reserves on the mountain.

Below: With New Zealand advice and guidance Samoan park staff built this visitor centre in traditional style.

The objectives of New Zealand assistance were defined following a preliminary visit by John Mazey, supervising ranger of New Zealand National Parks in 1978. Yet another chief ranger of New Zealand parks was established in Western Samoa, with his family, for much of 1979 and 1980. Rex Mossman's work was devoted to the building of a reserves-orientated operating group within Western Samoa's reserves management.

As in Peru, day-to-day situations were the training material, with a strong emphasis on park interpretation and public relations. A visitor centre, complete with displays, was designed and built within the national park. Interpretative pamphlets were designed and produced. A later outcome of Mossman's experience has been a training manual orientated more generally to the needs of South Pacific island situations.

Whether in Western Samoa, Peru or Nepal, there was a particular 'style' to the work of the New Zealanders; chief rangers who knew about mixing concrete, led by example and were themselves pleased to officiate at a concrete mixer. Practicality of approach, helpfulness and cultural sensitivity were all mentioned with appreciation during discussions on technical aid in national park development at the third World Congress on National Parks.

Assistance given in Western Samoa lay within a general initiative in the Pacific carried forward by both New Zealand and Australia. In 1971, at the suggestion of the Minister of Lands, Duncan McIntyre, a presentation on national parks was given to the leaders of South Pacific nations, meeting in Wellington. The first South Pacific Conference on National Parks and Reserves, in 1975, was hosted jointly by the South Pacific Commission and the New Zealand Government. Between 1976 and 1979, when the second South Pacific Conference was organised by the Australian and New South Wales Governments, the two countries conducted joint seminars. The third South Pacific Conference was held in Apia in 1975, arranged by the Government of Western Samoa. Mossman organised the post-conference course on training — the central theme of the New Zealanders' contribution, wherever they had been.

And it was McCaskill's interest in training that had taken him to the United States half a century before the meeting in Samoa. In December 1985 his daughter Margery Blackman, at a ceremony in Dunedin, received the Peter Scott Merit Award made to her late father. The award by the Species Survival Commission of IUCN recognised 'highly significant achievements in conservation'.

Chapter 17

The World Scene in the 1980s

*Ours may be the last generation able to choose
large natural areas to protect.*
— Bali Declaration, 1982

I f the concept of national park, as stated in 1872, struggled to find its
definition in the United States, it met even more difficulty in the world at
large. In the first thirty years only Canada, Australia, and New Zealand followed the American example. The turn of the century saw a step towards the
idea in Southern Africa with the establishment of some game reserves. By the
time of the First World War two of the European nations had created a
different interpretation in the form of strict nature reserves. Foundations were
laid in Africa and action was taken by some Central and South American
nations in the period between the wars, but it was only after the Second
World War that a slow but steady worldwide expansion began, fostered by
a growing recognition of the connection between expanding population and

Glacier National Park in Montana
contains some of the most spectacular
scenery and primitive wilderness of the
Rocky Mountains region. It joins
Canada's Waterton Lakes (one of the
earliest-established parks) across the
border. Both parks lie within the
Nearctic biogeographical realm.

technology on the one hand, and declining wild nature on the other. Growth accelerated after the first World Conference on National Parks in 1962.

It is notable that it was the 'frontier' countries that led in the establishment of parks. On the frontier, quite literally, lay the cutting edge of nature's destruction. Canada set up Glacier National Park in 1886 and Banff in 1887, and Australia established the Royal and Ku-ring-gai Chase parks in New South Wales in 1886 and 1894.

In 1870 the world's population was one thousand three hundred million, that of the USA, about forty million, and of New Zealand three-quarters of a million. The British Empire was at its zenith and British rule in India appeared secure. An accommodation had long been reached with the maharajahs and princes, some of whose hunting reserves were later to become the nuclei of national parks in India. Africa was a vast and largely unknown continent, its people living in islands surrounded by a sea of nature. The journeys of Burke, Speke and others to find the source of the Nile took place in the 1870s and 1880s.

In Europe, save for the French Republic, monarchies and aristocracies governed society. Their hunting reserves encompassed a few of nature's remnants. Some of these, too, were later to become national parks. But by and large, original nature had departed. The landscape was basically cultural. The battle of humanity and nature had been fought out, fortunately in pre-technological times. Prior to 1914 European initiatives in conservation were few and, with the exception of two governments, came from the private sector. The British National Trust began acquiring land for nature reserves in 1895. A similar movement started in the Netherlands in 1905 and four years later in Germany. In 1912 a French group purchased a modest eighty-two hectares for the Les Sept-Îles bird reserve.

The Swedes and the Swiss acted at government level. North of the Arctic Circle, in areas traversed by nomadic Sami, Sweden established four national parks in 1909. These represented all existing habitats of Lapland and contained most species of flora and fauna typical of the northern subarctic and arctic regions. These national parks are today larger than any others in Europe

The Swiss National Park (1914), one of the first in Europe, is an example of the strict nature reserve with scientific objectives. Such reserves contrast with the Yellowstone approach, which seeks to manage for public enjoyment as well as science and preservation.

and, with additions that bring the total area to over eight hundred thousand hectares, comprise the largest wilderness in Europe. Stora Sjöfallet, in central Sweden, was also established at that time.

The Swiss National Park — seventeen thousand hectares enclosing fifteen valleys separated by mountains up to three thousand metres — was created in 1914. Conceived as an alpine field laboratory for sustained biological research in an area to be unaffected by human action, the Swiss initiative was an important conceptual shift from the Yellowstone model: this park was to be dedicated to science. A strong research emphasis was also given to the objectives of the Swedish national parks.

Research was certainly part of the Yellowstone intention but an even stronger emphasis was given to public use. The Swiss defined, for the first time, one of the three dominant purposes, which operate singly or together: conservation for recreational, educational or cultural benefit; conservation of species, ecosystems and landscapes; or conservation for scientific studies of unaffected nature. This latter 'European' model belongs also to the policies of the Soviet Union.

The Czarist regime of Russia had long given protection to Askania-Nova in the Ukraine, now a fragment in a vast agricultural region. Bialowieza, on the Polish border, with the last forest of its kind in Central Europe and a refuge for the European bison since the fourteenth century, had enjoyed some form of protection for much longer. Indeed, it may be the oldest reserve in the world. The present Bialowieza National Park, created in 1919, extends across the border to become the most famous national park in Poland.

Forty years after Yellowstone, as the First World War engulfed Europe, the concept had won through in some of the 'young' developing countries and some hard experience had been acquired. There were initiatives in Europe but Argentina was the only country to take action in South America, and, in Central America, only Mexico had acted. Worldwide, there was little government movement towards national parks. Whole continents were without either the concept or policy of reservation. Population growth and technical power were both accelerating. The internal-combustion engine, electrical engineering, the motorcar and aeroplane had all arrived. The world's population in 1914 was one thousand eight hundred million. About forty national parks had been created in forty years.

In the thick of war and revolution, between 1916 and 1920, Russia created four reserves, including one on the shores of Lake Baikal and the Astrakhan Reserve of the Volga Delta. By 1920 the Russian Revolution was a major fact of European life, to be followed, in the brief twenty-one years between the wars, by economic depression and the rise of German nationalism, which swept Europe and the world into the second conflict.

The period was less than propitious for nature reservation in Europe. Nonetheless, a number of small reserves were created in Britain, the Netherlands, Ireland, Denmark, Germany, France and Finland. Of greater significance were the first signs that governments were finding merit in the national park idea, even if proclamation was not a guarantee of funds and manpower. Spain declared two parks, in the Pyrenees and the Cantabrian Mountains; Italy four, including Gran Paradiso of the west Italian Alps, royal hunting reserve of the House of Savoy. The chamois and ibex would in future be preserved, not hunted. Iceland, site of Europe's largest glacier, created one

Plitvice Lakes National Park in Yugoslavia encompasses a series of lakes and beautiful forest and mountain scenery. First established in 1949, and within the Palaearctic biogeographical realm, Plitvice is now a World Heritage site.

park in its realm of ice and volcanic fire. To the east, the USSR continued to extend its reservation of ecosystems for scientific research. Romania established Retezat, an alpine park in the Carpathian mountains, in 1935.

This growing government support was important, indeed vital, and it continued to strengthen. But the greatest advance involved the African treasure-house of wildlife. Here, on the subdeserts and savannahs, in the bush veldts, and open forests, in the equatorial rainforest, around the salt water and fresh-water lakes and in the vast swamps of the mighty rivers, lived more vertebrate species than anywhere else on land. Offshore was Madagascar, whose distinct-ively different biology had arisen from twenty million years of isolation. Native peoples in the African cradle of man's evolution had long reached a balance with nature, but three hundred years of European influence had led to habitat destruction and large-scale slaughter of animals for commercial markets. In harsh and finely balanced environments, the benefits of medicine, fostering increase in both human and animal populations, and the intro-duction of cattle and goats, unsuited to the tropical environment, had created a deterioration and loss of carrying capacity. Notwithstanding, Africa was still at the turn of the century the dominion of the animals.

The first nature reserves dated to 1897, when game reserves were set up in Natal at Umfolozi and Hluhluwe, habitat of the white rhinoceros, third largest of the terrestrial mammals. Nearby, on the coast of the Indian Ocean, a reserve including Lake Saint Lucia, an immense saltwater estuary with a rich bird life, was established to conserve hippopotami.

The next moves in Africa involved both Yellowstone itself and the Euro-pean scientific model. King Albert of the Belgians visited Yellowstone in 1919. There must be something truly inspirational about the place. Out of talks there, came the Albert National Park in the Belgian Congo, now Virunga National Park in the Republic of Zaire. It was established in 1925, one of four in Belgian-administered Africa systematically planned for scientific research. Virunga, a huge area straddling the equator, home of the mountain gorilla, and ranging from equatorial lowland forest to the permanent snow of Ruwenzori, is a complete and intact ecosystem complex.

A year later South Africa created Kruger National Park from its Sabie game reserve, a large area of low veld, savannah and bushland south of the Limpopo River. Then came the institutional action that was urgently needed if the splendid initiatives were to be extended to encompass a sufficient represent-ation of habitats to give hope of survival for the animal wealth of the African treasure-house. The 1933 London Conference on the Conservation of African Flora and Fauna provided the launching pad for the general development of parks in Africa. Dinder, east of the Blue Nile and not far from the Ethiopian border, was one of three parks created in 1935 in the Anglo-Egyptian Sudan. Major progress awaited the ending of the Second World War.

The laying of foundations in Africa was one of the notable aspects of the inter-war period. There were similar stirrings on two other continents. In South America, Argentina expanded Nahuel Huapi in 1922, and added three new parks. Brazil established three, including the tropical forests and beautiful vistas of Itatiaia in the Sierra da Mantiqueira. Guyana (then British Guyana) incorporated its spectacular Kaieteur Falls, and, in a region stretching from the Caribbean Sea and over the Cordillera de la Costa, Venezuela reserved the rain forests and brilliant bird life of Henri Pittier National Park. Six new national parks created by Chile included the Juan Fernandez Islands.

Far to the north lay a more famous fleet of islands. Darwin's observations in 1835 of the differences between birds and other animals of the islands of Galapagos had been his strongest argument for the role of natural selection in the origin of species. Ecuador made the islands a national park in 1935, one hundred years after Darwin's visit, to be a part of the history of man's efforts to preserve the record of evolution.

Masked boobies in Ecuador's Galapagos National Park, which was declared in 1935, just one hundred years after the visit of the *Beagle*.

In Asia, too, vital first steps were being taken. The peninsula of Udjung Kulon, south-western Java, was reserved in 1937 by Indonesia to protect the rare Javan rhinoceros. The Baluran animal sanctuary was also established on Java. Fifteen national parks were established in the Philippines. India set up a national park and three wildlife sanctuaries. Malaya established a park, and in Cambodia the magnificent ruins of Angkor Wat were protected.

In 1939 war, the destroyer of resources and the antithesis of conservation, was forced on the world. There were some three hundred protected areas comprising perhaps sixty million hectares, a minuscule fraction of terrestrial areas. Little happened, either in further development of concepts or in the declaration of new national park areas, for over a decade.

The vehicle for future conservation progress was set in motion in the French forest of Fontainbleau in 1948. Here, ninety years earlier, the concern of a group of artists for the beauty of the forest had entered the history of reservation. Part of the forest became protected by law. The International Union for Protection of Nature, established in 1948 at Fontainbleau, was to become the key agent in world-wide reservation. This meeting was the ini-tiative of the Swiss League for Protection of Nature, together with the newly created UNESCO, and the government of France. And behind the Swiss league lay the vision of the naturalist Paul Sarasin, founder of the Swiss National Park.

The great Swiss naturalist Paul Sarasin was a leader in conservation in Europe. This memorial in the Swiss National Park remembers his work in connection with the founding of the park.

In 1948, a very important year, the declaration of the vast Tsavo National Park of two million hectares in East Africa was the first of thirteen superb reservations in a five-year period, including Serengeti in 1951. Here, in habitats ranging from arid, treeless plains to montane forest, was encapsulated something of the original character of eastern Africa within ecosystem areas large enough to sustain the elephant, lion, hippo, crocodile, fox, jackal, hyaena, buffalo, wildebeest, zebra (to mention a few) plus hundreds of species of birds and the smaller animals, reptiles, insects and plants of the region. To the wealth of nature was added scenic splendour: the parks included Murchison Falls, where the Victoria Nile cascades into Lake Albert, and 'the smoke that thunders', Victoria Falls, one of the greatest natural features on earth.

Fontainbleau's IPUN became IUCN, the International Union for Conservation of Nature and Natural Resources, which promoted the shaping of a worldwide system of national parks and protected areas through its Commission on National Parks and Protected Areas, established at Delphi in Greece in 1958, and through regional and international conferences.

In no field of endeavour is it more clear than in the national park movement that the vision of individuals precedes the actions of government: in the United States, Thoreau, Olmsted and John Muir; in Europe, Paul Sarasin. In 1958 it was Tsuyoshi Tamura, of Japan, who proposed the idea of a world conference to the IUCN general assembly. This conference, held in Seattle in 1962, is considered by many to be the birth of the world movement. Ten years later, at the second world conference, E. M. Nicholson, former director of the British Nature Conservancy, was able to look back at the significance of the Seattle meeting, and forward to the now acknowledged place of national parks and protected areas in world conservation strategy:

'I suggest that the birth of the world movement at Seattle in 1962 will rank as a landmark no less decisive than the campfire at Yellowstone. There was launched a close-knit network of parks and of parks people, bound by ties of common interest, co-operation and friendship. It represented a fresh and vigorous mutation of the utmost importance in the national park organism. We can no longer afford to be merely narrow technicians; we are operating at the meeting point between the land (with all the resources of the biosphere) and man (with all his potential and need for fulfilment).'

The second World Conference on National Parks was held at the birthplace of the idea, Yellowstone National Park, in 1972. One hundred years later the campfire was rekindled, symbolically, on a cold and stormy evening, as the lightning of a September storm flickered over the geyser basins and thunder rolled in the mountains that had so deeply impressed the members of the Washburn expedition. The technical sessions took place a little south of Yellowstone, in Grand Teton National Park. There were now some sixteen hundred protected areas covering over two hundred million hectares, a major advance on the eight hundred areas of one hundred and twenty million hectares in 1962. (But world population had grown from three thousand million to almost four thousand million in the ten-year period.) The conference discussed management, administration and education at a level of detail and experience inconceivable ten years earlier. It was a confident meeting, hosted by that most professional of bodies, the US National Park Service. Delegates had only to look from the conference centre to the snowshower banners of approaching winter sweeping across the jagged Tetons to be reminded that their concern was the wheel of nature. Out there the elk herds were moving off the mountains into the valleys. Park managers could talk about natural processes conscious that a huge seasonal movement was unfolding before their eyes.

The Seattle conference had been all enthusiasm and excitement, purpose, principles and values. The exchanges on management had been more a swapping of experience than technical discourse about the state of an art. There was major discussion on the role of international agencies. Alongside the IUCN, the United Nations Educational, Scientific, and Cultural Organisation (UNESCO), the Food and Agriculture Organisation of the United Nations (FAO), the United Nations Environment Programme (UNEP) and the World Wildlife Fund (WWF) were all to play a major role in the expansion during the next two decades.

The confidence of the second world conference was founded on major progress; nowhere more evident than in Africa. Here the newly independent states of Senegal, Cameroon, Chad, Malawi, Tanzania, Uganda, Kenya and Zaire had all set up new national parks. Often the motivation was tourism, which for some had become a major source of income. Action was proposed in other parts of Africa, and Ethiopia had reserved three new areas, including Semien, site of the most dramatic mountain scenery in Africa and habitat of the rare Walia ibex. There were thirty new parks in Latin America, substantial progress in Asia, from Turkey to Thailand, and there were achievements in South-east Asia. There was also progress in industrialised Europe, where public opinion had become more supportive of reservation, but where dense population and lack of original nature led to a variety of approaches — from the German 'Naturparks' to nature reserves and protected areas of fine cultural landscapes in which farming, forestry and recreational hunting and fishing could all be pursued.

That such approaches could be called 'national park', as in the United Kingdom, illustrated the confusion that had evolved since Yellowstone in 1872, as countries adapted their understanding of the concept to widely

Britain's Peak District National Park provides an outstanding example of cultural landscape. Many of Europe's parks are of this kind, in contrast with the philosophy represented in the Yellowstone approach, or by the strict nature reserve.

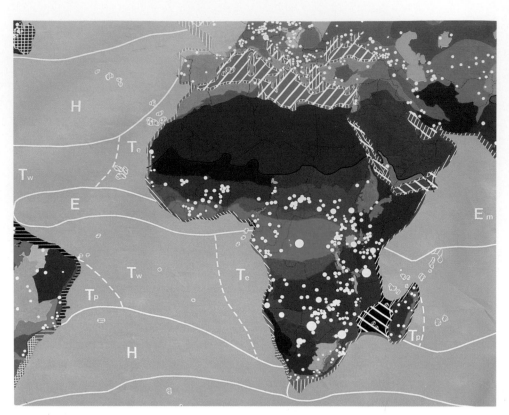

Biogeography and the national parks of Africa, or 'How well do the national parks represent the original ecosystems of natural regions?' Colours distinguish biogeographical provinces within the Afrotropical realm. From the white dots indicating the positions of national parks, a first impression of the representation of nature provided by the parks can be gained, but much scientific work is needed for a full assessment. Shaded areas extending into the oceans represent preliminary biogeographic classification in the seas.

varied circumstances. At its general assembly in New Delhi in 1969, the IUCN agreed to a definition of national park that has since become the broadly accepted statement of principles:

A national park is a relatively large area:
— where one or several ecosystems are not materially altered by human exploitation and occupation, where plant and animal species, geomorphological sites and habitats are of special importance, educative and recreative interest or contain a landscape of great beauty
— where the highest competent authority of the country has taken steps to prevent or to eliminate as soon as possible exploitation or occupation in the whole area and to enforce effectively the respect of ecological, geomorphological or aesthetic features that have led to its establishment
— where visitors are allowed to enter under special conditions, for inspirational, educative, cultural and recreative purposes.

The third World Congress on National Parks (curiously, 'Congress' replaced 'Conference'), held on the island of Bali in 1982, could again be presented with an account of progress: there were now two thousand two hundred parks in one hundred and twenty countries, with a combined total area of almost four hundred million hectares. Progress indeed, but for the first time the conference was able to assess this against a yardstick — the concept of 'biogeography', the result of a decade of work by biological scientists associated with IUCN. The national parks of the world had, on the whole, been selected in a piecemeal and opportunistic way. With the other protected areas, they had become the libraries of the original genetic stock of the planet. Now they could be examined critically as representatives of ecological regions.

Biogeography can be called the study of ecological similarity. Groups of ecosystems alike in appearance, composition and structure can be matched to vast geographic regions, or 'realms'. Significant differences in flora, fauna or vegetation structure occurring within the realms leads to a further sub-division into biogeographic 'provinces'. Within a province, still finer groupings arising from differences in ecosystems can be assigned to 'regions' and 'districts'. The grouping of the ecosystems is based primarily on vegetation, but because this is influenced fundamentally by climate and soil, their relationship is also expressed by the ecological groups. Climate, soil and vegetation also produce habitat, so biogeography draws the whole of the faunal world into its classification. The Bali conference was able to assess the representation (and the problems) of the eight vast biogeographic realms of the planet; the Nearctic (North American), the Palaearctic (North Asian), the Afrotropical (tropical African), the Indomalayan (India and South-East Asia), the Oceanian (Pacific Ocean), the Australian, the Antarctic (which includes New Zealand) and the Neotropical (Central and South America).

Some two hundred provinces were identified within the realms, and analyses of the number and extent of protected areas within each province permitted a crude assessment of areas that should have a priority for action. It was recognised that the tool for measurement provided by biogeography was less than perfect, suffering not least from the fact that far less than half of the world's species have ever been described. It was also recognised that time is running out for the protection of nature. The critical areas were clear: tropical forest systems in South-East Asia, India and the Himalayan slopes, East and West Africa, eastern South America and Central America, and the Pacific Islands; an urgent need to implement international action to combat the spread of deserts, including the establishment of protected areas as a means of understanding and control; wetlands were in danger in many places.

And there was the question of protection of the most fragile and sensitive ecosystems of all — the life and environment of Antarctica. This continent, larger than Europe, with an ice shelf the size of France, is in some respects, a paradox. The interior is a lifeless desert, which contains nine-tenths of the world's fresh water. The melted water from ice and snowfields freshens surrounding seas. Surface sea flows to the north, meeting warmer and saltier water at what is known as the Antarctic Convergence.

The nutrient flows created in these water masses support krill, a shrimp-like crustacean, in vast numbers. The largest school of krill ever tracked has been estimated to contain ten million tonnes. Krill, in turn, supports whales, seals, penguins, seabirds, fish and squid. It is estimated that one hundred million birds breed each year in the Antarctic region. Within the vastness of Artarctica, land suited to the breeding requirements of the birds, including penguins, and seals is very scarce. Competition is fierce and the vulnerability of animals of the Southern Ocean has already been shown by the dismal history of whaling and sealing. In the face of this record, international interest in the harvesting of krill and in mineral exploitation has become a matter of grave concern to conservation.

The Antarctic Treaty, which became effective in 1961, provides that the continent will only be used for peaceful purposes, with concentration on scientific research. The treaty's safeguards for conservation of flora and fauna have been effective. While acknowledging this, the second world conference promoted the vision of Antarctica and its surrounding seas as the first world park, under United Nations administration. By 1982, pressure for exploitation and the acknowledged consideration of a minerals regime made it clear that

Australia, the island continent, is a complete biogeographic realm in itself. The Great Barrier Reef Marine Park covers a vast three hundred thousand square kilometres. Its reefs are composed of over three hundred species of coral providing habitat for an unmatched range of marine life. The Great Barrier Reef Marine Park was made a World Heritage site in 1981.

The future and protection of the fragile and sensitive ecosystems of the Antarctic and its surrounding oceans are matters of great concern to science and conservation. The second World Conference on National Parks promoted the concept of a World Park under United Nations administration.

the vision was politically unattainable. The conference sought enhanced conservation status that would ensure long-term protection, maintain intrinsic values, ensure compatibility of human activities and establish an internationally protected area appropriate to the unique character and values of Antarctica.

The vision of a World Park of the Antarctic had met the realities of pressures on resources, politics and population — the emerging groundswell facing the conference in every direction. But success stories there were: Project Tiger in India, conservation of vicuña in the Pampa Galeras of Peru, national park policy in Alaska and the use of biogeographic principles in the selection of national parks in Indonesia.

At the turn of the century the population of tigers in India had been estimated at forty thousand. In 1972 there were fewer than two thousand of the striped grace that had inspired such fear, admiration and poetry. Indira Gandhi, in launching Project Tiger in 1973, went to the core of the problem: 'Its habitat, threatened by human intrusion, commercial forestry and cattle grazing, must first be made inviolate.' In the next seven years US$10,000,000 was spent by the Indian national and state governments. Tiger reserves were selected, with large core areas, surrounded by buffer zones, representing as many biogeographic types as possible in the range of tiger habitat and in areas where concentrated conservation action was feasible.

Management plans sought to eliminate human exploitation and disturbance from core areas, to restore ecosystems to natural functions and to monitor changes. Poaching was halted — not without assaults, ambushes and loss of life. Forty villages and sixty thousand people were resettled and fully rehabilitated. In 1979, the census of tigers was above three thousand.

The vicuña, one of two species of wild South American lamoids, had populated the Peruvian highlands in the times of the Inca Empire. In yet one more example of the mismanagement of ecosystems by an imported culture, these animals had declined after Spanish conquest to a quarter of a million in 1957 and fewer than ten thousand in 1968. Again the programme for recovery focused on habitat. The Reserve Nacional de Pampa Galeras was established in 1967, poaching was controlled and local people were involved in both the management and the benefits of the programme. Five centuries after the Incas, it again became possible to contemplate the vicuña drives that had once been a custom of the people of the area.

The Alaskan National Interest Lands Conservation Act of 1980 was the result of ten years of planning and politics. In this single piece of legislation the United States Congress gave permanent protection to forty-two million hectares of outstanding natural areas as national parks (including national reserves), national forests, wild and scenic rivers and wildlife refuges. These protected areas provided habitat for an estimated four hundred million birds and mammals, including caribou, grizzly, brown and polar bears, muskoxen, wolves, wolverines, moose, Dall sheep, mountain goats, seals, sea otters, walrusses and whales. While conservation planning, all too often, can only be focused on remnants uncommitted to development, the basis of the Alaskan Act had been studies based on extensive resource data, which identified both developmental potential and conservation objectives, giving weight to conservation and seeking to resolve conflicts.

Project Tiger and the saving of the vicuña were both rescue operations; case studies of human population pressure and the management of habitat, of situations all too common in Asia, Africa and South America. In contrast was the Alaskan initiative; conservation as it can now be practised in only a few places. The biogeographic planning of a reservation system in Indonesia, a very populous country, pointed to a government's determination to build the representation of its ecosystems into national land use, as a basic element of conservation strategy in recognition that action deferred in the face of pressure on resources is to lose the base from which recovery can be built.

These examples stood out from a general background. Population pressure on resources, worldwide, was remorselessly closing the door to the ideal of adequate representation of species diversity, not only in the making of new reservations but also in the maintenance of existing parks. A world population of under five thousand million in 1982 was expected to reach six thousand million within eighteen years — in the year 2000.

The difficulties were greatest where population growth was fastest. In Africa the 1972 population of four hundred million became five hundred and fifty million in 1982. United Nations projections anticipated a doubling of

Vicuña in Pampa Galeras National Reserve in the Peruvian Highlands.

Tanzania's famous Serengeti National Park supports the greatest concentration of plains animals left in the world, and the migrations of the great herds are one of the most inspiring of wildlife spectacles. Serengeti is a World Heritage site in the Afrotropical biogeographic realm.

Tourists approaching a rhino in Nepal's Royal Chitwan National Park. Tiger, leopard, sloth bear and marsh crocodile as well as rhino are among Royal Chitwan's important animal populations. This national park is a World Heritage site in the Indomalayan biogeographic realm.

1972 figures to nearly nine hundred million by the turn of the century. Here, the poverty-driven effort to extract more food and fuel from poor-quality land was turning this to barren land. Barren land was turning to desert. In North Africa the annual loss to desertification was one hundred thousand hectares. Half of the population south of the Sahara was dependant on wildlife, including fish, insects and snails, as a source of protein. The forests of both West and East Africa were being converted rapidly by forest farming, timber exploitation and, in East Africa, by the demand for firewood. While some post-independence African governments had strongly affirmed and progressed the conservation established by former colonial administrations, others had squandered previous effort. The destruction, poaching and administrative vacuum accompanying political upheaval and civil war had ruined or regressed many national parks that had formerly been jewels of Africa.

The Indomalayan biogeographic region of southern and eastern Asia is one of great biotic richness. The forests of Indonesia, for example, are estimated to contain as many as twenty-five thousand species of higher plants, five hundred species of mammals, fifteen hundred species of birds and possibly one million species of vertebrates and invertebrates. Protected areas of the region numbered some three hundred and covered twenty-two million hectares in 1982. Population, almost three thousand million in 1982, had grown almost as rapidly as that of Africa, from under two thousand million in 1962. It was expected to be approaching four thousand million by the year 2000. There were forecasts that the forests of Thailand, Malaysia and Nepal will vanish in this century. Barely two per cent of India's forests approach natural richness. The Food and Agriculture Organisation of the United Nations attributes the loss of some five million hectares of Asian forest, annually, to burning and temporary cultivation. The habitat destruction of the Vietnam War had been added to the pressures of subsistence living and conversion to man-made forest. The national parks of the Indomalayan region were in danger of becoming islands whose maintenance and protection was increasingly difficult. The prospect of further expansion seemed remote.

The magnificent cataracts of Iguazu lie within a World Heritage site comprised of two national parks, one in Brazil, one in Argentina, which abut along the Iguazu River. The setting of semi-tropical forest and the thunder of waters are long remembered by tourists to this representative of the Neotropical biogeographic realm.

If forecasts for the third region of high population growth, the Neotropical realm of South America, were less gloomy, no more confidence could be given to the long term. The continental average of under two per cent in reserved areas, which had resulted from rapid progress through the 1970s, was still far too low, and this included Venezuela and Chile at about ten per cent, and Peru at seven per cent. While Brazil had greatly expanded protection in the Amazon region to over ten million hectares, with planned extensions of almost seven million hectares, the habitats of the endemic birds, plants, and primates from the forests of the Atlantic coasts had suffered great destruction. Endangered populations of marmosets, lion tamarins and several species of monkeys were at precarious levels. The general drive for economic development in South America had created threats to existing parks from highway construction, colonisation, mining, oil exploration, native populations, pollution, dams and timber extraction.

Venezuela's three-million-hectare Canaima National Park is the setting of the Angel Falls, the world's highest waterfall.

Threats to national parks from developmental projects were a growing problem, nowhere better illustrated than in the Everglades National Park of the United States. The Everglades was once an immense freshwater drainage system, over two hundred kilometres long, flowing across the southern third of Florida into the Gulf of Mexico. The fluctuating seasonal water flows into the great swamps supported a diverse ecosystem, particularly abundant with fish and wading birds. Damming, water diversion and drainage in the source areas of Everglades water has greatly reduced bird and fish populations, creating the prospect of colonisation of the former swamps by foreign plants and setting the stage for change of the ecosystem. The US National Park Service has a team of resource managers and research scientists engaged in monitoring and the planning of proposals for recovery. Elsewhere in the United States, and around the world, the manipulation of water resources, air pollution, including acid rain, grazing, timber extraction, oil and gas exploration, over-pressure of tourism, hunting, roading and incompatible use of adjacent lands are among the human activities that can destroy the remaining three per cent of the world's inheritance of wilderness.

Whether population growth, progress with protection, or the growing threats to the integrity of the national parks, the Bali congress was presented with a bleak picture.

From the invention of agriculture had come the first civilisation and cities of six thousand years ago. Civilisation, the product of wilderness, had spread from Asia Minor across Europe to the New World. Here the idea of national park had been discovered; an institutional statement about man and nature arising from the realisation of the values of declining wilderness. Explored, extended and modified, the idea had evolved over time into a period of accelerated resource use. Now there was three per cent left globally, in a variable and imperfect representation of ecosystems. The vision of principle that might have been represented in an International Park of the Antarctic had failed.

As many as one million species may become extinct by the end of the century. The next decade would probably provide the last opportunity to conserve adequately large samples of relatively undisturbed biomes and ecosystems. So much for five hundred million years of evolution.

'In wilderness is the preservation of the world,' said Henry David Thoreau. His intuitive statement stood confirmed by the insights of the years since Yellowstone. As the preservation of natural ecological processes and of species and their diversity, it can be understood readily when so many plants and animals are endangered. In preserving species and their diversity, we preserve the wild genetic resources. Far less than half of the world's species have ever been described, so the genes are retained in the library, as it were, for future study. Wild genes have been used to improve many crops — one of the most notable examples being the resistance to disease and increase of yield of rice conferred by a wild species. As the cultivars of the wild rice *Oryza nivara* are grown over thirty million hectares of east Asia, the benefit of this wild gene is enormous. In the gene libraries of the world's protected areas lie incalculable future potential and benefits for pharmaceuticals, to pest resistance, and to faster growing and taller forms of plants.

Less readily appreciated is the value of the protected area in retaining the natural regulation, resilience, diversity and production of ecosystems. Manipulation of water flows entering the Florida Everglades causes a severe reduction in the numbers of wading birds and adversely affects a productive fishery. Habitat destruction causes decline of the tiger. The introduction of cattle and goats, animals foreign to African ecosystems, causes decline of habitat and reduces the total yield of the ecosystems, including the availability of protein.

While the practical values of erosion control, flood protection and preservation of water quality are plain, the spiritual and cultural values of protected areas are less evident. A national park or protected area is of a country's essence — the combination of parent rock, soil, landscape, climate and plant and animal species that have evolved over time and occurs nowhere else. As cultures derive from the interaction of people and land, and as a protected area is by definition a place of history, the cultural importance of a national park is profound. It is profound in another sense, identified by the 'Primitives', and asserted in the character of Robinson Crusoe. It is connected with the vigour, initiative, imagination and long-term survival of a people. This derives from the opportunities to engage the wilderness on nature's terms.

That national parks and protected areas provide for research, education, inspiration and less hazardous forms of recreation than scaling a mountain face, is well known. There are economic values, whether calculable or not, in all human contact with, and use of, protected areas. Tourism, the value of which is more readily calculated, is sometimes perceived as the only source of income. Even so, this can be sufficient, as for a period in Kenya, to be a major source of national wealth. Well managed, the income from tourism, and all the other less calculable incomes, can be derived in perpetuity. This contrasts with the view of the exploiter — that protection involves 'locking up' the resource. Rather, it is a screening process to sift out the activities that would destroy the sustainable incomes. The last value of the national park is 'existence', the benefit comforting people who may never go to the park. History shows that they are willing to pay nonetheless because to them the national park invokes the whole of nature.

From the wealth of information presented at the Bali conference, a sobering summary of the world scene in the 1980s emerged. The demands of the world's still-growing population on the resources of the planet are such that adequate reservation of wild nature may not now be possible. The declaration of the congress concluded that: 'Ours may be the last generation to choose large natural areas to protect.' Against this background, the fundamental importance of protected areas to conservation strategy stood out boldly.

Chapter 18

The Future

Wilderness is the raw material out of which Man has hammered the artefact called civilisation. Wilderness was never an homogeneous raw material . . . and the resulting artefacts are very diverse. These differences in the end-product are known as cultures.
— Aldo Leopold, 1949

Study how a society uses its land, and you can come to pretty reliable conclusions as to what its future will be.
— E. H. F. Schumacher, 1973

The story told here is a story of voyages — of Polynesians to Aotearoa, and of their thousand-year voyage of discovery in a land like no other, of the shaping of Polynesian into Maori culture by the nature of the land. Humans had come very late into fully evolved ecosystems in which mammals had no part. Maori culture evolved from an interaction that had no parallel, since in all the continental world the interdependence and interrelationship of humans and nature had proceeded already for millenia, if not for millions of years.

The City of Wellington from Mount Victoria.

The chemical methanol plant in the Waitara Valley is one of several large modern industrial installations processing natural gas.

This story is also one of European voyages, first of Tasman, Cook and the other explorer navigators, then of European migration, and of another period of learning and shaping. This time the clash between culture and land was powerful, and the changes great.

Most of these changes have taken place in just one hundred and fifty years. New Zealand's forested landscapes have been transformed to grassland. The plants and animals of a world from which the islands had been long separated have been introduced. Modern towns and cities, the products of Western technology and European tradition, have been built, great industries established and a transportation network put in place. A multi-cultural society of more than three million people has emerged.

The period has witnessed more change than had occurred previously in all the thousands of years since the advent of agriculture. The technology of the Industrial Revolution has transformed the earth and human society. Motor transport, the application of electricity, aircraft, telecommunications, enormous increases in the application of energy, and widespread use of chemicals and fertilisers all belong to the period. Recent decades ushered in the Information Revolution. The ability of the computer to process enormous amounts of data, generate useful information and control machines is, according to some, still in early stages. The computer and dazzling advances in telecommunications go hand in hand.

Like technical development, population growth appears still to be accelerating. Most forecasters attempt to lift the veil and to peer cautiously only as far as a projection of trends of the recent past can be taken by judgement and prudence. In 1887 the world's population was fewer than one and a half billion; 1987 finds it approaching five billion. United Nations experts anticipate a world population of more than six billion by the year 2000. A population in excess of nine billion by 2050 is possible. Most of the increase will take place in Africa, the Middle East, Latin America and southern and eastern Asia. An estimated growth of one and a half billion by the turn of the century in these regions compares with an estimated one hundred and forty million for Europe, the Soviet Union, North America, Japan, Australia and New Zealand.

The inexorable pressure of growing population in Africa, southern Asia and South America, together with the knowledge that only three per cent of terrestrial areas were protected, led the 1982 World Congress on National Parks to the conclusion that: 'Ours may be the last generation able to choose large natural areas to protect.' Of the regions with a relatively low population growth, however, Europe and large parts of the Soviet Union cannot consider reservation of 'natural' areas because few natural or near natural ecosystems still exist. The national parks of Europe are the finest examples of cultural landscape, but they do not contain original nature. Of the remainder, those of North America and Australia represent continental situations that have been influenced by many thousands of years of human and animal modification, while Japanese social and economic development programmes have impacted heavily on its natural environment. Unmodified or even partially modified original nature is rare indeed.

While gloomy predictions have been made about the undeniable facts of world population growth, it is management of the land and sea resources available to sustain the people of the planet that will determine whether or not forecasts of gloom prove to be correct. Some believe that resource pressures will be unbearable, and that the outcome will be the chronic environmental degradation revealed in accelerated soil erosion, aggravated flooding, reduced crop harvest, declining air and water quality and loss of wild species.

They point to destruction of tropical rainforest, currently running above ten million hectares per year, to the fact that one-fifth of the world's cropland is losing top soil, and that twenty-five thousand plant species and more than three thousand animal species are threatened with extinction. As a result of the use of fossil fuels, the carbon dioxide content of the atmosphere is growing, while loss of forest reduces the assimilative capacity of the earth's systems. A doubling of carbon dioxide content could induce significant climatic change by the middle of the next century, with considerable modification of wind and rainfall patterns. This scenario translates into poverty, hunger, economic decline and social disintegration on a vast scale.

Critics of such projections say that they are trend projections of the conditions likely to develop if there was neither change in public policy nor advances with the technologies that can ameliorate the trends.

Two worldwide initiatives aimed at fostering the public policy which would counteract such adverse trends have been launched. The first of these was the World Conservation Strategy of the IUCN endorsed by the General Assembly of the United Nations in 1979. The strategy has three main goals: to maintain essential ecological processes and life-support systems, to preserve genetic diversity and to ensure the sustainable utilisation of species and ecosystems.

These objectives are pursued through national conservation strategies developed by individual states from study of their own circumstances, and by international conventions to which nations bind themselves by treaty. The conventions deal, among other issues, with international trade in endangered species of wild fauna and flora, with conservation of migratory species of wild animals, and with the unique natural and cultural areas that are of such international value they are part of the heritage of all mankind — the World Heritage Convention.

The Ross Shelf and Mount Erebus.
   While New Zealand has been classified as a province of the Antarctic biogeographical realm, many other associations with Antarctica confer a special responsibility for conservation on the white continent and in the Southern Ocean.

The second of the world policy initiatives is the World Charter for Nature, which elaborates the obligations of interdependence between humans and nature implied in the World Conservation Strategy. Appropriately, the charter is displayed near the Declaration of Human Rights in the headquarters of the United Nations in New York, suggesting correctly that the stewardship of nature is a precondition for the rights of humanity.

The inspiration for the charter came not from the West but from Zaire. 'The seas, the oceans, the upper atmosphere belong to the human community . . . I would suggest the establishment of a Charter for Nature . . . If Zaire were asked to be a pilgrim for environmental protection, this we would be willing to be,' said President Sese Seko Mobutu at the opening of a general assembly of the IUCN in Kinshasa in 1975. New Zealand was one of the first countries to give full support in the United Nations debates, emphasising the need to include the marine environment and to recognise 'the contribution that can be made by non-government organisations working in conjunction with governments, in developing a national environmental strategy'. Given the involvement of the citizen in the history of conservation in New Zealand, this was an appropriate comment. New Zealand support for the charter was justified alike by an active involvement in the work of the IUCN, by the aid programmes that have assisted international nature protection and by the international standing of New Zealand's national parks and their administration.

Support for the World Conservation Strategy, the Charter for Nature, the conventions, and global efforts to anticipate and contain future dangers is no more than the duty of a responsible member of the international community. New Zealand, however, faces a challenge to culture and conservation that lies beyond the discharge of such responsibilities, a challenge deriving from a unique inheritance, a responsibility to its biogeographic region (the Antarctic realm) and a position of extraordinary advantage derived from the world scene and the history that has been described.

Against the world background, New Zealand's advantages and opportunities stand in clear relief. In one hundred years a superb system of national parks has been constructed. The Protected Natural Areas programme has the potential to enhance a protected areas system reflecting the ecological diversity of our country's ancient biological inheritance. Such a system, taken together with the national parks and the third major element represented by the nature reserves of the offshore islands, would be something of which any nation could be proud.

Very soon New Zealand may have among the best remaining relatively unbroken areas of rainforest in the world. In world terms these are the forests of a separate stream of evolution, an inheritance of antiquity, a kind of time capsule. Scientists of the world authority consider Waipoua Forest Sanctuary, Whirinaki State Forest and Pureora State Forest to be the most magnificent to be seen anywhere, in every sense national treasures, and a superb part of the natural heritage of mankind.

With nearly twenty per cent of its territory under nature protection or recreation availability policies, it would seem that New Zealand possesses already endowments beyond the dreams of many nations. It must always be remembered, however, that much of the heritage lies in the mountains, where protection is essential for soil and water conservation, and hence, in the long term, for our survival.

Waitutu State Forest, under investigation in 1987 as a possible extension to Fiordland National Park, is a forty-five thousand hectare tract lying between Lakes Hauroko and Poteriteri and the southern coast. There are few, if any, comparable areas left. This, and the continuity of natural ecosystems, gives Waitutu major national representational significance.

The heritage is, in fact, strongly biased towards mountain and other unproductive land. The history of European settlement and agriculture in New Zealand has ensured that the protected area system is lacking in its representation of lowland forest, that extensive lowland areas have been swept clean of their distinctive biological signature, that only scattered remnants remain in other farming areas, and that the small areas of lowland forest that are left may be too small for long-term viability. As well as lowland forest, representation of the heritage is deficient in wetland reservation, in coastal, especially sand-dune communities, mangrove reservation and in the tussock grasslands that once covered vast areas of the South Island.

In our cultural landscapes — the landscapes of production — the losses have been already far too great, and these are as much a part of the story of Aotearoa as the national parks and reserves. After one hundred and fifty years, learning by loss has run its course.

If we are to transform European conservation into New Zealand conservation, if we are to honour the trust of Te Heuheu Tukino, and if we are to discharge our heritage responsibility to our multicultural future, we must strike out in a new cultural direction and take some specific actions without further delay. Schumacher's assertion that a people's future is foretold in the use of their land can also be read to mean that the path to a great culture, or to mediocrity and extinction, is shaped by land policy. That message can be read back from the now-arid heartlands of ancient civilisations, from African famines and from advancing deserts.

Love of land has on many occasions enriched the pragmatic history of the reservation system. There was an immense symbolism in the action of Te Heuheu Tukino and his people. The gift of Tongariro sprang from the values of one thousand years of interaction with Aotearoa. The gift symbolised the handing on of these values. They could not be explained to Europeans, who after another hundred years can only, and with effort, begin to sense the totality of Maori 'oneness' with the land. Subsequent history has been a story of a slow, step-by-step wakening to individuality and distinctive beauty: immense seascapes, soaring mountains, floods, avalanches, harsh light, the wind, and always at the centre of controversy — the biological signature of the

Extensive stands of kahikatea were once a distinctive feature of lowland New Zealand, but in most areas these have been reduced to scattered remnants. Only on the West Coast does the opportunity remain to protect relatively large tracts of New Zealand's tallest tree.

The native sedge plant, pingao, once provided splashes of green and gold along our coastline and was highly prized by Maori people for weaving. Introduced marram grass today crowds out this beautiful plant, which now is found extensively only on the most isolated coasts.

Birchwood Ponds, Ahuriri Valley, North Otago.

High-country wetlands such as these include valuable habitat for animals and plants. Decline of wetlands throughout New Zealand has reached a serious position. In the high country, as in the lowlands, there is an urgent need to survey and protect key areas — an objective of the Protected Natural Areas programme.

Mangrove swamps are a distinctive natural feature north of Kawhia Harbour on the west coast of the North Island and Whakatane on the east. Very often their significance has not been realised and they have become a cheap source of stock food or the site of rubbish dumps.

Right: Kapuatai Peat Dome in the Hauraki Plains.
  Protection of this scientifically important feature contributes to landscape character in a production area.

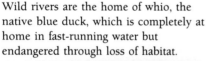

Wild rivers are the home of whio, the native blue duck, which is completely at home in fast-running water but endangered through loss of habitat.

inheritance — the forest of no other land; the plants of a lonely voyage through unimaginable spans of time.

Yet there is a precondition without which there will be, in the long term, no conservation future at all. The precondition is faithful maintenance of the ethic embodied in the National Parks Act. Earlier chapters have tracked the path of history from the passing of the Scenery Reservation Act — the European reaction to destruction of the forest that was to the first generation of European New Zealanders, the essence of the character of their country. When bird life declined, offshore islands became sanctuaries. It became evident that deer and goats were a serious threat to the forests and the soil and water values dependent on them. A requirement for extermination of introduced plants and animals was built into the ethic.

Later came the realisation that the whole of reservation was skewed towards scenic values in mountain lands, and that beneath the groundwork of scenery lay the ecosystems. These had been shaped and honed by at least eighty million years of isolation, and they could not be recreated. Reservations of ecosystems became a requirement of the ethic. Loss of coastline values led to an emphasis on coastal reservation. When the wild rivers, foaming in the sombre browns and greens of their forests, so distinctive of wet, steep New Zealand, had become too few, there was yet another reaction to loss fuelled by the reassessed values of a new generation. A means of identifying and preserving wild and scenic rivers was created.

There is still much to do, and with time running out, if an opportunity of extraordinary significance is to be secured. Nationally, it is to do with the future of multi-cultural New Zealand. Will a culture worthy of the distinctiveness and beauty of the ancient islands grow with understanding and pride in the inheritance around it? Internationally, the opportunity is to do with the ever-increasing attraction the inheritance of original nature must have to a world that is losing it, with the environmental image supporting our exports, and with the opportunity to emerge as a leader and example in conservation.

The reservation system, with all the symbolic meaning of its Maori gift, and with all it has to say in the landscape about distinctive New Zealand, and with all its deficiencies of ecological representation, can be the springboard both for the immediately necessary actions and for the total land ethic on which to base the next hundred years of cultural development.

All this is the story told in the national parks and associated reserves, themselves an outcome of our history, the prizes won from the dangerous process of learning by loss. It is dangerous because the benchmark is always the present, and the present includes what has been lost already.

The challenge posed at the end of the first century is the creation of a sign-post as prescient and potent in its practical initiative as the gift of Te Heuheu. It is not enough to talk hopefully about very obvious measures like completing the Protected Natural Areas programme and strong, imaginative and positive progress with marine reservation, or even developing the will to carry them out.

The end of a century is the time to look out over another century, to perceive the attainability of great goals, and to put in place the policies that will move us steadily towards the goals. In the analogy of voyages, it is time to fix our position, to do some urgent reassessment and to replot the course of a navigation that has already some distinction.

What will New Zealand be like in 2087, at the second centennial of Te Heuheu's gift? It could be argued that the possibilities of nuclear accident, a major volcanic incident, or simply the time span make speculation uncertain and profitless. But in one of few ethical statements in legislation, the National Parks Act enjoins 'preservation in perpetuity'. As well, we know that losses of New Zealand's original nature are forever. So a construct of a possible New Zealand of 2087 will allow some judgement of the pressures that heritage land will feel, and give some sense of the energy and will with which we should shape a course into the future.

Recent forecasts indicate that New Zealand's population could lie between five and seven million. A high proportion, certainly more than half, could be concentrated in urban centres in the Auckland, Waikato and Bay of Plenty regions. Auckland's conurbation could host three million people. New Zealand society would be, ethnically, much more mixed than it is today and diversified further by a steady flow of Polynesian immigration and by a small but steady influx in search of better living quality. Both English and Maori would be widely spoken.

The pattern and structure of industry would be greatly changed. Rising fertiliser costs and the realisation that the future of our land-based exports lies in specialised market niches has long shifted the focus of land production towards high-quality soils and away from marginal hill country. Agriculture and horticulture would be supported by expertise in bio, genetic, and food technologies. The best land would be used intensively for a diverse range of production: fruits, crops, vegetables and a wide range of animal products. Shelter belts would pattern the landscape in these areas, as the trees of agro-forestry regimes would dominate the landscape of lesser-quality soils and the easier hill country. The remainder of economic output, apart from tourism, and a very much greater proportion than at present, would be sustained by small, highly specialised automated (probably robot controlled) manu-facturing, directed like the food products at market niches. While hydro-electricity could still provide a large proportion of the country's energy, the

Modern shelter patterns.

bulk of energy production would be dependent on coal, gas reserves being long expended.

Island insularity would have been reduced greatly by immense advances in the technologies of transport and communications. Communications from the home would be made readily with any part of the world. World information and entertainment would flow to home terminals. Reduction in working hours has put emphasis on occupation (arts, crafts, education). On the one hand, more time would be spent at home, but on the other, more time would be available for outdoor recreation.

The challenge of the future, then, is to accept that land policy shapes culture, that a New Zealand land ethic can be developed, and to shape the direction of our culture through the land ethic and the policies expressing it. What would be the planks of such a policy? First would be the determination that the whole of our landscape, whether in production or reservation, would reflect the distinctive character of New Zealand. Implicit in such a policy would be rejection of an 'island' mentality, and the perception of protected areas as an integral part of the mosaic of land use in their practical value as land protection, their visual affirmation of distinctive New Zealand and their scientific value as a library of gene stock. The studied use of native plants for practical purposes (for example, shelter belts and land stability) and the equally studied attempt to recreate vegetation mixes appropriate to particular regions, at both small and large scale, would be implications of such a policy.

The understanding of regional character must occupy an important place in the ethic. Ecological diversity is one of the strongest features of New Zealand character. The protected natural areas of a region offer a key element in landscape expression of regional character.

Maori land knowledge and cultural values are a vital component of a New Zealand land ethic. This knowledge and these values grew from a unique interaction — how shall we express it? There is a danger that land knowledge will be lost — how shall we as a society ensure that this does not happen? In a sense, Te Heuheu's gift was to protect the culture of his people. Those concerned in protected area planning have a special responsibility to ensure that policies, interpretation and management combine to record, preserve, protect and interpret the land knowledge and cultural values of the Maori people.

How the parks can, and should, relate to Maori culture is clear. Less evident is their expression of one hundred and fifty years of European cultural adjustment to distinctive New Zealand. The two philosophical outcomes of this particular voyage of discovery are the ethic, discussed above, on the one hand, and the 'parks of the people' concept, on the other. Both are indigenous — each a product of historical evolution. 'Parks of the people' began with Te Heuheu's gift 'for the use of both Maoris and the Europeans'. The idea can be traced through Vogel, the Scenery Preservation Act, Vosseler, and Michael Joseph Savage to the joint shaping of the National Parks Act by government and the people. Will the parks still be 'of the people' in 2087? Will the unique partnership, attracting interest (and envy) internationally, survive the resource ambitions and political pressures of the future? The crux of that role is that the people remain responsible, as they are now, for making policy and for general oversight. The answer lies with the people. It lies with the sense of inheritance and with the sense of responsibility to the future. It is vital that those who serve on the people's administration understand the values they are responsible for and keep the long term steadily in view. Understanding land values means knowing land — from being in it and from study of information about it. Those who do not know the land will make bad decisions, and there is no place for such.

If the citizen role and responsibility in 'the parks of the people' is to be preserved it must be understood clearly that the concept will need periodic defence. It must be understood also that the responsibility for the people's role in the partnership carries an obligation for performance and a burden of accountability for that performance. Prior to the National Parks Act 1980, accountability was clear, as appointments to the parks and reserves boards were made on the recommendation of the National Parks Authority. This procedure should be continued as one step towards the future. The complementary step needed is the insurance that people with skill and land knowledge will continue to be available to serve in the citizen administration.

The history of land reservation, essentially one of reactive protection and 'learning by loss', explains a dismal performance in marine reservation. One hundred years after the Gift, the heirs to a great voyaging tradition, the administrators of one of the largest extended economic zones in the world, an island race whose involvement with their coastline is total, whose yachtsmen brave the Southern Ocean, have a record as laggard in marine reservation as that for the land is advanced.

The problems of exploitation are legion and infamous: from boom-bust raids on crayfish and toheroa, to the saga of the inshore schnapper fishery, to the controversies that embroil various attempts to discharge sewerage to the sea, to those about management of estuaries — replete with ecological ignorance and the view that mangrove swamps are wasteland.

The apparent refusal to contemplate the sea as a functioning ecology that is part of and related to events on land was reinforced long ago by the

Demoiselle and sponges — typical deepwater fauna in the Poor Knights Marine Reserve.

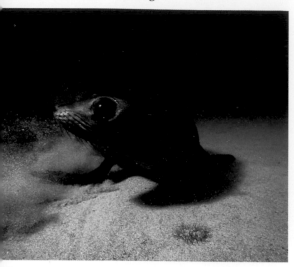

Young fur seal in Dusky Sound.
  The length and variety of the New Zealand coastline translates into a richness and diversity in the sea that is quite the equal of that on land.

insertion of a mental block, an administrative device terminating terrestrial administration at mean high-water mark. This was an effective statement that land administrations had no onus for what happened in the sea. We were effectively shielded from that responsibility as also from the knowledge that products from the land may damage the ecology of the sea, that soil erosion is a double-edged disaster; loss of productivity on the land, for example, being echoed by blanketing the shellfish beds of the estuaries.

The waters of the fiords that give Fiordland National Park its name, and are an integral part of the character of the great wilderness, are not part of the national park. Other administrations than those governing national parks can give rights and make decisions that would breach the integrity of the national park and disorganise its management.

In plotting a course to the future, the setting in place of a system of marine reservation must belong with the strategies of the land ethic and the protection and confirmation of national and regional landscapes based on indigenous ecological character.

But we have talked of the need for marine reservation for most of the past two decades. The history told in this book demonstrates that most conservation strategies are implemented too late, and that they derive from strong public initiatives led by people of vision. Conservation leadership within, or by, governments as institutions has been rare.

Red coral and tiger shell in Dusky Sound.
  Regional ecological differences apply in the sea as well as on the land.

In discussing the future, the lesson of history must be borne in mind. It applies particularly in 1987 because 'too late' signals are once more flying clearly in the winds of change, and clearly visible in the diverging trends of funding and staffing on the one hand, and forecasts of tourism on the other. While the interest of New Zealanders in their parks will increase, it is probable that overseas visitor numbers will double or treble in the short thirteen years to the end of the century. Very great pressure will be applied to the Hermitage area of Mount Cook National Park and Milford Sound in Fiordland National Park. Preserving the quality of such areas requires financial and staff resources, planning and a lead time of two to three years in order to install facilities. Urgent action is required to cope with the short-term situation.

Neither tourism increase nor a steady growth in recreation demand for New Zealanders will cease at the year 2000. 'House full' signs are inevitable unless a major emphasis to strategic national and regional tourist planning is given now, in 1987 — strategic planning that will diffuse tourism and provide alternative interests and destinations to the current focal points of interest and impact.

It is against the longer-term prospect that the relevance of cultural and land ethic strategy, and of fostering overall indigenous landscape character, nationally and regionally, becomes most evident. It is against the long-term prospect also that the urgency of completing and implementing policies for the protection and management of the rare resources of original nature and unique evolution becomes plain. The present situation has a similar capacity for the breach of fundamental conservation strategy as had the fire storms of the 1890s.

Looking outwards from 1987 to great goals it is plain that economic interest and conservation interest are one. Beneath the umbrella of the land ethic, there is urgent short-term planning of a detailed nature and equally urgent mid-term strategy planning to be done. There are a number of incomplete programmes that can be considered to be endangered. The resources required for implementation are not great; the long-term value in their achievement will be immense. To realise the value, these must be carried through without delay:

(i) The Protected Natural Areas programme is the vital base for national and regional landscape policy, as also for scientific representation and cultural identity.

(ii) A system of wilderness areas was recommended by a Wilderness Advisory Group (following an initiative from the Federated Mountain Clubs) in the early 1980s. Wilderness is a policy of particular significance in the New Zealand 'unique nature' situation.

(iii) In 1987, although the appropriate law exists for the declaration of wild and scenic rivers, progress with this policy has been slow.

(iv) We have no record of the changes occurring in our protected lands; whether vegetation composition is shifting, for example, or new plant successions taking place, or whether air and water quality are changing. Monitoring to follow the scientific history of our rare inheritance would be of enormous benefit.

Determined implementation of these programmes is no more than 'fire-fighting', the restoration of vision span to perceptions dimmed by over-concentration on the short term. Some other action in 1987 is needed to

Kawarau Gorge in the 'Old Man'
ecological district, Central Otago.

  A series of ecological reserves has been
recommended to cover altitude
sequences from the vegetation of the
arid gorge area to the wet tundra of the
alpine tops. The surveys were part of the
Protected Natural Areas programme.

demonstrate, one hundred years later, that the Gift is understood and that Te
Heuheu's years of trial are comprehended. Te Heuheu Tukino knew in his
soul where he stood; he, his land and his culture were one. Can New
Zealanders of 1987 have equal confidence?

  To establish the base, and the goals for the next century, a national reassessment of heritage is needed, region by region — to inventory, discuss,
value and set goals. Each region has heritage: Maori heritage, European heritage, heritage of other cultures and the heritage of regional biological distinction. All the heritage agencies (Historic Places Trust, Walkways Commission, Queen Elizabeth II National Trust, the new Department of Conservation,
and the boards of our national parks and reserves) should be involved with
the Maori community and central and regional government in a programme
designed to culminate in a national forum that does indeed look out to the
long-term future.

*I plead on behalf of New Zealand that whilst we are laboriously
endeavouring to improve the country by means of great public works, we
shall not overlook the value and importance of those great natural features,
without care for which, however attractive we may otherwise make the
country, we cannot make it attractive as the home of an industrious
population, nor can we hope to preserve its character and its intrinsic
value.*
— Julius Vogel, 1874

*He kura tangata e kore e rokohanga, he kura whenua ka rokohanga.
Only the land endures.*

Bibliography

Introductory material

Grace, J. Te H. *Tuwharetoa: The History of the Maori People of the Taupo District.* Wellington, 1959

Te Heuheu Tukino. Letter to the Minister of Lands. National Archives of New Zealand, MA, MLP 1, 1903/118

Chapter 2

Abel Tasman National Park. *A Park for All Seasons: The Story of Abel Tasman National Park.* Auckland, 1985

Department of Lands and Survey. *New Zealand National and Maritime Parks.* Wellington, 1985

———— *New Zealand's Subantarctic Island Nature Reserves.* Wellington, 1981

Statutes of New Zealand. 1977, 1980

Chapter 3

Champion de Crespigney, R., and Hutchinson, H. G. *The New Forest.* London, 1903

Clark, D. E. (ed.). *National Parks of the West.* 2nd ed. San Francisco, 1965

Evelyn, J. *Sylvia.* London, 1644

Everhart, W. C. *The National Park Service.* New York, 1972

McCaskill, L. W. 'How it all Began: The Story of the First National Park.' Unpublished MS, n.d.

Manns, T. R. 'The Birth and Evolution of the National Park Idea.' Paper presented at the 19th International Seminar of Parks and Protected Areas, Yellowstone, 1986

Marsh, G. P. *Man and Nature.* Cambridge, Mass., 1965

Nakamura, H. *The Idea of Nature, East and West: The Great Ideas Today, 1980.* Chicago, 1980

Nash, R. *Wilderness and the American Mind.* Rev. ed., New Haven, 1973

Simmons, R. C. *The American Colonies.* London, 1976

Sutton, A. and M. *Yellowstone.* New York, 1972

Chapter 4

Andrews, J. H. R. *The Southern Ark: Zoological Discovery in New Zealand 1769–1900.* Auckland, 1986

Cheeseman, T. F. *Manual of the New Zealand Flora.* 2nd ed. Wellington, 1925

Dennis, A., and Potton, C. *The Alpine World of Mount Cook.* Wellington, 1984

Froude, V., Gibson A., and Carlin, B. *Te Whaonui o Tane: Indigenous Forests of New Zealand.* Wellington, 1985

Gage, M. *Legends in the Rocks: An Outline of New Zealand Geology.* Christchurch, 1980

Given, D. R. *Rare and Endangered Plants of New Zealand.* Wellington, 1981

Molloy, L., and Enting, B. *The Ancient Islands: New Zealand's Natural Environments.* Wellington, 1982

National Parks handbooks

Sibson, R. B. *Birds at Risk: Rare and Endangered Species of New Zealand.* Wellington, 1982

Stevens, G. *Lands in Collision: Discovering New Zealand's Past Geography.* Wellington, 1985

Williams, G. R. (ed.) *The Natural History of New Zealand.* Wellington, 1973

Williams, K. *Volcanoes of the South Wind: A Field Guide to the Volcanoes and Landscape of Tongariro National Park.* Wellington, 1985

Chapter 5

Anderson, A. *When all the Moa-ovens Grew Cold.* Dunedin, 1983

Barton, P. L. 'Maori Geographical Knowledge and Mapping: A Synopsis.' *Turnbull Library Record* (13,1) May 1980: 5–25

Bellwood, P. *Man's Conquest of the Pacific: The Prehistory of Southeast Asia and Oceania.* Auckland, 1978

Brailsford, B. *Greenstone Trails: The Maori Search for Pounamu.* Wellington, 1984

———— *The Tattooed Land: The Southern Frontier of the Pa Maori.* Wellington, 1981

Cumberland, K. B. '"Climatic Change" or Cultural Interference? New Zealand in Moa-hunter Times.' In *Land and Livelihood: Geographical Essays in Honour of George Jobberns,* edited by M. McCaskill. Christchurch, 1962

———— *Landmarks.* Sydney, 1981

———— 'Man in Nature in New Zealand.' *New Zealand Geographer* (17,2) October 1961: 137–154

Davidson, J. *The Prehistory of New Zealand.* Auckland, 1984

Herries Beattie, J. *Maori Lore of Lake, Alp and Fiord.* Dunedin, 1949

——— *The Maoris and Fiordland.* Dunedin, 1949

Howe, K. R. *Where the Waves Fall: A New South Seas Islands History from First Settlement to Colonial Rule.* Sydney, 1984

Leach, H. *1000 Years of Gardening in New Zealand.* Wellington, 1984

Mead, S. M. (ed.) *Te Maori: Maori Art from New Zealand Collections.* Auckland, 1984

Oliver, W. H., and Williams, B. R. (eds). *The Oxford History of New Zealand.* Wellington, 1981

Orbell, M. *The Natural World of the Maori.* Auckland, 1985

O'Regan, T. Interview with M. Neazor, Wellington, January 1985

Peart, J. D. *Old Tasman Bay.* Nelson, 1937

Reed, A. W. *Treasury of Maori Exploration.* Wellington, 1977

Chapter 6

Banks, J. *The* Endeavour *Journal of Joseph Banks.* Edited by J. C. Beaglehole. 2nd ed. Sydney, 1962

Beaglehole, J.C. *The Exploration of the Pacific.* 3rd ed. Stanford, 1966

────── *The Life of Captain James Cook.* London, 1974

Begg, A. C. and N. C. *James Cook and New Zealand.* Christchurch, 1969

────── *Port Preservation.* Christchurch, 1973

Burns, P. *Te Rauparaha: A New Perspective.* Wellington, 1980

Carr, D. J. (ed.) *Sydney Parkinson: Artist of Cook's* Endeavour *Voyage.* Wellington, 1983

Darwin, C. *The Voyage of the Beagle.* Edited by L. Engel. Garden City, N.Y., 1962.

Fiordland National Park Board. *Fiordland National Park.* Te Anau, 1973

Forster, J. R. *The* Resolution *Journal of Johann Reinhold Forster, 1772–1775.* Edited by M. E. Hoare. London, 1982

Grace, R. 'Dusky's Big Guns.' *Aorangi* (4,1) 1984: 15–18

Hall-Jones, J. *Early Fiordland.* Wellington, 1968

Lyte, C. *Sir Joseph Banks: Eighteenth-Century Explorer, Botanist and Entrepreneur.* Wellington, 1980

McClenaghan, J. *Fiordland.* Wellington, 1966

Mackay, D. *In the Wake of Cook.* Wellington, 1985

McNab, R. *From Tasman to Marsden.* Dunedin, 1914

────── *Murihiku and the Southern Islands.* Invercargill, 1907

────── *The Old Whaling Days.* Christchurch, 1913

Oliver, W. H., and Williams, B. R. (eds). *The Oxford History of New Zealand.* Wellington, 1981

Reader's Digest Services (ed.) *Wild New Zealand.* Sydney, 1981

Rogers, L. M. (ed.) *The Early Journals of Henry Williams.* Christchurch, 1961

Sharp, A. *Duperry's Visit to New Zealand in 1824.* Wellington, 1971

Sinclair, K. *A History of New Zealand.* Rev. ed. Harmondsworth, 1984

Smith, B. *European Vision and the South Pacific, 1768–1850.* Oxford, 1960

Stanbury, D. (ed.) *A Narrative of the Voyage of HMS Beagle.* London, 1977

Villiers, A. *Captain Cook.* London, 1967

Dumont d'Urville, J. S. C. *New Zealand 1826–1827.* An English translation of the *Voyage de l'Astrolabe in New Zealand Waters* by Olive Wright. Wellington, 1950

Chapter 7

Allan, H. H. *Flora of New Zealand.* Wellington, 1961

Arthur's Pass National Park Board. *Handbook to the Arthur's Pass National Park.* 3rd ed. Christchurch, 1966

Bagnall, A. G., and Peterson, G. C. *William Colenso.* Wellington, 1948

Belich, J. *The New Zealand Wars and the Victorian Interpretation of Racial Conflict.* Auckland, 1986

Bidwell, J. C. *Rambles in New Zealand 1839.* Christchurch, 1952

Cheeseman, T. F. *Manual of the New Zealand Flora.* 2nd ed. Wellington, 1925

Clark, A. H. *The Invasion of New Zealand by People, Plants and Animals: the South Island.* New Brunswick, 1949

Cowan, J. *The New Zealand Wars: A History of Maori Campaigns and the Pioneering Period.* Wellington, 1923

Cumberland, K. B. *Landmarks.* Sydney, 1981

Dennis, A. *The Paparoas Guide.* Nelson, 1981

Dieffenbach, E. *Travels in New Zealand.* Christchurch, 1974

Dobson, A. D. *Reminiscences.* Auckland, 1930

Druett, J. *Exotic Intruders.* Auckland, 1983

Fleming, C. A. 'The Influence of Early German Naturalists and Explorers in New Zealand.' Address to the Humboldt Society, 1983

Fox, W. *The War in New Zealand.* Christchurch, 1973

Glenn, R. *The Botanical Explorers of New Zealand.* Wellington, 1950

Grace, J. Te H. *Tuwharetoa: The History of the Maori People of the Taupo District.* Wellington, 1959

Haast, M. F. von. *The Life and Times of Sir Julius von Haast* Wellington, 1946

Johnston, J. A. 'The New Zealand Bush: Early Assessment of Vegetation.' *New Zealand Geographer* (37) April 1981: 19–24

King, C. *Immigrant Killers.* Auckland, 1984

Lee, J. *I Have Named it the Bay of Islands.* Auckland, 1982

McClymont, W. G. *The Exploration of New Zealand.* London, 1959

McKay, D. *In the Wake of Cook: Exploration, Science and Empire 1780–1801.* Wellington, 1985

McLintock, A. H. (ed.) *An Encyclopaedia of New Zealand.* 3 vols. Wellington, 1966

Natusch, S. *The Cruise of the Acheron.* Christchurch, 1978

Nelson Lakes National Park Board. *Nelson Lakes National Park* Rev. ed. Nelson, 1974

Oliver, W. H., and Williams, B. R. (eds). *The Oxford History of New Zealand.* Wellington, 1981

Orange, C. 'The Covenant of Kohimarama.' *NZJH* (14,1) April 1980: 61–82

Parsonson, A. 'The Expansion of a Competitive Society: A study in Nineteenth-Century Maori Social History.' *NZJH* (14,1) April 1980: 45–60

Pascoe, J. *Great Days in New Zealand Exploration.* Wellington, 1958

Pears, N. 'Familiar Aliens: The Acclimatisation Societies' Role in New Zealand's Biogeography.' *Scottish Geographical Magazine* (98,1) April 1982: 23–34

Platts, U. *The Lively Capital.* Christchurch, 1971

Shepard, P. *British Reaction to the New Zealand Landscape Before 1850.* Wellington, 1969

Simpson, T. *Te Riri Pakeha: The White Man's Anger.* Martinborough, 1979

Sinclair, K. *A History of New Zealand.* Rev. ed. Harmondsworth, 1984

Stafford, D. M. *Te Arawa.* Wellington, 1967

Taylor, N. M. (ed.) *Early Travellers in New Zealand.* Oxford, 1959

Temple, P. *New Zealand Explorers: Great Journeys of Discovery.* Christchurch, 1985

Torrill, W. B. *Royal Botanic Gardens, Kew.* London, 1959

Wilson, O. *From Hongi Hika to Hone Heke.* Dunedin, 1985

Chapter 8

Appendices to the Journals of the House of Representatives. 1874

Arnold, R. 'The Virgin Forest Harvest and the Development of Colonial New Zealand.' *New Zealand Geographer* (32) 1976: 105–126

Brown, L. *Captain Inches Campbell-Walker — New Zealand's First Conservator of Forests.* Wellington, 1966
———— *The Forestry Era of Professor Thomas Kirk.* Wellington, 1968
Burdon, R. M. *The Life and Times of Sir Julius Vogel.* Christchurch, 1948
Conly, G. 'Kauri.' *Landscape* (4) 1978:20–25
———— *Tarawera: The Destruction of the Pink and White Terraces.* Wellington, 1985
Dalziel, R. *Julius Vogel: Business Politician.* Auckland, 1986
Dobson, A. D. 'On the Destruction of Land by Shingle-Bearing Rivers and Suggestions for Protection and Prevention.' *Transactions of the New Zealand Institute* (4) 1871:153–157
Everhart, W. C. *The National Park Service.* New York, 1972
Fleming, C. A. 'Nature Conservation in New Zealand, The Conservation of Natural Resources.' Unpublished MS, n.d.
Green, W. S. *The High Alps of New Zealand.* London, 1883
Haast, M. F. von. *The Life and Times of Sir Julius von Haast.* Wellington, 1946
Kerry-Nicholls, J. H. *The King Country.* London, 1884
Kirk, T. 'The Displacement of Species in New Zealand.' *Transactions of the New Zealand Institute* (28) 1895: 1–27
McLintock, A. H. (ed.) *An Encyclopaedia of New Zealand.* 3 vols. Wellington, 1966
New Zealand Herald. 11 June 1886
New Zealand's Heritage: The Making of a Nation. Edited by R. Knox. 21 vols. Wellington, 1971
New Zealand Parliamentary Debates. 1868
Potts, T. *Out in the Open.* Christchurch, 1882
Reischek, A. *Yesterdays in Maoriland.* Fac. ed. Auckland, n.d.
Savage, P. *The Government Gardens.* Rotorua, 1980
Statutes of New Zealand. 1874, 1880, 1881, 1885
Union Steamship Company. *Maoriland.* Melbourne, 1884
Wynn, G. 'Conservation and Society in Late Nineteenth-Century New Zealand.' *NZJH* (11,2) October 1977:124–136

———— 'Pioneers, Politicians and Forest Conservation.' *Journal of Historical Geography* 1979: 171–188

Chapter 9

Appendices to the Journals of the House of Representatives. 1886, 1889
Cooper, B. *Te Mata O Tauponui A Tia: The Head of the Lake.* Turangi, n.d.
Cowan, J. *Sir Donald MacLean.* Dunedin, 1940
———— *The Tongariro National Park.* Wellington, 1927
Department of Lands and Survey. *The Restless Land: The Story of Tongariro National Park.* 2nd ed. Wellington, 1982
Grace, J. Te H. *Tuwharetoa: The History of the Maori People of the Taupo District.* Wellington, 1959
Harris, W. W. 'An Analysis of the Origins and Evolution of the New Zealand National Parks Movement.' Unpublished M.A. Geography thesis. University of Canterbury, 1974
Maori Land Court Minute Books (Taupo). Vols 5–9. Microfilm. University of Auckland.
New Zealand Herald. 28 January, 12 February, 1880
New Zealand Parliamentary Debates. 1887
Scholefield, G. H. (ed) *New Zealand Dictionary of Biography.* Wellington, 1940
Stafford, D. M. *Te Arawa.* Wellington, 1967
Statutes of New Zealand. 1863

Chapter 10

Appendices to the Journals of the House of Representatives. 1895–1899
Arnold, R. D. 'The Virgin Forest Harvest and the Development of Colonial New Zealand.' *New Zealand Geographer* (32) 1976: 105–126
Bates, A. P. *A Pictorial History of the Wanganui River.* Wanganui, 1985
Begg, A. C. and N. C. *Dusky Bay.* Christchurch, 1966
———— *Port Preservation.* Christchurch, 1966
Brown, L. *Captain Inches Campbell-Walker: New Zealand's First Conservator of Forests.* Wellington, 1966
———— *The Forestry Era of Professor Thomas Kirk.* Wellington, 1968
Burdon, R. M. *King Dick.* Christchurch, 1955
Carle, C. J. *Forty Mile Bush: A Tribute to the Pioneers.* Masterton, 1980
Dendy, A. 'Plants and Animals of Canterbury.' In *Canterbury Old and New.* Christchurch, 1900
Hall-Jones, J. *Fiordland Explored.* Wellington, 1976
Heerdegen, R. G. 'Land for the Landless.' *New Zealand Geographer* (23) 1967: 34–49
———— 'Some Aspects of the Settlement of the North Island Bushlands.' Paper presented at the 41st ANZAAS Conference, Adelaide, 1969
Jourdain, J. W. R. *Land Legislation and Settlement in New Zealand.* Wellington, 1925
King, M. *The Collector: A Biography of Andreas Reischek.* Auckland, 1981
New Zealand Parliamentary Debates. 1881, 1884, 1887–1896
Noonan, R. *By Design: A Brief History of the Public Works Department Ministry of Works 1870–1970.* Wellington, 1975
Pears, N. 'Familiar Aliens: The Acclimatisation Societies' Role in New Zealand's Biogeography.' *Scottish Geographical Magazine* (98,1) April 1982: 23–34
Statutes of New Zealand. 1880, 1881, 1885, 1892
Wynn, G. 'Conservation and Society in Late Nineteenth-Century New Zealand .' *NZJH* (11,2) October 1977: 124–136

Chapter 11

Appendices to the Journals of the House of Representatives. 1901–1920
Bates, A. P. *A Pictorial History of the Wanganui River.* Wanganui, 1985
Dennis, A., and Potton, C. *The Alpine World of Mount Cook.* Wellington, 1984
Dingwall, P. R. 'Ecological Considerations Shaping Tongariro National Park.' *Landscape* (13), November 1983: 27–31
———— 'Harry Ell's Vision in Nature Conservation.' *Landscape* (10) November 1981: 23–27
Hall-Jones, J. *Fiordland Explored.* Wellington, 1976
New Zealand Parliamentary Debates. 1902, 1903, 1905
Noonan, R. *By Design: A Brief History of the Public Works Department Ministry of Works 1870–1970.* Wellington, 1975
Oakley, L. *Harry Ell and his Summit Road.* Christchurch, 1960
'Obituary — Freda du Faur.' *New Zealand Alpine Journal* (6,23) June 1936: 388–391
Roche, M. M. 'Securing Representative Areas of New Zealand's Environment: Some Historical and Design Perspectives.' *New Zealand Geographer* (37,2) 1981: 73–77

Statutes of New Zealand. 1900, 1903, 1906, 1907, 1914

Thomson, A. P. 'George Malcolm Thomson and the 1913 Royal Commission on Forestry.' *New Zealand Journal of Forestry* (30,1) 1985: 18–27; (30,2) 1985: 186–195

Chapter 12

Adams, G. *Jack's Hut.* Wellington, 1968

Bagnall, A. G. 'Heather at Tongariro: A Study of a Weed Introduction.' *Review* (41) December 1982: 17–21

Burrell, R. *Fifty Years of Mountain Federation.* n.p., 1981

Department of Lands and Survey *Land of the Mist: The Story of the Urewera National Park.* Gisborne, 1983

Forest and Bird. 1923–1940, 1955

Knox, R. (ed.) *A Thousand Rivers Shining: Stories from New Zealand's Mountain World.* Wellington, 1984

New Zealand Parliamentary Debates. 1922

Pearce, D. G. 'Tourist Development at Mount Cook Since 1884.' *New Zealand Geographer* (36,2) 1980: 79–84

Statutes of New Zealand. 1921, 1922, 1928

Syme, R. 'Federated Mountain Clubs and the 1952 National Parks Act.' Unpublished MS. 1985

Thomson, J. *Origins of the 1952 National Parks Act.* Wellington, 1976

Chapter 13

Files of the Department of Lands and Survey (Nelson). 1941

Nelson Evening Mail. June–August 1941, November–December 1942, May 1943.

Syme, R. 'Federated Mountain Clubs and the 1952 National Parks Act.' Unpublished MS., 1985.

Chapter 14

Appendices to the Journals of the House of Representatives. 1952–1964

Cleland, R. L. 'Experiences in the 1950s and 1960s'. Unpublished MS., n.d.

Forest and Bird. 1953–1964

McCaskill, L. W. 'Lessons for Our Parks from Overseas'. Unpublished MS., 1966

———— 'National Parks.' Unpublished MS., 1985

———— 'National Parks Authority.' Unpublished MS., 1985

———— 'Scenic Reserves and the National Parks Authority.' Unpublished MS., 1985

Report by the Department of Lands and Survey on the administration of Wanganui River reserves. 1954

Report by the National Parks Authority on the proceedings of the National Park Rangers Forum held at Arthur's Pass, November 1959

Thomson, A. P. 'History of Forest Parks and FMC Involvement.' Presented to FMC meeting, 1981

Thomson, J. *Origins of the 1952 National Parks Act.* Wellington, 1976

Chapter 15

Appendices to the Journal of the House of Representatives. 1967, 1969

Campbell, J. L. *Poenamu: Sketches of the Early Days in New Zealand.* Auckland, 1973

Chapman-Taylor, R. *Education in National Parks.* Wellington, 1976

Communication and correspondence with the author: Hutchins, L.; Lucas, P. H. C.; McFarlane, J.; McKerchar, D.; MacMillan, G.; O'Brien, J. D.; Thomson, A. P.; Wetere, K. T.; Young, V. S.

Dominion. 27, 28 January 1970

Evening Post. 27 January 1970

Files of the Department of Lands and Survey (Auckland). 1967

McMahon, C. K. (ed.) Reports, Papers and Proceedings of the Physical Environment Conference, Wellington, 1970

Mason, B. J. *Back Country Boom.* Wellington, 1974

Mitchell, I. B. 'Marlborough Sounds Maritime Park and Coastal Reserves.' Paper presented at the 'Between the Tides' symposium, Nelson, 1978

Morton, J., Thom, D. A., and Locker, R. *Seacoast in the Seventies.* Auckland, 1973

New Zealand Parliamentary Debates. 1967

New Zealand Weekly News. 12 January 1970

Reports of the Hauraki Gulf Maritime Park Board. 1967–1985

Reports, minutes and agendas of the National Parks Authority. 1965–1980

Reports of National Parks boards. 1970–1980

Thompson, A. P. 'The Great Bowen Falls Debate: A Chapter in Fiordland History.' Unpublished MS., 1986

Chapter 16

Communication and correspondence with the author: Clarborough, M.; Cleland, R.; Croft, P.; Jacobs, H.; Lucas, P. H. C.; McCaskill, L. W.; Mossman, R.; Nicholls, G. E.; Sheridan, P.

Dennis, A. *Arthur's Pass National Park.* Christchurch, 1979

Everhart, W. C. *The National Park Service.* New York, 1972

Fuchs, V., and Hillary, E. *The Crossing of Antarctica.* London, 1958

Hunt, J. *The Ascent of Mount Everest.* London, 1953

Jacobs, H. Reports to the Secretary of Foreign Affairs, Wellington, on the technical co-operation programme between New Zealand and Peru. 1977

Jefferies, B. E. 'Sagarmatha National Park: The Impact of Tourism in the Himalayas.' Paper delivered at the the third World Congress on National Parks, Bali, 1982

Lee, R. F. *Family Tree of the National Park System.* Philadelphia, 1972

Lucas, P. H. C. An account of the 27th session of the Commission on National Parks and Protected Areas of IUCN at San Carlos de Bardoche, Argentina 1986

———— *Conserving New Zealand's Heritage.* Wellington, 1970

———— 'New Zealand and International Conservation.' Address to the Wellington Branch of the Royal New Zealand Forest and Bird Protection Society. 1981

———— Report on technical co-operation between Peru and New Zealand.

———— 'Thinking Globally, Acting Locally.' Address to the Pukeiti Rhododendron Trust. 1982

Mossman, R. 'Training for Conservation in a Developing Country — Western Samoa.' Dissertation presented as part requirement for the Diploma of Parks and Administration. Lincoln College.

Nash, R. *Wilderness and the American Mind.* New Haven, 1967

Nicholls, G. E. 'A New Zealander Looks at National Parks and

Reserves in North America.' Wellington, 1968
——— 'Sagarmatha National Park.' *Nepal Nature Conservation Society's Annual.* Kathmandu, 1977

Chapter 17

Adams, A. B. (ed.) *First World Conference on National Parks.* Washington, DC., 1962

Barnes, J. N. *Let's Save Antarctica.* Richmond, 1982

Borrie, W. D. *Population, Environment and Society.* Auckland, 1973

Cahn, R. '"Islands in a Storm" Five articles about threats to the National Parks of the United States.' *Christian Science Monitor.* 1982

Communication and correspondence with the author: Molloy, L. F.; Thorsell, J.

Champion de Crespigney, R., and Hutchinson, H. B. *The New Forest.* London, 1903

Curry-Lindah, K., and Harroy, J-P. (eds). *National Parks of the World.* 2 vols. New York, 1972

'A Concise Guide to National Parks' *National Geographic* (156) 1 July 1979: 111–124

Darwin, C. *The Voyage of the Beagle.* London, 1961

Demeny, P. 'Can World Population Forecasts Come True?' *People* (2,1) 1984

Elliott, H. (ed.) *Second World Conference on National Parks.* Lausanne, 1974

The World's Greatest Natural Areas: An Indicative Inventory of Natural Sites of World Heritage Quality. Compiled by IUCN's Commission on National Parks and Protected Areas. Gland, 1982

McNeely, J. A., and Miller, K. R. *National Parks, Conservation and Development: The Role of Protected Areas in Sustaining Society.* Washington D.C., 1984

Moore, R., and the editors of *Life* magazine. *Evolution.* Amsterdam, 1964

Morcombe, M. *Australia's National Parks.* Melbourne, 1977

Osten, R. van *World National Parks, Progress and Opportunities.* Brussels, 1972

Simmons, R. C. *The American Colonies.* London, 1976

Sutton, A. and M. *Yellowstone.* New York, 1972

Chapter 18

Barnes, J. N. *Let's Save Antarctica.* Richmond, 1982

Boshier, J. F. *et al. Four Futures: Energy Implications of Social and Economic Change.* Auckland, 1986

Communication and correspondence with the author: Adams, R.; Atkinson, I.; Bamford, D.; Cleland, R. L.; Davison, J. J.;Edmonds, A.; Fleming, C. A.; Garratt, K. J.; Given, D.; Green, P.; Hutchins, L.; Kelly, G. C.; Jefferies, B.;Jones, B.; McFarlane, J.; McSweeney, G.; McKerchar, D.; Mark, A. F.; Molloy, B.; O'Connor, K.; Park, G. N.; Rennison, G.; Salmon, G.

Conservation Foundation *National Parks for the Future.* Washington D.C., 1972

Davison, J. J. 'Policy Implications of Trends in Supply and Demand for Natural Areas for Protection and Recreation.' Unpublished thesis, University of Canterbury, 1986

Department of Lands and Survey. *Seminar on People and Parks: The Human Side of Managing New Zealand's Parks and Protected Areas.* Wellington, 1984

Department of Scientific and Industrial Research. *Land Alone Endures: Land Use and the Role of Research.* Wellington, 1980

——— *The New Zealand Protected Areas Programme: A Scientific Focus.* Wellington, 1986

Dingwall, P. R. (ed.) *Protection and Parks: Essays in the Preservation of Natural Values in Protected Areas.* Wellington, 1984

Forster, R. R. *Planning for Man and Nature in National Parks.* Morges, 1973

Kerr, G. M., Sharp B. M. M., and Gough J. D. *Economic Benefits of Mount Cook National Park.* Christchurch, 1986

King, K. J., Bailey, K. N., and Clark, M. J. *Coastal and Marine Ecological Areas of New Zealand.* Wellington, 1985

Lucas, P. H. C. 'The World Conservation Strategy.' *Forest and Bird*, May 1980: 13–18

Morton, J. *et al. To Save a Forest: Whirinaki.* Auckland, 1984

Queen Elizabeth II National Trust. *The Waipa County Landscape.* 2 vols. Wellington, 1982

US National Parks Centennial Commission. *Preserving a Heritage.* Washington D.C., 1973

Index

Illustration Credits

It will be plain that I am indebted to many persons and institutions for illustration material. I am most grateful to them all, but the record draws attention particularly to one institution and three photographers.

The Alexander Turnbull Library has helped greatly with historical illustration, as with other information. Many photographs are the work of Tony Lilleby, of the Department of Conservation's Interpretation, Planning and Design Centre. Lloyd Homer, of the New Zealand Geological Survey, provided the series of aerial photographs of the fifteen parks appearing on pages xv to xix. Ann and Myron Sutton, of Montana, USA, gave invaluable assistance with material from their worldwide collection.

For information used as a basis for the maps I am indebted to the following:

For 'Reduction of New Zealand's indigenous forest' (page 40), to *Te Whaonui o Tane*, published by the Commission for the Environment. The map as presented is indicative. At the scale used, it cannot, of course, be precise.

For 'Pacific settlement' (page 44), to Kerry Howe's *Where the Waves Fall*.

For 'Routes of Maori trade in the northern South Island' (page 50), to Barry Brailsford's *Greenstone Trails*.

For 'Maori tribal locations' (page 52), to assistance from Te Warena Taua.

For 'The shaping of Tongariro National Park' (page 96), to Paul Dingwall.

In order to identify the specific location of an illustration on a page, the following code has been used: A indicates Above; AL, Above Left; AR, Above Right; C, Centre; and B, Below.

Photographic essays of individual parks

Tongariro (pages 98–100): Bruce Jefferies
Egmont (pages 127–30): John Clay except 127A, Tony Lilleby; 127B, Chris Rudge; 128C, 130, Interpretation, Planning and Design Centre, DOC
Arthur's Pass (pages 144–6): Peter Simpson except 144A, Tony Lilleby; 145A, 146BL, Andy Dennis
Abel Tasman (pages 152–4): Tony Lilleby
Fiordland (pages 164–7): 164A, 164B, 165BL, Interpretation, Planning and Design Centre, DOC; 165A, 165BR, David Thom; 164C, 166A, Fiordland National Park collection; 166B, Paul Green
Mount Cook (pages 168–71): Ray Slater
Urewera (pages 172–4): John Blount except 172C and 173A, Tony Lilleby

Nelson Lakes (pages 175–7): 175A, Peter Croft; 175BL, 177 Tony Lilleby; 175BR, 176A, 176BL, Interpretation, Planning and Design Centre, DOC; 176BR, David Thom
Westland (pages 178–81): Murray Reedy
Mount Aspiring (pages 182–4): Bill Hislop except 182BL, David Thom; 182BR, 184A M. Burke; 183A, P. McGraham
Hauraki Gulf (pages 199–201): Rex Mossman
Marlborough Sounds (pages 202–4): 202A, K. Heather; 202C, 202B, 203A, 203B, 204A Department of Conservation (Picton); 203C, Kerry Johnson; 204B, David Mazey
Bay of Islands (pages 205–7): Shaughan Anderson except 205, 206BL, 207B D. P. Taylor; 207A, R. Grose
Whanganui (pages 208–10): Fiona Lundy except 209AR, 210A, J. R. Lythgoe; 209B David Thom
Paparoa (pages 211–14): Grahame Champness

Text illustrations

Auckland Institute and Museum 5B, 138, 139A, 162, 163
Alexander Turnbull Library 3, 27, 46, 48, 49B, 53, 55, 56, 62B, 66A, 67, 68, 69, 70, 71, 72, 73, 74, 75, 76, 77, 80, 81, 82, 84, 87, 93, 95, 103, 104, 105, 106, 109, 111, 112, 114B, 116, 118, 119, 124, 136, 142
Canterbury Museum 107AL, 114A, 115, 125, 134, 135
Department of Lands and Survey 17BR, 78
Great Barrier Reef Marine Park Authority 233
Hawke's Bay Art Gallery 66B
Hocken Library, University of Otago 2A, 107AR, 108B, 113
Interpretation, Planning and Design Centre, DOC 31, 32A
National Art Gallery 108A
National Museum of New Zealand xx, 1, 83, 85, 86, 88
New Zealand Forest Service 6, 139B
New Zealand Herald 159
New Zealand Historic Places Trust 94
New Zealand Railways Corporation 110, 122
New Zealand Wildlife Service 18, 37C, 37B, 38A, 39B, 41B, 42
Royal Forest and Bird Protection Society of New Zealand 140, 141, 148
Tongariro National Park collection 33C
Twentieth Century Photography (NZ) Ltd 160
Whanganui National Park collection 2B

Dave Bamford 4A
Gary Blackman 156
Mark Bellingham 246AL
Barney Brewster 245B, 252
Hazel Chapman 8, 133
John Coster (Department of Lands and Survey) 48B

Andy Dennis   4BL
Roger Grace   13C, 13B, 61, 249, 250
David Gregorie   196B
Gerard Hutching   245C
Les Hutchins   58B
Harold Jacobs   222A, 235
Bruce Jefferies   9, 220B, 221A, 234, 243, 246B
Tony Lilleby   4BR, 7, 10, 11, 12, 13A, 14, 15, 16, 17A, 17BL,
    19, 33A, 33B, 34, 35AL, 35B, 36, 38BL, 38BR, 39A, 40B,
    41A, 47AL, 49A, 51, 54, 57, 58A, 60, 62A, 63, 195B, 241,
    242, 246AR, 247
P. H. C. Lucas   191, 231
Helen MacGibbon   188
David McKerchar   23B
Gerry McSweeney   245A
John Mazey   5AR

Kenton Miller   232
Rex Mossman   223B, 224
John Parsons (Alpha Photography)   92
Chris Rudge   197
Pat Sheridan   222B, 223A
Neil Simpson   35AR
Brian Smith (Interpretation, Planning and Design Centre,
    DOC)   37A
Ann and Myron Sutton   22, 23A, 24, 29, 30, 215, 219, 220A,
    225, 228, 229, 238
Douglas Sutton (University of Auckland)   47AR
Warwick Teague (Royal Forest and Bird Protection
    Society)   157
David Thom   21, 193, 195A, 196A, 237, 244
James Thorsell   226, 230, 236
David Wakelin   221B

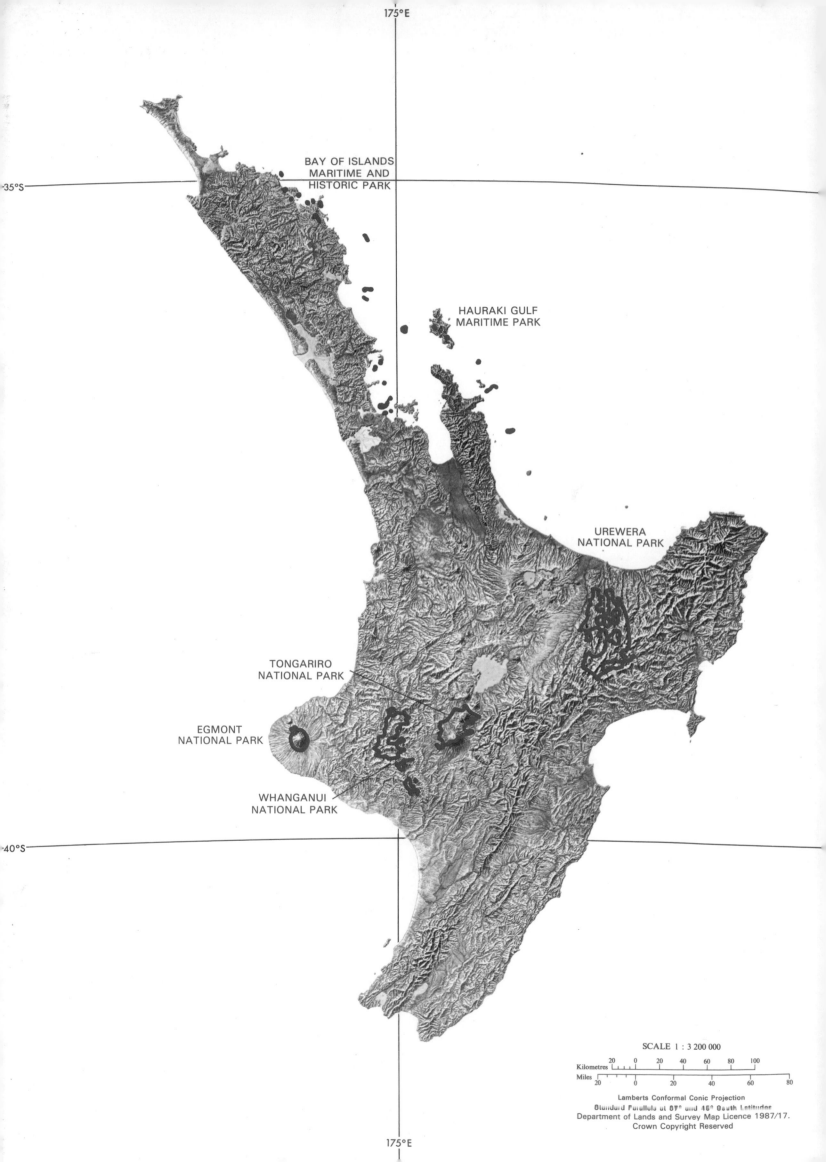

175°E

-35°S

BAY OF ISLANDS
MARITIME AND
HISTORIC PARK

HAURAKI GULF
MARITIME PARK

UREWERA
NATIONAL PARK

TONGARIRO
NATIONAL PARK

EGMONT
NATIONAL PARK

WHANGANUI
NATIONAL PARK

-40°S

175°E

SCALE 1 : 3 200 000

Kilometres 20   0   20   40   60   80   100

Miles 20   0   20   40   60   80

Lamberts Conformal Conic Projection
Standard Parallels at 37° and 45° South Latitudes
Department of Lands and Survey Map Licence 1987/17.
Crown Copyright Reserved